David James Burrell

The Religions of the World

An Outline of the Great Religious Systems

David James Burrell

The Religions of the World
An Outline of the Great Religious Systems

ISBN/EAN: 9783337259303

Printed in Europe, USA, Canada, Australia, Japan

Cover: Foto ©Lupo / pixelio.de

More available books at **www.hansebooks.com**

THE

RELIGIONS OF THE WORLD.

AN OUTLINE

OF THE

GREAT RELIGIOUS SYSTEMS.

BY

DAVID JAMES BURRELL, D.D.

PHILADELPHIA:
PRESBYTERIAN BOARD OF PUBLICATION
AND SABBATH-SCHOOL WORK,
1334 CHESTNUT STREET.

COPYRIGHT, 1888, BY
THE TRUSTEES OF THE
PRESBYTERIAN BOARD OF PUBLICATION
AND SABBATH-SCHOOL WORK.

All Rights Reserved.

WESTCOTT & THOMSON,
Stereotypers and Electrotypers, Philada.

PREFACE.

A MAN who rejects all other religions and accepts Christianity ought to be able to give a reason for it (1 Pet. 3 : 15). To this end, obviously, he should have at the least a general acquaintance with the systems of religion which have, at one time or other, claimed the world's mind and conscience. It is the purpose of this book to present an outline of the great systems measurably clear, concise and accurate—such as shall enable the reader to characterize each at sight and defend his faith against them all. For, as there is only one true God, there can be only one true religion. Christianity claims to be that one. It may verify that claim, on the one hand, by a setting forth of its own merits, and, on the other, by a comparison with other and rival faiths. In this comparison our religion, if true, has everything to gain and nothing to lose. We therefore rejoice in the fact that of late the science of Comparative Religion has rapidly pushed itself to the front.

The essays in this book were originally prepared in brief for a Bible-class of young men. They were afterward revised and extended for a university lecture course, and once more for an association of pastors in a summer assembly. It is at the request of some of the foregoing auditors that the essays have now been arranged for publication. It is the writer's hope that the book may prove interesting and profitable—not, perhaps, to those who are already more or less familiar with the science, so much as to the many common folk, who, cumbered with much serving in secular affairs, yet feeling the need of information on a subject which claims ever more and more of public thought, must have their reading in simple terms, clear outline and compact form.

The following conclusions will probably occur to the reader: (1) There is a measure of good in each of the great religions; (2) It is not true that "one religion is as good as another;" (3) The Christian religion alone is altogether good; (4) The false systems cannot be regarded as progressive steps toward the true; (5) The true religion derives little or nothing from the false: "It gives a light to every age; it gives, but borrows none;" (6) The false philosophies which are from time to time advanced against the Christian religion are nearly or quite all borrowed from the erroneous systems of the past; (7) Christianity is the absolute religion; that is, it is wholly free from error and contains all good; (8) It alone reveals the true God; (9) It alone presents the ideal man; (10) It alone suggests a plan for the reconciliation of guilty man and offended God; (11) It is the only moral system; (12) It is fair, therefore, to regard it as final; (13) It is destined to be the universal religion. Jesus shall reign where'er the sun doth his successive journeys run.

CONTENTS.

		PAGE
I.	FETICHISM	7
II.	THE RELIGION OF ANCIENT EGYPT	29
III.	ZOROASTRIANISM	59
IV.	BRAHMANISM	85
V.	BUDDHISM	119
VI.	THE RELIGION OF GREECE	163
VII.	THE RELIGION OF THE NORSEMEN	197
VIII.	CONFUCIANISM	231
IX.	ISLAM	263
X.	THE TRUE RELIGION	305

I.
FETICHISM.

The Fetich is any material thing, living or dead, not divine, to which reverence is paid on account of a supernatural influence proceeding from it.

Central Thought: A man is not the controller of his own affairs.

(1) His master is fetich, the fortune-giver.
(2) He may have many fetiches of divers kinds.
(3) Fetichism is (*a*) not Polytheism,
    (*b*) nor Henotheism,
    (*c*) nor Pantheism.
(4) It is, however, a system, having both a creed and a cultus.
(5) It is better than any form of materialism, because it holds to the reality of supersensible things.
(6) Providence *vs.* the modern fetich.

"*What shall I do to be saved?*"   No answer.

The Religions of the World.

I. FETICHISM.

The religion of Adam was the true one. He worshiped God in spirit and in truth. He had his theology direct from the divine lips. He "heard the voice of the Lord God walking in the garden." There was no such thing as spiritual ignorance or unbelief in those days. But Adam sinned and then fled shamefaced from the garden of delights. Night closed in around him—an Egyptian night, a darkness that could be felt. He was without God and without hope in the world. But he was not without memory. Amid the ruins of his former greatness walked the dim figure of his Creator. The prodigal could not forget his home and his Father, could not wholly forget that he was made after the divine image. A guilty wanderer, his soul cried out for God. In the darkness he groped after him. Oh, blessed reminiscence! The Moslem felt it when he wrote—

> "As thy beloved's eyes are mirrored in thine eyes,
> God's Spirit, painted so, within thy spirit lies."

And also when he wrote—

> "God and the soul are two birds free,
> And dwell together in one tree.
> *This* eateth various flavored fruits
> Of sense's thoughts and world's pursuits;
> *That* tasteth not nor great nor small,
> But silently beholdeth all."

In this deep night we come upon *Fetichism*, the religion of the abject masses of men, such as the Eskimos, the Australian bushmen, the jungle-dwellers of Africa. It is the lowest grade of religion. Comte, in his *Positive Philosophy*, makes it the primordial faith, or the initial stage in the logical evolution of religion.[1] We prefer to regard it as the farthest point—the point of arrest, as it were—in the retrogression of the soul from God.[2]

---

[1] "Fetichism is not only the most ancient, but it is also the most universal, form of religion. It furnishes incontrovertible proof that the lack of correct knowledge was the true and only cause of polytheism, and that for the uncultured savage everything is God or may be God." —Meiner's *History of Religion*.

[2] Altogether, the theory to which the facts appear on the whole to point is the existence of a primitive religion communicated to man from without, whereof monotheism and expiatory sacrifice were parts, and the gradual clouding over of this primitive revelation everywhere, unless it were among the Hebrews. Even among them a worship of teraphim crept in (Gen. 31 : 19-35), together with other corruptions (Josh. 24 : 14); and the terrors of Sinai were needed to clear away polytheistic accretions. Elsewhere degeneration had free play, "a dark cloud stole over man's original consciousness of the divinity, and in consequence of his own guilt an estrangement of the creature from the one living God took place: man, as under the overpowering sway of sense and sensual lust, proportionally weakened, therefore, in his moral freedom, was unable any longer to conceive of the divinity as a pure,

Max Müller says: "Fetichism, so far from being, as we are told by almost every writer on the history of religion, a primitive form of faith, is, on the contrary, so far as facts enable us to judge, a decided corruption of an earlier and simpler religion. If we want to find the true springs of religious ideas, we must mount higher. Stocks and stones were not the first to reveal the Infinite before the wondering eyes of men." The true order is, "In the beginning, God."

Definition.—The word *fetich* is from the Portuguese *fetisso*, a charm.[1] A fetich is defined by Waitz as "an object of religious veneration, wherein the material thing and the spirit within it are regarded as one;" by Schultze, as "any object whatsoever viewed anthropopathically or as endowed with human characteristics;" by Aug. Comte, as "a body animated in the same manner as the human body, and, like that, governed by a will;" by Peterson, as "a vehicle through which a

spiritual, supernatural, and infinite Being distinct from the world and exalted above it."—RAWLINSON'S *Ancient Religions*, pp. 175, 176.

[1] The first writer to employ the word *fetich* was De Brosses in his work *Du culte des dieux Fétiches*, which appeared in 1760, anonymously and without the name of the place of publication. As to the origin of the word, he mentions " . . . . certain deities whom Europeans call fetiches, a word formed by our traders in Senegal out of the Portuguese term *fetisso—i. e.* enchanted, divine, oracular."

It is from the Latin root *fatum, fanum, fari.*

Winterbottom, in his *Account of the Native Africans in the Neighhood of Sierre Leone*, derives the word from the Portuguese *faticeira*, witch, or *faticaria*, witchcraft. The negroes borrowed not only this, but also another word, *gree-gree*, from the Portuguese. According to Bastian, the universal name in West Africa for a fetich is *enquisi*. Another name is *mokisso*, or *juju*, also *wong;* among several American tribes, *manitu.—Fetichism*, FRITZ SCHULTZE, Ph.D., p. 24.

supernatural power makes itself felt;" by Tyler, as "a spirit embodied in or attached to, or conveying influence through, certain material objects."

All these definitions seem too broad. *A fetich is any material thing, living or dead, which, while not regarded as divine, is reverenced on account of a supposed supernatural influence proceeding from it.*[1]

Central Thought.—The savage has a clear perception of the fact that he is not his own master; he is controlled by a power or powers not himself. The most important business of his life is to discover those forces that hold him in their mysterious grasp.

(1.) He finds presently, as he supposes, that his good or ill fortune is associated with some material thing, as a stone or a crooked stick; this henceforth becomes his fetich or potent charm. He invokes its kind offices or placates its wrath, believing that his luck is made or marred by it.

He may have more fetiches than one; the number, indeed, may be indefinitely increased by the addition of anything whatever that in any way affects his fortune. He may believe in the mysterious animation of all sensible things. The world is full of potent life.[2] He fears to tread upon a plant or hurt a noisome rep-

[1] Webster's definition of *fetich* is as follows: "A material thing, living or dead, which is made the object of brutish and superstitious worship, as among certain African tribes." The objection to this definition is that it confuses the respective ideas of fetich and idol.

[2] "The negro carries the belief in an animated nature to its uttermost limits, but as his mind is too rude to conceive of *one* universal animated nature, his imagination leads him to regard every trifling object around him as endowed with life."—WAITZ, *Anthropology of Savage Tribes;* SCHULTZE, p. 3.

tile, lest it avenge itself upon him. An Indian salutes a snake by the wayside, "Hail, friend! take this gift of tobacco-dust; it will comfort you on your long journey." He may crush the reptile, but not until he has first placated it.

(2.) *He may have Many Fetiches.*—The kinds of fetich are innumerable. Trees, rivers and mountains are invested with the mysterious power.[1] The Australians worship the rock-crystal.[2] The aborigines of North

[1] Jacob Grimm gives a very full account of the worship paid to water in the spring, the brook, the river and the sea, and describes the religious observances of the people as they "offered their prayers, lighted lamps or made their sacrifices on the banks of the stream or on the margin of the spring;" and these usages he traces from the remotest antiquity down into the Christian era.

"The pure, flowing, bubbling evanescent water; the flaming, glowing, dying fire; the air, perceptible, not to the eye, but to the ear and to the touch; the earth, which maintains all things and to which they all revert,—these have ever been regarded by man as sacred and worshipful, and through them he has been wont to bestow a solemn consecration upon the customs, the pursuits and the events of his life. Their action upon the entire universe being steady and constant, the untutored mind pays them worship for their own sake, without any reference to a deity residing in them."—SCHULTZE, p. 66.

[2] The Ephesians worshiped a block of black stone having a remote resemblance to a human figure, which they called Diana. It was said to have fallen down from heaven, the fact being, probably, that it was a meteoric stone.

Keary says in his *Outlines of Primitive Belief*, p. 83: "The great typical instance is that of the Artemisium at Ephesus. Some remains of this wonder of the world have in quite recent days been recovered and brought to this country, and we may judge from them (if we were in doubt before) that in outward decorative art it was inferior to no production of its own age.

"In the holy of holies still stood the time-honored image of the Ephesian Artemis, that hideous figure, only part human, part bestial or worse, and part still a block. This had been the central object of all

America attached a peculiar virtue to the wampum-belt. There are negroes in the interior of Africa who know no god greater than a cord which they wear knotted about the calves of their legs. (The Jesuit missionaries are said to have substituted for this a rope of twisted palm-leaf which had been blessed on Palm Sunday.)

A star,[1] a cloud,[2] the "lights of St. Elmo,"[3] an

from earliest to latest days. For the sake of this the three temples had risen, one upon the site of the other. A real Greek Artemis might adorn the sculptures of the walls, might be allowed presence as an ornament merely, but the popular worship was paid to the deformed figure within."

[1] "The vices which degrade the moral character of the Romans are mixed with a puerile superstition that disgraces their understanding. They listen with confidence to the predictions of haruspices, who pretend to read, in the entrails of victims, the signs of future greatness and prosperity; and there are many who do not presume either to bathe or to dine or to appear in public till they have diligently consulted, according to the rules of astrology, the situation of Mercury and the aspect of the moon."—GIBBON's *Rome*, chap. 31.

On the 12th of December, 1680, John Evelyn writes: "This evening, looking out of my chamber window toward the west, I saw a meteor of an obscure bright color, very much in shape like the blade of a sword, the rest of the sky being very serene and clear. What this may portend God only knows. But such another phenomenon I remember to have seen in 1640, about the trial of the great earl of Strafford preceding our bloody revolution."—KNIGHT's *England*, vol. iv. chap. 22.

[2] All men had a touch of superstition. Evelyn looks with wonder upon "a shining cloud in the air in shape resembling a sword." After the battle of Edgehill, "in the very place where the battle was stricken, have since and doth appear strange and portentous apparitions of two jarring and contrary armies." So records a tract in which the apparitions and prodigious noises of war and battles are certified by a justice of the peace, a preacher and other persons of quality.—KNIGHT's *England*, chap. 3.

[3] "Toward the latter part of October they had in the night a gust of

elephant's tooth, a lion's tail, a bunch of hair from a white man's beard, a splinter of a tree struck by lightning, a curious stone, a heap of mud, birds and beasts of every kind,[1] dwarfs and albinos—in short, anything material in heaven above or earth beneath—may come to be regarded as a fetich.

This is not Polytheism.—Observe that this invest-

---

heavy rain, accompanied by the severe thunder and lightning of the tropics. It lasted for four hours, and they considered themselves in much peril until they beheld several of those lambent flames playing about the tops of the masts and gliding along the rigging which have always been objects of superstitious fancies among sailors. Fernando Columbus makes remarks on them strongly characteristic of the age in which he lived: 'On the same Saturday, in the night, was seen St. Elmo, with seven lighted tapers at the topmast; there was much rain and great thunder; I mean to say that those lights were seen which mariners affirm to be the body of St. Elmo, on beholding which they chant litanies and orisons, holding it for certain that in the tempest in which he appears no one is in danger.' "—IRVING's *Columbus*, book vi. chap. I.

[1] In the East India islands, as in Africa also, the shark is a mighty fetich along the sea-coast. Eels are worshiped in Cusaie and in the Marian Isles. In the Carolines the god Mani is represented as a fish. "At Eap there are kept in a pond of fresh water two fishes of extreme age, but yet only a span in length, which always stand in a right line, head to head, without moving. If any man touch them and they are made to stand at right angles with each other, an earthquake is the result."

The reverence paid by American Indians to the rattlesnake was the means of saving the life of the Count von Zinzendorf (1742): "The Cayugas, with whom he was staying, were about to put him to death, supposing that his presence was productive of ill-luck to them. The count was seated one night on a bundle of sticks, writing by the light of a small fire. Unknown to him, a rattlesnake lay alongside him. When the Indians who were to take his life approached and observed the snake, they withdrew, firmly convinced that the stranger was of divine origin."—SCHULTZE.

iture of all things with a living power is not Polytheism. The fetich is not an idol; that is, a symbol or image of the true God. No doubt, as we shall presently see, there are savages who believe in the Invisible One, but their fetiches, as such, are in no wise associated with him. The moment an object stands for God it ceases to be a fetich in any proper sense, and becomes an idol. Schultze says, referring to animal veneration, " They worship the animal itself *in propriâ naturâ*, and without any reference to any divinity which it may represent." [1]

Nor is it Henotheism.—Observe, again, that this is not what Max Müller calls " Henotheism;" that is, the worship of anything as a god in and of itself, without respect to the Supreme One. The fetich, we repeat, is not in any wise whatsoever regarded or treated as a god.

Nor Pantheism.—Once more observe: it is not Pantheism. It does indeed fill the earth with mysterious powers, but there is no blending or expanding of all into one. The savage cannot generalize in that way. He merely personifies, like a child playing with a doll.[2] His fetich is a living thing, with an influence

[1] " It is not as if the savage in his anthropopathic apprehension represented to himself a self-existent superior power, a self-existent soul which merely assumed for a time the external shape of the fetich No: the stone remains a stone, the river a river."—SCHULTZE, p. 21.

[2] " The little girl who in perfect seriousness regards her doll as a playmate, who strips and clothes it, feeds and chastises it, puts it to bed and hushes it to sleep, calls it by a personal name, etc., never imagines that all her care is expended on a lifeless thing; she does not make any such reflections as these: 'This is all merely an illusion that I indulge on purpose—a play that I engage in, but with the distinct understanding

all its own to make or mar his fortune; it is, in other words, a mascot taking the place of a god. It is not divine; it can scarcely be called supernatural. It is a material object supposed to be endowed with supernatural gifts. Its power is an unknown quantity which experience alone can estimate.

A Kaffir broke a piece off the anchor of a stranded vessel and soon after died. The Kaffirs thenceforth regarded that anchor as possessed of the mysterious influence, and saluted it as they passed by with a view to propitiating it.

If a fetich fails to stand the test of experience, it is scolded, flogged, imprisoned, dragged in the mire or cast into the sea.[1] It is not uncommon, after an epidemic, for an entire tribe to make a bonfire of their fetiches. These are obviously, therefore, not regarded as divine in any important sense, although they may be said to be esteemed by the savages as tentative powers to be cast aside when their insufficiency is shown, as, *e.g.*, their not being able to ward off a plague. When Xerxes ordered three hundred lashes to be administered to the Hellespont because it had broken up his bridge of boats, he manifestly had no flattering

that it is only play.' She has no thought that the doll is a lifeless thing; for her it is possessed of a human life."—SCHULTZE, p. 21.

[1] "In front of the American's house (in Shemba-Shemba, West Africa) there was a crowd of people assembled, in the midst of whom a fetich-priest was running up and down with loud cries, jerking hither and thither a wooden puppet decked with tatters of every color, and beating it with a switch on the face and shoulders. I learned that a knife had been stolen from one of the negroes, and he had applied for its recovery to this priest, who was the owner of a fetich in high repute as a detective of thieves."—SCHULTZE, p. 27.

opinion of its power; he did not regard the Hellespont as either a god or the symbol of a god; it was a fetich overpowered by the winds, and therefore to be treated with angry contempt.

The fetich is understood to be more or less familiar with the future. It is consulted on the chase and in time of war. In Lapland a ring is used for divination upon the head of a magical drum. The North American Indians foretell coming events by taking the direction of smoke from the wigwam of the great medicine-man.

Fortune-telling is a rudimental kind of Fetichism. The prospector who in these days in our mining districts wanders over the hills with a hazel switch poised in his hand searching for ore is a fetichist. Emerson wrote,

"Things are in the saddle,
And ride mankind."

This is evidently true of such things as horseshoes, hazel twigs and crooked sixpences.

The savage ascribes to his fetich the power of defending him from evil. He has one fetich against the thunder, another against lions, another against diseases, another to extract thorns from his feet. Potsherds are scattered around burying-places to keep off evil spirits, and the camp is surrounded with mussel-shells to cut the devil's feet. A beaver-skin or an earthen pot on a pole in the midst of the encampment is an effective "totem" to avert evil. Among certain tribes on the western coast of Africa it is the custom for a son to preserve the skull of his father as a great fetich. It is kept in a secret place where no one but himself is ever allowed to see it. He sets food and offers sacrifices before it. This attention secures him victory over all his foes.[1]

Here we have the most abject form of spiritual bondage. It is the harpy Superstition wielding a whip of scorpions. The infant at its birth is placed under the tutelage of a fetich. A vow of faithful service is made in its behalf by the fond parents and tattooed in hieroglyphics upon the tender flesh. The fetich thus chosen is called the great one, and is thenceforth the controlling genius of the life of this immortal being. He is accustomed from his earliest childhood to revere the terms of this parental covenant. He expects his fetich to preserve him from danger and misfortune, in return for which he renders an unquestioning and unfaltering service. Other fetiches he may have, but this is always the supreme one. An Indian lad upon the verge of manhood takes a new fetich. He retires to a lonely

[1] Rev. A. W. Marling, of the Gaboon mission, speaks as follows of a revolting form of worship prevailing among the Fang tribe of Western Africa: "It is called in their language *beatee*. It is practiced by the men only; the women are not allowed to know anything about it. When a man has been dead and buried for some time the skull is taken from the grave, given to his eldest son, who takes it to his own house and places it in some secret corner. Henceforth no one except himself, not even his wife, is allowed to see it. The spirit of his father is now supposed to have a special care for the son. If the latter be setting out on a journey, he has a fowl or a goat killed and food prepared. This he himself takes and deposits in private before the skull. The spirit is supposed to partake of the refreshment and to be propitiated toward the son, and to grant him protection in his journey and success in his undertaking, whatever it may be."—*Foreign Missionary*, June, 1885, pp. 21, 22.

place in the forest and dreams his life-dream, wherein his destiny is revealed to him. On awaking he tracks an animal to its lair and kills it, and its skin, worn thenceforth upon his person, is regarded as a magical protector. Should he lose it he receives an ignominious title, "The man without medicine." The skin serves him as his Providence. It stands him in the place of a god.

(3.) *It is a System.*—This rude form of religion—if religion it may be called—is found sometimes possessing the characteristics of a system. It has a creed and a *cultus*. It has an order of ministers, called gangas, magians, feticeros or medicine-men, etc., whose duties are to reveal the future, practice necromancy and juggling tricks, minister at the altar and guard the mysteries from profane eyes. They usually speak a language of their own, a dialect quite unintelligible to lay folk. They have temples also. One of these in Africa is thus described by Bastian: "The sacred place was quadrangular, constructed of straw matting, the entire front being of wooden framework with three arched doorways. Each of the two side-doorways was surmounted by a pyramid, while over the middle one rose a cupola, and the doorposts were adorned with figures in blue and green. Within was the fetich, a simple mound of earth, on which stood three forked sticks painted red and white in alternate stripes."

Such is Fetichism, the religion of the charm, the cabal, the talisman, the "mascot."

(4.) *It is Better than Materialism.*—There is this only to be said in its favor: it betrays an instinctive faith in the unseen. May we venture with Schleiermacher to call this the "God-consciousness"? No man created in the divine image ever yet sank so low in barbarism as to be a thorough materialist. The naked cannibal believes in the reality of invisible things. His Fetichism, if not worship, is a step taken through the darkness toward God.[1]

The Hindus have this proverb:

> "The wall said to the nail, 'What have I done
> That through me thy sharp tooth thou thus dost run?'
> The nail replied, 'Poor fool! what do I know?
> Ask him who beats my head with many a blow.'"

I say, therefore, that though he does obeisance to nothing better than a coil of dried intestines hung on the ridge-pole of his tent, the fetich-worshiper is nearer heaven than the fool (Ps. 14 : 1) whose university culture has emboldened him to say, "There is no God." The fetichist has something that serves him as a rule of faith and practice, though it be merely, as Bastian calls it, "a system of the universe in smallest twelvemo."[2] Better a philosophy of gorgons, hydras and

[1] "Primitive man has a belief in the great *thing*—the tree, river, mountain, or what not. This belief is an affection of the mind, very different from the simple sense that the thing is physically broad and high. Along with the physical sensation goes a subtler inward feeling, a sense not easily measurable, as physical sensations are, but still discoverable. We know it to be there by the answer which the material sensation has called out of man's heart, and which makes itself audibly known in his worship."—KEARY'S *Outlines of Primitive Belief*, p. 17.

[2] "The vow he has undertaken is for him the sum-total of religion. So long as things go pleasantly for him he is happy and contented under the guardianship of his mokisso; he feels strong in the assurance of

chimeras dire than what Carlyle calls a "religion of frog-spawn," a "philosophy of dirt." The fetichist believes in an overruling spiritualism, in presences more or less powerful, here and there and everywhere. Moreover, he believes in his own helplessness. His destiny is in the grip of these unseen and unknown presences. He must somehow keep on the right side of them or disaster will overtake him. He has little or no conception of sin or of virtue, as such. His chief end is to please himself, and all his aspirations are briefly comprehended in *good-luck*.[1] Give him success in the chase, victory in battle, rings and bracelets,

---

divine approval; ascribes to the divine complacency his days of sunshine; indeed, his judgment is strictly controlled by his wishes and desires. But if, unintentionally or involuntarily, he breaks his vow, the whole course of providence in his regard is at once and irrevocably altered. Then misfortune overtakes him; he is quickly overwhelmed with calamities, and his only escape lies through death and oblivion; for him there is no hope, no path leading to reconciliation and deliverance. The luckless wretch need not, in Africa at least, go far in search of death. The fiends who surround him in the shape of fellow-men quickly trample him to death, and with the last breath of the fetich-worshiper expires a system of the universe in smallest twelvemo."— BASTIAN, SCHULTZE, p. 39.

[1] "Certain Bushmen, being asked by a European what they meant by good and what by bad, could not give any reply, but they held fratricide to be perfectly harmless.

"The Kamtchatdales hold that an act is sinful which is unlucky; for instance, to visit hot springs; to brush snow off the shoes out of doors; to seize a red-hot coal otherwise than with the fingers when you would light your pipe; to bring home the first fox you have taken; to tread in the tracks of a bear, etc.

"The Orangoo negroes hold it sinful to spit on the earth, while the natives of Labrador regard nothing as sinful save only the murder of an innocent man."—SCHULTZE, p. 11.

and plenty of wives, and what more could a man want here below?[1]

(5.) *Providence* vs. *the Fetich.*—We have been long enough in this miasmatic valley; let us climb up the mountains and through the clear air of our Christian faith look away to the ineffable Throne. What infinite stretches of crag and chasm lie between the fetich and God!

On the clear heights of belief there is no chance. We are in the domain of providence:

> "All is of God! If he but raise his hand
> The mists collect, the rain falls thick and loud,
> Till, with a smile of light on sea and land,
> Lo! he looks back from the departing cloud."

To believe thoroughly in Providence is to be a very child of God. But, alas! there is something of fetich-worship in every one of us.[2] We believe in charms

---

[1] "In all negro languages the word *belly* is one of great import. Politeness requires that one inquire if all is well with his neighbor's belly. The South Sea Islanders call thoughts *words in the belly*. The stomach of one who dies is kept as a relic, and the Kroo negroes hold that the stomach ascends into heaven after death."—SCHULTZE, p. 12.

[2] "Why is it that sailors cling to port on a Friday and loose their ships and weigh anchor on Sunday? Why did the ancients build a temple to Fortune, consult oracles and venerate white stones rather than black stones? Why did our grandmothers dislike the assemblage of nine rooks, turn back when they met a dog crossing their paths and show an antipathy to black cats? Why does a Fijian, to propitiate his ugly wooden god, offer him a *bakolo*, the dead body of his brother? Why was it improper to eat beans and the seeds of the lupine? What magic makes the third time never like the rest? At the wicked little German towns where small grand-dukes improve their revenues by licensing gaming-tables you will find old gamblers begging the youngest in the company, often an English boy who has come to look about him,

and amulets, in magic numbers and unlucky days. Our grandmothers were afraid to walk over the sweepings of their rooms. There are those who cover up their looking-glasses in presence of the shrouded dead. Farmers are afraid to disturb the swallows that chatter under the eaves of their barns, lest so doing they blast the growing harvest. The sailor has a thousand superstitious fancies.

> "God save thee, ancient mariner,
> From the fiends that plague thee thus!
> Why look'st thou so?"—"With my cross-bow
> I shot the albatross!"

In the van of Peter the Hermit's army of crusaders was carried a sacred goose, on the life or death of which was thought to depend the issue of the campaign for the conquest of the holy sepulchre.[1]

In witchcraft we find a stupendous relic of Fetichism, the fires of which are scarcely yet extinguished. The red string which a lad ties around his fingers to cure warts is a fetich.[2] The Holy Grail was a fetich; so are

to take for them the first throw of the dice. Why so? Why is a fresh hand more likely to throw the three sixes than an old one?"—*The Gentle Life.*

[1] "Above eighty thousand ranged themselves under the banner of Peter the Hermit, who walked at their head with a rope about his waist and sandals on his feet. Peter's lieutenant was Walter the Pennyless, and in the van of his troops were carried a *sacred goose and a goat*, which (monstrous to believe!) were said to be filled with the Holy Ghost. This immense and disorderly multitude began their march toward the East in the year 1095."—TYTLER'S *History,* book vi. ch 9.

[2] "A pulled tooth is to be driven into a young tree and covered with the bark. If the tree be cut down the ache comes back. If you break a twig off a willow and drive it into the aching tooth until the blood

bones of the saints, splinters of the true cross and similar relics, as well as all charms, talismans, rosaries and images blessed by priests.[1] We are thus continually tempted to push aside Providence and make way for strange influences.[2]

> "And still from Him we turn away,
>   And fill our hearts with worthless things;
> The fires of avarice melt the clay,
> And forth *the fetich* springs!
> Ambition's flame and passion's heat
> By wondrous alchemy transmute
> Earth's dross, to raise some gilded brute
> To fill Jehovah's seat."

The brazen serpent, cherished for its sacred associations, came to be regarded at length as a fetich, and was

comes, and then restore the twig to its place, drawing the bark over it, the toothache goes away."—SCHULTZE, p. 61.

[1] One of the most familiar fetiches of the Roman Catholic Church is the *scapular*. It is related that the Virgin Mary, appearing to St. Simon Stock, presented him with a "scapular," or brown woolen jacket, at the same time informing him that it would protect the wearer from all possible danger of the flames of hell. The scapular received the formal sanction of Pope Clement X. It was furthermore announced by Pope John XXII. in his bull 'Sabbathine' that any person dying with the scapular upon his person would remain in purgatory only until the Saturday following his death. The Carmelite monks were granted a monopoly of the trade in scapulars, and they reaped immense profits from it.

[2] "In 1608, John Smith was preserved by the Indians who had butchered his companions. He exhibited a pocket compass and showed how it always pointed to one quarter. He requested that a letter should be conveyed to Jamestown, and when it was known that he could so endue a piece of paper with intelligence as to speak to his distant companions, he was beheld with superstitious awe."—KNIGHT's *England*, vol. iii. ch. 22, p. 344.

destroyed; "'Nehushtan!' cried Hezekiah; that is to say, '.It is nothing but brass.'" The bread of the sacramental feast when invested with supernatural virtues becomes a fetich; so does the Bible when printer's ink and paper claim the reverence due to the spirit of the Word. It is much to be feared that prayer itself, when used as a mere herb or balsam for healing disease and in return for a stipulated fee, is a fetich and nothing else. The Jews made a great fetich of Mount Zion, and the Samaritans of Gerizim, and the discourse of Jesus was aimed at both when he said, "Believe me, the hour cometh, when ye shall neither in this mountain, nor yet at Jerusalem, worship the Father. . . . God is a Spirit; and they that worship him must worship him in spirit and in truth."

The man who believes in charms and talismans, in magic or divination or witchcraft, in sacred relics or images, or the consecrated wafer, is a spiritual kinsman of him who does obeisance to formless stocks and stones.

"*What shall I Do to be Saved?*"—The fetich-worshiper is a believer in immortality, but his sensual mind is so absorbed in the gratification of present needs that he thinks little or nothing of the everlasting future. To him salvation is a word in an unknown tongue. In his rude philosophy there is nothing to bridge the chasm between the sinful soul and the offended Lawgiver.[1] The man who rejects Providence

---

[1] "A draught of *fetich-water* can discover in the heart the proofs whether of guilt or of innocence, and it is therefore but natural that it should have also power to banish *moral ills*. During the festival of the

can have no Saviour, for our Christ is simply the best of providences, the Special One.

Two practical thoughts by way of application:

I. Let us honor Providence. We live beneath the glowing light of the Sun of Righteousness. We know that God liveth and ruleth over all. Let us take heed, therefore, and beware of investing anything whatsoever, or any person whomsoever, with wisdom or power that belongs to God alone. His is the eye that never sleeps beneath the wing of night. Good-fortune is his smile, and " our midnight is his smile withdrawn."

II. The abject servitude and helplessness of the millions who are not only without God, but without symbols of him, appeal as with articulate voices to all that is humane within us. We pity the idolaters, such as worship graven images of Deity, but there are vast multitudes still lower down who are absolutely without so much as an image of God. Ours is the grave responsibility—shall we not rather say the glorious privilege?—of sending the good news of life and immortality to those lying in darkness and the shadow of death. A great missionary once wrote: " Whosoever shall call upon the name of the Lord shall be saved. How, then, shall they call on Him in whom

first-fruits the men of the Creek tribe of American Indians used to take, after a prolonged fast, the war-medicine, being strong emetics and drastic agents, while the women bathed and washed themselves. All offences, with the exception of murder, were thus blotted out. It is beyond question that the idea of purification from sin attached to these ceremonies, but especially to the bath and the drinking of the black draught, as it was called, an infusion of dried cassine-leaves."— SCHULTZE, p. 34.

they have not believed? and how shall they believe in Him of whom they have not heard? and how shall they hear without a preacher? And how shall they preach, except they be sent? as it is written, How beautiful are the feet of them that preach the gospel of peace, and bring glad tidings of good things!"

God help us to know our opportunity and to embrace it! From the wretched abodes of superstition, darkened by the overhanging shadow of death, comes a cry for help. He that hath ears to hear, let him hear!

II.
THE RELIGION OF ANCIENT EGYPT.

I. *The Sacred Books:*
   Forty-five in number.
   "Book of the Dead."
II. *Theology:*
   (1) God.
       Ammon-Ra and the Divine Dynasties.
       Zoölatry.
   (2) Immortality.
       The *ka.*
III. *Morals:*
   Maat.
   The Religion of Sadness.
CENTRAL THOUGHT: Life.
"*What shall I do to be saved?*"   Observe the *Maat.*

II. THE RELIGION OF ANCIENT EGYPT.

THE river Nile, so long hiding its source among the mountains in the interior of the Dark Continent, flows northward three thousand miles and empties through seven divergent mouths into the Mediterranean Sea. It is the great life-sustaining artery of Egypt. In September, at the rising of the dog-star, its waters begin to swell, covering the land with a gradual inundation, until as the nilometer marks ten, twelve or fourteen cubits the hearts of the people are gladdened with the sure hope of a plentiful harvest. For Egypt is merely a narrow strip of black loam lying for hundreds of miles on either side of the river.

"The pulse of Egypt beats but once a year."

A difference of six cubits in the annual overflow determines whether or not the lean kine of famine shall devour the fat. If the nilometer mark twelve cubits, after the subsidence of the waters in November the valley begins to assume the appearance of a garden, and is soon "covered with verdant crops, enameled with flowers and interspersed with groves of luxuriant palms."

The Nile is the most historical of rivers. On its banks Joseph built his granaries and watched the slow-plying rafts that floated downward laden with corn. In the rushes along its edge was hidden away the child who, rescued by a king's daughter, was presently to turn these waters into blood at the behest of an offended God. On its still surface rocked the gilded barge of Cleopatra with its silken sails, and here, centuries afterward, Napoleon dreamed his vain dreams of universal empire.

A Land of Ruins.—But the history-making days of Egypt are past. It is now a land of solitude and decay. Thebes, Karnak, Dendara, Memphis—what visions of golden splendor their names suggest! To-day they are only sand-swept ruins. Yet the world has no such ruins elsewhere—temples carved out of the solid rock, reached by long avenues of sphinxes; immense columns and porticos; obelisks towering high in the air and covered with hieroglyphics depicting the mighty deeds of sovereigns who died before Abraham! What think you of an obelisk weighing three hundred tons? or of a monolithic temple weighing not less than five thousand tons, which must have been transported from the mountain-quarries down the entire length of the Nile to its delta?

Egypt has been rightly named "the wonder-land." Her pyramids, standing near the ancient site of Memphis, are the oldest as well as the most stupendous of earth's monuments. Imagine, if you can, what scenes have transpired within their shadow. When the patriarch Jacob went down to visit Thebes he must have looked upon these very pyramids with wondering eyes, for they were then already two thousand years old.

There they stand, tombs of history, with their blank, immobile faces looking out upon the endless wastes of Sahara, as if to say: "Behold, O eyes of the living, the magnificence of past days! Boast not of your achievements, for the greatest of all is dead and buried greatness!"[1] In Dr. Robinson's story of the pyramids he confesses to a momentary disappointment when the Arab guides pointed them out in the distance: "But as we approached them, and looked upward along their mountain-sides to the summit, their huge masses seemed to swell into immensity and the idea of their vastness was absolutely overpowering. Vain pride of human pomp and power! The monuments remain unto this day the wonder of all time, but their builders, their history and their very names have been swept away in the dark tide of oblivion."

The Rosetta Stone and its Revelations.—The multitudinous ruins of Egypt are covered over with inscriptions, detailing the rise and fall of dynasties and the mighty deeds of the Pharaohs. But anything like an exact interpretation of these was quite impossible until the beginning of the present century. In 1799, while a French officer, Champollion, was erecting works at a place called Rosetta, on the Nile, a slab of black basalt was dug up whereon was inscribed in parallel columns of Greek and hieroglyphics a decree conferring divine honors on Ptolemy V., who reigned in the second century B. C. The Greek, which was easy of translation, afforded a means of interpreting the hieroglyphics. Thus the key was found by which the treasure-house

[1] RENOUF, *Religion of Ancient Egypt.*

of ancient Egypt, locked for thousands of years, has at length been opened to the light. Its pillars and obelisks no longer speak to us in an unknown tongue.

And what are their revelations? As to the civilization of Egypt, they portray her advancing torch in hand when as yet the nations universally were sitting in darkness and the shadow of death. We are coming to think of Egypt as the cradle of civilization. The more we study her monuments, the less can we glorify the so-called progressive spirit of modern times. Here is "the fountain from which the Assyrian, the Greek and the Hebrew drank." "It is certain," says Renouf, "that at least three thousand years before Christ there was in Egypt a powerful and elaborately organized monarchy, enjoying a material civilization in many respects not inferior to that of Europe in the last century." It was not without reason that the Egyptian priests were wont to say sneeringly to the philosophers of Athens, "You Greeks are mere children; you know nothing of the past." The beginnings of the culture and enlightenment of Egypt, stretching back beyond all annals and traditions, are lost like the sources of her great river—in darkness. Here "was nursed and educated that intellect which, receiving a divine wisdom from on high, gave birth to the social and national institutions which have unfolded out of their bosom the Christian Church." It is evident from her monuments that Egypt in the very dawn of her historic era was far advanced in science, familiar with very many conveniences which we assign to the inventive genius of modern days, and was not to be despised in respect to her literature. Her artisans were acquainted with hydraulic engineering. Rameses II. opened a watercourse between Bubastes and the Red Sea at an expense of one hundred and twenty thousand lives and treasure incalculable, which gave to the French engineer Lesseps the suggestion of the Suez Canal. As to her advancement in art, we may take the testimony of Rawlinson, who says, among other eulogistic words: "The life-sized statue of Phra-Kephren, discovered in the temple of the Great Pyramid, in its majestic simplicity of character will bear comparison with that of Watt by Chantrey in Westminster Abbey."

It is fortunate for the gratification of our curiosity that the Egyptians were fond of writing. They covered the walls of their homes, tombs and temples with inscriptions which the dry air and drifting sands together have kept legible to this day. In the marshy grounds along the borders of the Nile grew the papyrus (whence our word *paper*), out of which was manufactured a cheap parchment, which, with the reed stylus, made writing a common art. Rolls of papyrus are unwound among the linen bands of mummies whereon the red and black characters are as plain as when, stained with tears, they were put out of sight long centuries ago with the beloved dead. From these we discover that the literature of ancient Egypt embraced, in a wonderful degree, the arts, sciences and philosophies of later ages. It is difficult to realize that the golden period of Egyptian letters was in the reign of the Pharaoh of the Exodus, fifteen centuries

B. C. His palace was in hundred-gated Thebes, where men of genius ever found liberal patronage. There was a great library there over whose door was written "Dispensary of the Soul." The court-librarian, or master of the scrolls, was Kagabu the elegant, illustrious as a novelist and poet.[1] There is extant an epic poem by Pentaour, who may have been the laureate of that golden age, which celebrates the prowess of Rameses the Great in war. We have also a novel called the *Story of Two Brothers*, which is probably the oldest work of fiction in the world, having been written by the minstrel Enna "for the amusement of the crown-prince, who afterward perished with his host in the Red Sea." There are many other complete tales and poems, as well as historical documents, biographies and annals, copied from the hieroglyphics on temple walls or from papyrus preserved in mummy crypts.

How strange to read these productions—the "Romance of Setna," the "Garden of Flowers," the "Tale of the Doomed Prince "—knowing as we do that they represent the tears and laughter of forty centuries ago! Here are some verses taken from a monumental tablet found among the ruins of Thebes, and purporting to have been addressed by the god Amen or Ammon to King Thotmes III.:

"I am come! To thee have I given to strike down Syrian princes;
Under thy feet they lie throughout the breadth of their country.
Like to the Lord of light I made them see thy glory,
Blinding their eyes with light, the earthly image of Amen.

[1] QUACKENBOS'S *Oriental Literature.*

"I am come! To thee have I given to strike down Asian people;
Captive now thou hast led the proud Assyrian chieftains.
Decked in royal robes, I made them see thy glory,
All in glittering arms and fighting aloft in thy war-car.

"I am come! To thee have I given to strike down Libyan archers;
All the isles of the Greeks submit to the force of thy spirit.
Like a lion in prey I made them see thy glory,
Couched by the dead he has slain down in the rocky valley.

"I am come! To thee have I given to strike down the ends of the ocean;
In the grasp of thy hand is the circling zone of waters.
Like the soaring eagle I made them see thy glory,
Whose far-seeing eye there is none can hope to escape from."[1]

In this, a fair illustration of inscriptions found in the sepulchres of kings, we detect a true poetic stateliness. It will be observed that nearly all the literature of Egypt is religious in its tone. The people are referred to by Herodotus as "surpassing all others in the reverence they paid the gods." So Professor Maury remarks: "Everything among them took the stamp of religion. Their writing was so full of sacred symbols that it could scarcely be put to any purely secular use."

I. *The Sacred Books.*—The sacred or hermetic books of Egypt, as we are informed by Clement of Alexandria, were forty-five in number. Though denominated sacred, they were in great part taken up with disquisitions on philosophy and the sciences. One only of these books is still extant. It is a collection of prayers and magic rites used in the burial service, its title being "Book of the Dead," literally, "Book of the *peri em*

[1] QUACKENBOS, *Oriental Literature.*

hru;" that is, of the "coming forth by day." It is a mythological work in which the continuous theme is the conflict between darkness and light. This was probably the most venerated of the sacred books, for which reason it was often transcribed on papyrus to be wrapped about the embalmed bodies of illustrious or holy men. Here is an extract from the book, given simply by way of illustration. (The soul is supposed to have journeyed through the dark valley which intervenes between time and eternity, fighting its way through hosts of opposing dragons and monsters of evil. It then appears for trial in the dreaded judgment-hall of Osiris, where the heart is placed in an immense balance and weighed against the feather of truth. It is at the moment of its appearance in the judgment-hall that the soul speaks): "O ye lords of truth, let me utter truth. I have privily done evil against no man. I have not been idle, given to intoxication nor unchaste. I have not exacted of the laborer more than his daily task. I have caused none to hunger, made none to weep. I have murdered none, defrauded none. I have not eaten the sacred bread of the temple. I have not cheated in weights or measures. I have not slandered. I have not netted the sacred birds. I have offered to the gods the sacrifices that were their due. I have given food to the hungry, drink to the thirsty and clothes to the naked. I am pure! I am pure!" (Happy would we be if at the judgment-bar, with honest hearts, we might present that plea, "I am pure!" But, alas! in the light of our gospel who can presume?)

There are fragments of another sacred book called *Shait en Sensen,* or "Breaths of Life," which consisted of thoughts on immortality. Its precepts were wrapped around the mummies of priests. Here is a quotation:

> "Hail to thee, departed one!
> Thine individuality is for ever;
> Thy body is indestructible;
> Thy mummy doth germinate.
> Thou art not exiled from heaven, neither from earth;
> Thou dost breathe for ever.
> Thy flesh is upon thee
> As on thine earthly form.
> Thou dost eat and drink with thy lips;
> Thou receivest bread with the souls of the gods;
> Thy soul doth breathe for ever and ever."

Let us inquire now as to *the distinguishing marks* of the religion of Egypt. What was its theology? What were its forms of worship? What light, if any, did it throw upon the problems of the future world? What were its effects on personal character and the conduct of every-day life? For by such crucial tests the value of all religions must be known.

II., *Theology.—What did it Declare concerning God?* On this subject its teaching is twofold. It is important that we should understand this at the beginning: we are dealing with a *religio bifrons.* One face it turns toward the priesthood, and another toward the people. This is scarcely to be wondered at when we remember the vast gulf of separation which lay between the educated or priestly class and the servile, ignorant, unambitious masses. The former were permitted to know and speculate concerning religious things; the latter were told that God was mystery, and that must content them.

To the priestly mind God was, pre-eminently, the source and author of life or power. The general name for deity was *nutar*, which, as Renouf argues, means power, that being also the meaning of the Hebrew *el*. "The extremely common Egyptian expression *nutar nutra* exactly corresponds in sense to the Hebrew *El Shaddai*, the very title by which God tells Moses that he was known to the patriarchs: 'And God spake unto Moses, and said unto him, I am Jahve (or Jehovah), and I appeared unto Abraham, unto Isaac, and unto Jacob by the name of *El Shaddai*, but by my name Jahve was I not known to them.' There can be no doubt who that Power is which, in our translations, we do not hesitate to call God. It is unquestionably the true and only God, who 'is not far from any one of us, for in him we live and move and have our being,' whose 'eternal power and godhead' and government of the world were made known through 'that Light which enlighteneth every man that cometh into the world.'"

In searching for an apt symbol it was inevitable that the Egyptians should fix upon the sun, which is the fountain of universal life and power. On many of the monuments the deity is thus represented. The symbol was no doubt oftentimes allowed to obscure the idea of the thing symbolized, yet we cannot doubt that in the philosophy of the Egyptian priests—that arcanum of mysteries whose doors were open only to the stoled and mitred few—back of all names and symbols was the thought of *one supreme and only God*. We find it on the tomb of Rameses, where the triumphant king is represented as declaring, "Ammon-Ra hath been at my right and left hand in battle. He hath brought the universe to my feet." So also in the name *Nuk-pu-Nuk*, found written on embalming-cloths, wherein is a wonderful likeness to the meaning of the name Jehovah, "I am that I am." And not less in the following hymn, ascribed to the time of the earliest of the Pharaohs:

" Glory to thee, who hast begotten all that is;
　Who hast created man;
　Who hast made the gods and all creatures of the field;
　Who makest man to live;
　Who hast no being second to thyself!
　Lord of generation! thou givest to the living breath;
　Thou makest the world to move in its seasons;
　Thou orderest the course of the great river whose ways are secret;
　Thou art the Light of the world!"

Ammon-Ra.—Two names were given interchangeably to the Supreme One—Ra and Ammon: sometimes they are combined into a single name, *Amn-Ra*. The meaning of the word Ammon is *concealment*. This is the face which God turned toward the people. Ra means the sun; that is, God as the author of life. He is represented as a hawk-headed man, his forehead encircled with the solar disk. There are countless inferior deities also, bearing to Ra the same relation as the stars to the sun, borrowing all their splendor from him.[1]

[1] " Ra is not only the name of the sun-god; it is the usual word for

Minor Gods.—We are informed by Herodotus that these subordinate gods were divided into various ranks or orders. Manetho speaks of them as divine dynasties. They were all originally designed to represent God in different phases as the Creator of life. Here is the central thought of the pantheon—*life;* and this must be our clue to the mysteries of the religion of Egypt.

We are accustomed to say of God that he is a Being "without body, parts or passions." To the Egyptian mind this was not necessary to the conception of him. Their gods had bodies; they suffered from hunger, thirst, disease and old age. "They perspired, their limbs quaked, their head ached, their teeth chattered, their eyes wept, their nose bled. They were stung by reptiles and burnt by fire. They howled with pain and grief." And they were forced by threats and imprecations to grant the prayers of men.

Osiris.—One of these gods, Osiris, deserves a passing

sun. In other mythologies the sun-god is borne in a chariot or on horseback; in Egypt his course across the sky is made in a boat. The sky (Nu) is accordingly conceived as an expanse of water, of which the Nile is the earthly representative. Ra is said to proceed from 'Nu, the father of the gods.' His adversary is Apap, who is represented as a serpent pierced with the weapons of the god. The conflict is not between good and evil, but the purely physical one between light and darkness. Shu and Tefnut are the children of Ra; Shu is air, and Tefnut is some form of moisture, probably dew.

"Whatever may be the case in other mythologies, I look upon the sunrise and sunset, on the daily returns of day and night, on the battle between light and darkness, on the whole solar drama in all its details, that is acted every day, every month, every year, in heaven and in earth, as the principal subject of Egyptian mythology."—RENOUF'S *Religion of Ancient Egypt*, p. 113.

mention.[1] He is represented as a mummied figure with a crocodile's head, wearing on either side an ostrich-feather, which is the symbol of truth, and holding in his hands a shepherd's crook and a flail. The tradition is that Osiris came down from heaven as an incarnation of God and reigned over Egypt, conferring many incalculable benefits upon her people. But he was murdered by his enemy, Typhon, who cut his body in pieces and threw it into the Nile. His faithful wife Isis with many tears sought these fragments,

[1] "The parents of Osiris are Seb and Nut, and about these there can be no mistake. Seb is the earth, and Nut is heaven. Seb is identified with the earth in the older texts, and in the later ones 'the back of Seb' is a familiar term for the earth. Seb is also the Egyptian name for a certain species of goose, and in accordance with the *homonymous* tendency of the mythological period of all nations the god and the bird were identified; Seb was called 'the great cackler,' and there are traces of the myth of a 'mundane egg' which he 'divided' or hatched. Nut is the name of a female goddess frequently used synonymously with the other names of the sky, and she is as frequently pictured with her arms and legs extended over the earth, with the stars spread over her body. The marriage of heaven and earth is extremely common in mythologies: what is peculiar to the Egyptian myth is that earth is not represented as the mother of all things, but the father, and heaven is here the mother. From the union of Seb and Nut sprang the mild Osiris, the sun, the Isis, the dawn, wedded before they were born, and the fruit of their marriage was Horus, the sun in his full strength. Set the destroyer is also the son of Seb and Nut, but his triumph is in the west; he is darkness, and his spouse Nephthys, a deity of mixed character, is the sunset. There are traces of a legend according to which Osiris mistook Nephthys for his wife Isis. Nephthys, who loved him, encouraged the illusion, and from their embrace Anubis was born. Anubis, like his mother, is a deity of a mixed character, partly belonging to the diurnal, partly to the nocturnal, powers. It is said of him that 'he swallowed his father Osiris.' I believe that he represents the firelight or dusk immediately following the disappearance of the sun."—*The Religion of Ancient Egypt*, p. 115.

and when they were placed together, lo! Osiris was alive again; and he liveth for evermore, enthroned in the judgment-hall of the invisible world. This has been justly pronounced "a wonderful forefeeling of the gospel narrative"—an outline, though dim, of the incarnation, life, suffering, vicarious death, resurrection and exaltation of Jesus the Christ.

Mystery.—But this truth, in common with all the spiritual truths that centred in the pantheon of Egypt, was only for the initiated: "This is the hidden mystery. Tell it to no one; let it be seen by no eye, heard by no ear. Only thou and thy teacher shall possess the knowledge of it." Before this holy of holies hung a veil which priests only might draw aside, and which never, like the curtain of Zion's holy place, was torn in twain. "What is God?" the people asked. And the keepers of the oracles answered, "Mystery."—"And what is truth?"—"Mystery."—"And what lies beyond the threshold of the eternal world?"—"Mystery. It is not given unto you to know. Bow down with closed lips before your appointed gods." Says James Freeman Clarke: "The priesthood enveloped in mystery every truth, just as they swathed the mummies fold above fold in preparing them for the tomb." Not always can even we, on whom the light with its healing beams has arisen, solve the problems of the spiritual world;

> "No victory comes of all our strife;
> From all we grasp the meaning slips;
> The Sphinx sits at the gate of life
> With the old question on her awful lips;"

but to the Egyptians the very foundations of truth were shrouded in darkness. The eyes of the people, dying in their sins, were so holden that they saw not the God who stood beside them with the balm of Gilead in his hands. "I do not know," says a recent writer,[1] "whether it has ever struck you, as you look into the faces of the Egyptian images at the museum, that they are full of wonder and awe—as children amazed at something that holds them in its spells, rather than as men of intellect and resolution who see the mystery, but are minded to explore it or die." The same wondering and far-off look is seen even upon the face of the immovable Sphinx and in the grim features of the rams that line the avenues of the temples. The pyramids point up to heaven as if to say, "We are searching for it," and the labyrinths wind in and out among crypts and silent vaults as if to say, "Thou shalt never find it." The Nile seems with its sluggish flow to murmur, "I am the god of this valley, the producer of its life, first-born of the sun, which is the fountain; yet thou knowest not whence I came; my source and overflow alike are wrapped in darkness, and I am the genius of Egypt."

Zoölatry.—What, then, did the people worship? Not the sun, and certainly not the unseen principle of life of which the sun and stars were but luminous shadows. Nay, they worshiped whatever the priests were pleased to set before them; and, mindful of the look upon the Sphinx's face, they asked no questions. The priests said, "We are the custodians of the higher

[1] BALDWIN BROWN.

modes of truth; they are not for you. Be content to know that God is life, and whosoever worships life in any form worships him. Look about you on the towering palm, the growing barley, the leek and the onion: there is life in all. Or go down to the river: the ibis is there and the crocodile, the lizard and the snake. These be your gods!" In this manner the people came to worship trees and birds and every living thing that creepeth upon the face of the earth, and Egypt became the land of zoölatry. Among these living things, which her people regarded with reverence because they conceived them to be manifestations of the divine life, were, notably, the bull, the Mendesian ram, the luminous-eyed cat, the crocodile, the serpent and the ibis. These all received divine honors and were embalmed by the priests. The chiefest of them was the bull Apis, representing life in its highest form as the productive force of nature. A few years ago an arched gallery two thousand feet long was discovered near Memphis filled with the mummies of sacred bulls. It will readily be imagined that the worship of this god was celebrated with rites of a most obscene character. And, indeed, if the entire Egyptian ceremonial could be described or reproduced before us, we would turn away in shame and confusion of face; for of all the great religions of the world this is the most abject.

Picture a man of Egypt, burdened with a sense of wrong-doing and urged on by a vague desire for reconciliation with an offended Deity, visiting one of the temples of his national faith. By a vast avenue of sphinxes he reaches a portico of massive monolithic columns. He hears afar off weird strains of music; the air is heavy with floating incense; processions of shaven priests pass silently by. As he advances among innumerable statues of grotesque divinities the avenues grow narrower, the figures less colossal. He passes out of one great columned chamber into another, each less imposing than the former. At length he finds himself in a narrow cell; this is the adytum, or holiest of all. And yonder, in the dim light, he discovers the gleaming eyes of a cynocephalous ape or of a mummied cat, or mayhap it is nothing but an onion. These be thy gods, O son of the Pharaohs!

I say, man bowing at such an idol shrine as this has reached his most utter degradation. It matters not what spiritual truth may lie at the basis of his worship; here is an immortal soul brutalized and lower than the creeping thing it worships, for it is a true saying that no worshiper is ever better than his god.

"Who does not know," asks Juvenal in one of his satires, "what kinds of monsters demented Egypt worships? One part adores the crocodile, another quakes before the ibis gorged with serpents. The golden image of a sacred long-tailed ape glitters where the magic chords resound from mutilated Memnon, and ancient Thebes lies in ruin with her hundred gates. There whole towns venerate cats, here a river fish, there a dog, but no one Diana. It is impiety to violate and break with the teeth the leek and onion. O holy races to whom such deities as these are born in their gardens!"[1]

[1] RENOUF.

Immortality.—Let us not conclude, however, that there was nothing good or wholesome in the religion of Egypt. It spoke with no uncertain voice concerning the great doctrine of immortality and judgment after death. The very architecture of the Pyramids had its creed; no man can look upon their massiveness without the conviction that its builders hoped to live for ever. The lotus-flower opening with the early sun, and the phœnix rising from its ashes, teach more beautifully than any formulated dogma the resurrection of the body. And why should the Egyptians have so carefully embalmed their dead, wrapping them in spices that have warded off the tooth of time during these forty centuries, had not they believed that the soul was destined to reanimate them?

They conceived of this present life as the mere vestibule of the endless one. Diodorus says: "The Egyptians call their houses hostelries, on account of the short time during which they inhabit them, but the tombs they call eternal dwelling-places." Renouf, commenting upon this remark of Diodorus, says: "The latter part of it is strictly and literally true: *pa t'eta*, 'eternal dwelling-place,' is an expression which is met with at every instant in the inscriptions of the earliest periods descriptive of the tomb. The word *anchiu*, which literally signifies the 'living,' is in innumerable places used emphatically for the 'departed,' who are enjoying everlasting life. The notion of everlasting life, *anch t'eta*, is among the few words written upon the wooden coffin, now in the British Museum, of King Mykerinos of the third pyramid. *Neb anch*, 'lord of life,' is one of the names given to the sarcophagus. In the very ancient inscription of Una the coffin is called *hen en anchiu*, 'the chest of the living.' It is only evil spirits who are spoken of in the sacred writings of the Egyptians as 'the dead.'" It is obvious from this, that whatever other virtues were lacking in this religion, it did give a due prominence to the doctrine of life beyond death, as certain of our own poets have written:

> "To die is to begin to live : it is to end
> An old, stale, weary work, and to commence
> A newer and a better : 'tis to leave
> Deceitful knaves for the society
> Of gods and goodness."

The Suten-hotep-ta.—The usual inscription over the lintel of the tomb is this : " A royal table of propitiation grant Anubis, who dwells within the divine house. May sepulture be granted in the nether world, in the land of the divine Menti, the good, the great, to the departed one who is faithful to the great God !" On later tombs the inscription is as follows : " A royal table of propitiation grant Osiris, dwelling in Amenti, lord of Abydos. May he grant the funeral oblations, bread, beer, oxen, geese, wine, milk, oil, incense, wrappings, all gifts of vegetation, whatever heaven gives or earth produces, to enjoy the Nile, to come forth as a living soul, to come in and go out at the Ristat, that the soul may not be repulsed at the gates of the nether world, to be glorified among the favored ones in presence of Un-nefer, to receive the aliments on the altars of the great God, to breathe the delicious breezes of the north wind, and to drink from the depth of the river." [1]

This prayer for the dead was called the *Suten-hotep-ta;* it was the Paternoster of the Egyptian ritual, and was supposed to have been given by divine revelation. The most meritorious of works was to repeat a considerable number of *Suten-hotep-tas* in behalf of the departed.[2] In the moral writings great stress was placed upon the service in behalf of the dead. Among the *Maxims* of Ani it is written: "Give the water of the funeral sacrifice to thy father and mother who repose in the tomb; renew the water [3] of the divine oblations.

[1] Renouf.

[2] "Innumerable inscriptions call upon the passers-by to invoke the gods in behalf of the departed: ' O all ye who are living upon earth,' 'who love life and hate death,' 'you who are in the service of Osiris or Anubis,' 'priest, prophet, scribe, spondist, ministrant, male or female, every man and every woman, passing by this tomb, tablet, statue, or shrine, whether you be passing northward or southward,—as you desire to enjoy the favor of the king, or as you desire your name to remain upon earth or to transmit your dignities to your children, or as you love and obey the gods of Egypt, or as you wish to be blessed by the gods of your cities, or by your wish to possess a part of the divine abode of Osiris who dwells in Amenti, or to be faithful to the great God, or as you wish to flourish upon earth and pass on to the blessed,—say a Suten-hotep-ta,' etc. (Here follows the entire formula of the Suten-hotep-ta.)"—*The Religion of Ancient Egypt*, p. 143.

[3] "The lustral water offered on earth to the dead had its counterpart in the other world. The most usual representation of this is the picture in which the goddess Nut pours out the water of life to the deceased from the interior of a sycamore tree. In a picture published by M. Chabas the deceased kneels before Osiris and receives from him the water of life from a vessel under which is written *anch ba*, 'that the soul may live.' The picture is taken from the mummy of a priest who lived twelve hundred years before Christ. But the same idea occurs in a Greek inscription found at Saqara by Mr. C. Wescher. 'She lived twenty-

Neglect not to do it even when thou art away from thy dwelling. Thy son will do it in like manner for thee."

Retribution.—On many of the tombs are pictured the scales of judgment—a human heart in one side, a feather in the other, while the god Anubis stands by watching. Here is plainly the doctrine of retribution: "For we must all appear before the judgment-seat, that every one may receive according to that he hath done, whether it be good or bad." It was not lawful to bury the dead until sentence had been passed upon their character by a board of forty-two assessors (this being the number of classified sins), who must determine whether they were worthy of a resting-place in the sepulchre. If not, their mummies were placed on the margin of the lake, "their culprit ghosts waiting and wandering along its shores for a hundred years." And this was but an earnest of a more solemn trial which awaited every one in the shadowy regions of Amenti.

The Ka.—A curious feature of the Egyptian religion was its doctrine of the *ka*. A man was regarded as having a double personality. His *alter ego*, or spiritual double, was called his *ka*. By this he swore, as the Roman by his *genius* and the Persian by his *fravashi*. On the monuments of Egypt the royal *ka* is represented close beside the king himself. The worshiper was accustomed to offer sacrifice to the *kau* of the dead. The common belief was that the disembodied personality of each individual on being ushered into

five years,' the inscription says, ' and Osiris beneath the earth gave her the refreshing water.' "—*Ibid.*, p. 147.

the unknown world was provided with a substantial body, and at once entered upon pursuits which were strikingly similar to those of this present life.

Heaven.—The life of the blessed is thus described: "He has the use of all his limbs; he eats and drinks, and satisfies every one of his physical wants exactly as in his former life. His bread is made of the corn of Pe, a famous town of Egypt, and the beer he drinks is from the red corn of the Nile. The flesh of cattle and fowl is given to him, and refreshing waters are poured out to him under the boughs of sycamores which shade him from the heat. The cool breezes of the north wind breathe upon him. The gods themselves provide him with food; he eats from the table of Osiris at Ristat and from the tables of the sun-god Ra. He is given to drink out of vessels of milk or wine; cakes and flesh are provided for him from the divine abode of Anubis. The gods of Heliopolis themselves bring the divine offerings. He eats the bread which the goddess Tait has cooked, and he breathes the sweet odors of flowers. He washes his feet in silver basins which the god Ptah of Memphis, the inventor of all arts, has himself sculptured. Fields also are allotted to him in the lands of Aarru and Hotep, and he cultivates them. It is characteristic of an industrious and agricultural population that part of the bliss of a future state should consist of such operations as ploughing and hoeing, sowing and reaping, rowing on the canals and collecting the harvests daily. We are told that the height of corn in the fields of Aarru is seven cubits, and that the length of the ears is two cubits. This blissful place is surrounded by a wall of steel, and it is from its gate that the sun comes forth in the eastern sky."[1]

Hell.—Should the *ka*, or soul, of an Egyptian fail to secure a favorable verdict at the court of Osiris, it wanders forth into *Tuat*, the nether world, to encounter and be overcome by a thousand calamities, such as "being turned away from its own door," breathing a fiery atmosphere, going to *Nemmat*, the headsman's block, being forced to eat filth and suffering corruption. The comprehensive title of these is "the second death."

The *kau* of the departed were enabled to defend themselves from the dangers of the nether world only by the use of charms and talismans. Hence the custom of covering the mummies with cabalistic phrases and images of animal gods. Such words as the following are frequently found inscribed upon the tomb: "Back, crocodile of the west! there is an asp upon me; I shall not be given to thee. Dart not thy flame upon me!" There was supposed to be great virtue in a golden asp or scarabæus or a buckle of red quartz typifying the blood of Isis.

Assimilation with the Gods.—The doctrine of immortality, as held by the priests, was to this effect: that when a man dies and becomes *maa-cheru*, or justified, by safely passing the ordeal of judgment, he is identified or assimilated in some mysterious way with Deity itself. In some cases, indeed, he is assimilated with many gods, taking the hair of one, the eyes

[1] RENOUF.

of another, the lips of a third, and so becoming a sort of animated pantheon; and all this without losing his personal identity. He still remembers his former life among men, and from his place in the mummy crypt, assuming the name of some beneficent god, he speaks comfortable things to his mourning friends.

It was held also among the initiated that the dead have power to assume all kinds of living shapes, as the turtle-dove, the serpent, the hawk, the crocodile, the heron, the lotus-flower, and in such strange guise to range the universe at will.

"*What shall I Do to be Saved?*"—The thought of salvation, as held among Christian people, had little or no place in this religion. Mercy was an unknown word; there was no forgiveness with the gods. The sum and substance of the doctrine of destiny was this: "Whatsoever a man soweth, that shall he also reap." If one would reach the land of Amenti and abide in peace, let him hold himself in readiness to have his heart weighed against the feather of truth. The only answer possible to a sinner's cry, "What shall I do to be saved?" was this: "Prepare for the judgment of Osiris by observing the rules of right conduct."

Morality.—It remains for us to note briefly the influence of this religion on the character of the people. They were familiar with a rule of right living called *maat*.

Maat.—This word, which is of frequent occurrence, signifies "a perfectly straight and inflexible rule." It is from the root *ma*, meaning to stretch out, and, like our word *right*, has reference primarily to law and order. "*Maat*," says Renouf, "is Law, not in the forensic sense of command issued either by a human sovereign authority or by a divine legislator, like the law of the Hebrews, but in the sense of that unerring order which governs the universe, whether in its physical or in its moral aspect. This is surely a great and noble conception."

An Elaborate Code.—But beyond this the Egyptians had an elaborate code of injunctions and prohibitions as to particular sins. "Besides the crimes of violence and theft, different offences against chastity are mentioned; not only evil-speaking and lying, but exaggeration, chattering and idle words, are condemned; he who reviles the king, his father or his god, the evil listener, and he who turns a deaf ear to the words of truth and justice, he who causes pain to another or who in his heart thinks meanly of God,—all these fail to satisfy the condition of admission into the ranks of the triumphant dead."[1]

The Maxims of Ptah-hotep.—One of the sacred books, a fragment of which is preserved in the Imperial Library at Paris, was an extended treatise on practical morality. It purports to have been written by Prince Ptah-hotep, whose sayings partake less of the wisdom of Solomon than of the rude sagacity of Poor Richard.

"The man is happy," wrote he, "who lives upon his own labor."

"Love thy wife; flattery will serve thy purpose with her better than churlish words."

"Curse not thy master before God."

[1] RENOUF.

"The bad man's life is nothing better than death."

"What we say in secret is known to Him who created us."

"Gossip is abominable."

"Walk not with a fool."

Aside from this volume of proverbial philosophy there were thirty commandments, of which no traces remain. Thus the Egyptians were not without lights to walk by.

M. Chabas says of the Egyptian code of morals: "None of the Christian virtues were forgotten in it. Piety, charity, gentleness, self-command in word and action, chastity, the protection of the weak, benevolence toward the humble, deference to superiors, respect for property in the minutest details,—all were expressed there." In the "Book of the Dead" the soul of the righteous is represented as saying, "I did that which was right and hated the wrong; I was bread to the hungry, water to the thirsty, clothes to the naked, a refuge to the needy; and that which I did unto him the great Ra hath done unto me."[1] It must be remembered, however, that the moral precepts of any people are always better than their practical morals; their sacred books are better than their lives.

No Egyptian Heroes.—It is a notable fact that Egypt had no heroes. The religion of the Bull and the Ibis could not but beget in its disciples a gross animal life. The poor labored for meat; the rich and learned had their ambition smothered in wanton luxuries. Other empires have left us great men who, though their

[1] RENOUF.

graves are forgotten, still tread the earth with stately steppings; but Rameses and Sesostris are names and nothing more.[1] Their souls were wrapped up with their bodies in mummy-cloths and laid away in endless rest. There was nothing in their religion to stimulate the doing of immortal deeds.

The Religion of Sadness.—Another significant fact is this: that while the Egyptians were the most mirthful people on earth, they were the saddest of worshipers. Apuleius says:[2] "The gods of Greece rejoice in dances, but the gods of Egypt in lamentations." And another says: "The Egyptians offer tears on the altars of their gods." Is not this the old story of the golden calf? They who worship Apis must ever drink the dust of their idol mingled with bitter waters. There is no spiritual joy save in the worship of that Supreme One at whose right hand are pleasures for evermore.

An illustrious lady, the wife of Pasherenptah, is represented as thus addressing her husband from the grave: "O my brother, my spouse, forbear not to eat and drink, to drain the cup of joy, to enjoy woman's love and make holiday of life; for as to Amenti, it is the land of slumber and darkness, an abode of sorrow

[1]   "All the kings of the nations lie in glory;
    Cased in cedar and shut in a sacred gloom;
    Swathed in linen and precious unguents old,
    Painted with cinnabar and rich with gold.
      Silent they rest, in solemn salvatory,
    Sealed from the moth and the owl and the flittermouse—
    Each with his name on his brow."
                          JEAN INGELOW.

[2] Quoted by James Freeman Clarke.

for all. We wake no more to see our loved ones. The dwellers on earth have waters of life, but thirst is for ever with me. I weep for the waters that pass by."[1]

The religion of Egypt is dead. It has utterly vanished from the face of the earth. "On the walls of her tombs," says Draper, "still remain Pthah the Creator and Neph the divine spirit sitting at the potter's wheel turning clay into the forms of men; and Athor, who receives the setting sun into her arms. The granite statues have outlived the gods."

From this, as from other false systems, we turn with a feeling of ineffable relief to the glorious gospel of the blessed God. Here is no worship of birds and four-footed beasts and creeping things. Here is no mystery along the path that leads to eternal life. Nay, it is so plain that the wayfaring man need not err therein. What simplicity is here, and yet what grandeur! A cross, an open sepulchre, a God with outstretched hands. For God so loved the world that he gave his only-begotten Son, that whosoever believeth in him should not perish, but have everlasting life. This is that great "mystery of godliness," deeper and more wonderful than any behind the veil of Isis, which God in Jesus Christ has revealed to the least of his little ones.

[1] RENOUF.

III.
ZOROASTRIANISM.

I. *The Sacred Book:*
   Zend-Avesta.
   The Poets.
II. *The Central Thought:*
   Dualism.
   Ormuzd and Ahriman.
   Prayer.
III. *Three Distinguishing Features:*
   (1) Fire-worship.
   (2) The Idea of Conflict.
      Moral Code: The Four Laws.
   (3) The Fravashis; Philosophy of the Future.
      "*What shall I do to be saved?*" Repeat the Patet.

III. ZOROASTRIANISM,

THE RELIGION OF ANCIENT PERSIA.

"AND behold there came wise men from the east to Jerusalem, saying, Where is he that is born king of the Jews? for we have seen his star in the east, and are come to worship him." These "wise men" were Magi, or fire-worshipers. It is their religion which is now to engage our attention. We turn our eyes toward Persia, the most magnificent of empires, symbolized by the silver breast of the great Babylonian image. What memories are awakened by her name! Years have not dimmed the crowns of Cyrus, Xerxes and Longimanus, or of the beautiful queen who reigned in Shushan, the palace of the lily. Max Müller says: "There were periods in the history of the world when the religion of Zoroaster threatened to rise triumphant on the ruins of the temples of all other gods. If in the battles of Marathon and Salamis Greece had succumbed to Persia, the state religion of the empire of Cyrus might have become the religion of the whole civilized world." But there is no room for any "if." History is not a fabric of happenings. All its events are singly spun and woven together in the loom of Providence. The Weaver breaks no threads, loses none, misweaves none.

Of Persepolis, the wonder of the world for its magnificence, naught remains save heaps of ruins. "The spider hangs her veil undisturbed in the halls of Kai Kosrou, the owl stands sentinel on Haroun-al-Raschid's fallen palace-towers, the dromedary browses in the lonesome gardens of Babylon."

A Dead Religion.—And the religion of Zoroaster has shared the doom of the great empire that espoused it. What can be sadder than the thought of a dead religion? We lament the lost arts; we stand regretful among the crumbling porches of old systems of philosophy; we read not unmoved the epitaphs of fallen thrones and dynasties. These, however, are merely losses to the world's material possessions. But the decay of a religion involves the ruin of countless inestimable hopes and incalculable destinies. It is as if a costly-laden ship went down with immortal souls clinging to every rope and spar.

The sum-total of the followers of Zoroaster to-day is not more than one hundred and fifty thousand. These are for the most part congregated in and around the city of Bombay. By their Mohammedan neighbors they are called *Guebres*, or infidels. They still feed with sandal-wood the sacred fire which tradition says has never been extinguished on the altar of the Sun. And still, white-robed and white-turbaned, they circle the altar, singing hymns like the following, which their fathers sang when Medo-Persia was mightiest among the empires of the earth:

> "Praise to Ormuzd, great Creator!
> With our life and bodies praise;

> Purer than the purest, fairest,
>   Bright through never-ending days!
> What is good and what is brilliant,
>   That we reverence in thee—
> Thy good spirit, thy good kingdom,
>   Wisdom, law and equity."

These are the only adherents of the mighty power that once, towering in pride, hewed out the mountain-clefts for temples, branded her mark in the servile foreheads of the Jews, and equipped the most formidable fleets and armies ever seen that she might hurl them against the floating battlements of Alexander.

The religion of Zoroaster had, at its best, no great measure of vital tenacity. In the second century of the Christian era it bowed submissively and wellnigh yielded up the ghost at the bidding of the idolatrous Parthian priests. From this it recovered only to tremble and succumb again at the shaking of Mohammed's sword. Perhaps its very strength has been its weakness. Lacking the vital inspiration of heaven-given truth, it was yet possessed of so many of the humble graces and gentle courtesies of true religion as to be unfitted for standing against the brute forces of falsehood.

Before proceeding to a more minute exposition of the characteristic features of this religion it is proper that somewhat should be said about *its prophet* and *his book*.

Zoroaster.—Zoroaster, if born at all (for there are those who question his real existence, holding that the name represents merely a divine principle), was born in Bactria not less than three thousand years ago, and how much earlier none can tell.[1] Tradition says that

> "As soon as born he laughed a merry laugh,
> Though other children weep when first the air they quaff;
> His parents then, Dogdûyah and Purshasp,
> Cried out, ''Tis some great prophet in our arms we clasp.'"

The meaning of the name given him is "golden splendor." His earlier years are a blank. He first appears as a priest ministering in the temple of the Sun. His heart is distressed by the gross idolatries of the people, and not less by the bitter sense of his own ignorance and weakness. There by the altar he utters his cry, the first prayer to Ahura-Mazda:

"I believe thee, O God, to be the best of all, the source of light for the universe. All shall choose thee as the fountain of light, thee, thou holiest Mazda!

[1] "The historic statements that have come down to us on the subject of the age of Zoroaster, with whose name the origin of Iranic cultivation is by common consent regarded as intimately connected, are so absolutely conflicting that they must be pronounced valueless. Eudoxus and Aristotle said that Zoroaster lived six thousand years before the death of Plato, or B. C. 6348. Hermippus placed him five thousand years before the Trojan War, or B. C. 6184. Berosus declared of him that he reigned at Babylon toward the beginning of the twenty-third century before our era, having ascended the throne, according to his chronological views, about B. C. 2286. Xanthus Lydus, the contemporary of Herodotus and the *first* Greek writer who treats of the subject, made him live six hundred years only before the invasion of Greece by Xerxes, or B. C. 1080. The later Greeks and Romans declared that he was contemporary with Darius Hystaspis, thus making his date about B. C. 520–485. Between the earliest and the latest of the dates assigned by these authorities the difference (it will be seen) is one of nearly *six thousand years!*"—*Origin of Nations*, p. 97.

"I ask thee—oh tell it aright, thou living God!—by what means is this universe supported and who is the promoter of life?

"I ask thee—oh tell it aright, thou living God!—who was in the beginning the creator of truth? Who made the sun and stars, the waxing and waning moon?

"I ask thee—oh tell it aright, thou living God—who holdeth the earth and the skies overarching it? Who made the rivers and the trees? Who begat light and darkness, kindly sleep and the awaking?

"Who hath made the mornings, noons and nights, those wayside sentinels who remind us of duty? Oh tell us aright, thou living God."

In answer to that cry came, as he supposed, a revelation from Ahura-Mazda, pointing out for him the career of a reformer, and promising all needed supplies of light and divine countenance. His reforms were aimed, on the one hand, at Pantheism with its priesthood corrupt, mercenary and shameless, and on the other at the worship of idols.[1] As against these he rose up to testify for Ahura-Mazda, the Lord of light.

A picture has been drawn by Bunsen of an assembly of the people called together by Zoroaster on one of the hills adjacent to the primeval city of Bactria to

---

[1] "In the early nature-worship idolatry had been allowed, but the Iranic system pronounced against it from the first. No images of Ahura-Mazda or of the Izeds profaned the severe simplicity of an Iranic temple. It was only after a long lapse of ages that, in connection with a foreign worship, idolatry crept in. The old Zoroastrianism was in this respect as pure as the religion of the Jews."—RAWLINSON'S *Seven Monarchies*, ii. 48.

determine whether they would worship many gods or one. Standing before the multitude, he addressed them in these words, as found in the Zend-Avesta:

"I will proclaim to all listeners the praises of the all-wise God. Hear now what is best, that every man may choose his creed before the coming of judgment.

"There were two ancient spirits, twins, who revealed the evil and good. Of these the bad spirit chose the evil; the other, he whose garment is the eternal arch of heaven, chose the right. So will all who faithfully serve Ahura-Mazda.

"Let us be counted among those who benefit the world. O Ahura-Mazda, bliss-conferring truth! let our minds abide in the dwelling-place of wisdom.

"O men, clinging to these commandments of the great Mazda, which are a torment to the wicked and a blessing to the good, ye shall gain the victory over all."

I. *The Sacred Book.*—Such hymns, or invocations, compose the larger part of the ZEND-AVESTA, which is the one sacred book of the Fire-worshipers. The meaning of Zend-Avesta is "living word."[1] It is believed to have been addressed to men by Ahura-Mazda through the lips of Zoroaster his prophet. It consists of four parts—Yazna, Vispered, Vendidad and Yesht. These contain little or nothing as to theology or as to the conduct of daily life, but an endless multiplicity of prayers and hymns. The book is simply a liturgy.

---

[1] So Maurice. According to Rawlinson, "Avesta" means *text*, and "Zend" means *comment;* so that the full title, Avesta-u-Zend, or, as contracted, Avesta-Zend, means "text and comment."

Its opening hymn is entitled "The Archangels' First Anthem; or, The Revealed Thought, Word and Deed of Zarethustra." Many of these hymns are exceedingly beautiful, as this fragment: "In the name of God, the Giver and Forgiver, rich in love, praise to the name of Ormuzd, the God that hath the title, who always was, always is and always will be! Praise to the omniscience of God, which hath sent us that wisdom of wisdoms which finds an escape from hell for the soul at the bridge and leads it over into Paradise, the fragrant home of the pure!" There are many unintelligible things in the Zend-Avesta—many that suggest mysticism and dense profundity. And little wonder, if they took their rise, as Müller says, in that "period of mystic incubation when India and Egypt, Greece and Babylonia, were sitting together and gossiping like crazy old women, chattering with toothless gums and silly brains about the dreams and joys of their youth."[1]

Though the liturgy of the Zoroastrians can be found only in the hymns of the Zend-Avesta, their doctrines

[1] "The result, however brought about, which must always remain doubtful, was the authoritative issue of a volume which the learned of Europe have now possessed for some quarter of a century, and which has recently been made accessible to the general reader by the labors of Spiegel. This work, the Zend-Avesta, while it may contain fragments of a very ancient literature, took its present shape in the time of Artaxerxes, and was probably then first collected from the mouths of the Zoroastrian priests and published by Arda-Viraf. Certain additions may since have been made to it, but we are assured that 'their number is small,' and that we have no reason to doubt that the text of the Avesta in the days of Arda-Viraf was, on the whole, exactly the same as at present."—*Seven Monarchies*, lii. 272.

and the precepts by which their daily lives were guided must be sought elsewhere, chiefly among the poets. Persia is the warm mother-land of poets. There is that in the air—fragrance of vineyards and rose-trees, songs of the nightingale, dalliance of color and warm sunlight—which awakens all genius. Apart from Zoroaster, who stands among the Persian bards as Saul among the prophets, there were Hafiz and Saadi and many other immortal names. "In all ages and languages," says Alger, "the poet is a preacher." Doubted; yet certainly the literature of Persia "reveals *her* poets as the keenest, tenderest, sublimest, most versatile of preachers;" and the religion of Persia has no existence apart from the afflatus of the Zoroastrian bards. Where else but under those clear shining skies could fancies like this be born?—

> "The firmament is God's love-letter writ for man;
>   The sun is the seal stamped on its envelope of air;
>   The confidential night tears off the blazing seal,
>   And lays the solemn star-script, God's handwriting, bare."

Let us now note the peculiar and distinguishing features of this religion, as derived not only from the Zend-Avesta, but from the actual life and beliefs of the fire-worshipers.

II. *The Central Thought: Dualism.*—Its teaching is, that there are two gods—Ormuzd or Ahura-Mazda, and Ahriman or Angra-Mainyu—and these two are equal.[1]

[1] "Dualism proper, or a belief in two uncreated and independent principles, one a principle of good and the other a principle of evil, was no part of the original Zoroastrianism. At the same time we find,

"Ormuzd and Ahriman: Devotion's dazzling child,
And Doubt's demoniac son, false, filthy, black and wild;
The moment they were born creation they began:
Ormuzd all good things made; all evil, Ahriman."

The latter, "false, filthy, black and wild," has no altars, and, though recognized as an equal antag-

even in the Gathas, the earliest portions of the Zend-Avesta, the germ out of which dualism sprung.

"The Iranians came to believe in the existence of two coeternal and coequal Persons, one good and the other evil, between whom there had been from all eternity a perpetual and never-ceasing conflict, and between whom the same conflict would continue to rage through all coming time.

"The dualistic principle being thus fully adopted, and the world looked on as the battle-ground between two independent and equal powers engaged in a perpetual strife, it was natural that the imagination should complete the picture by ascribing to these superhuman rivals the circumstantials that accompany a great struggle between human adversaries. The two kings required, in the first place, to have their councils, which were accordingly assigned them, and were respectively composed of six councilors. The councilors of Ahura-Mazda—called *Amesha-Spentas*, or 'immortal saints,' afterward corrupted into Amshashpands — were Vohu-Mano, Asha-Vahista, Khshathra-Vairya, Cpenta-Armaiti, Haurvatat and Ameretat. Those of Angra-Mainyu were Aku-Mano, Indra, Caurva, Naonhaitya and two others whose names are interpreted as Darkness and Poison.

"As the two principles of good and evil have their respective councils, so have they likewise their armies. The good spirit has created thousands of angelic beings who everywhere perform his will and fight on his side against the evil one; and the evil one has equally on his part called into being thousands of malignant spirits, who are his emissaries in the world, doing his work continually and fighting his battles. These are the devas or dives so famous in Persian fairy mythology. They are 'wicked, bad, false, untrue, the originators of mischief, most baneful, destructive, the basest of all beings.' The whole universe is full of them. They aim primarily at destroying all the good creations of Ahura-Mazda; but if unable to destroy, they content themselves with perverting and corrupting. They dog the steps of men, tempting

onist of the good Ormuzd, no divine honors are paid to him.

Ormuzd.—A brief quotation from a child's catechism printed for use among the modern Parsees will suffice to show that, while possessing a dualistic theology, they practice a monotheistic worship. The first question is:

"Whom do we Zoroastrians believe in?"

"We believe in one God, and in none beside him.

"Who is that God?

"The God who created the heavens and earth, the sun, moon and stars, the angels and the four elements. Him we believe in; him we worship, invoke and adore.

"And do we not believe in any other?

"Whoso believes in any other God is an infidel, and shall suffer the penalties of hell."

Ahriman.—Nevertheless, throwing his shadow over this faith in the one, stands the other—Angra-Mainyu, the evil-minded. There is a divergence here from the biblical thought of Satan in this, that in the latter case there is a divine foot upon the serpent's head, while in the former two Titans of equal birth, majesty and power stand opposing each other. Satan is a worm at God's

---

them to sin, and, as soon as they sin, obtaining a fearful power over them.

"At the head of Ahura-Mazda's army is the angel Serosh, 'the sincere, the beautiful, the victorious, the true, the master of truth.' He protects the territories of the Iranians, wounds, and sometimes even slays, the demons, and is engaged in a perpetual struggle against them, never slumbering night or day, but guarding the world with his sword, more particularly after sunset, when the demons have the greatest power."—*Seven Monarchies,* ii. 51-54.

feet; Ahriman is Ormuzd's equal. It remains yet to be seen which shall pluck the world, the costly guerdon of their struggle, from his rival's hands. Yet nowhere is there a clearer hope than under these blue splendid skies of Persia that good shall finally prevail, and the earth shine as a jewel in the crown of the "all-perfect, all-powerful, all-glorious."[1]

Traces are seen everywhere among the poets, who are the truest preachers of the Zoroastrian creed, of warm desire and aspirations after nearness to this God behind the dazzling veil. There is said to have been one whose supreme desire was to approach the sun so near as to be consumed by it. Thus it is written:

> "Blest time that frees me from the bonds of clay
> To track the lost one in his airy course!
> Like motes exulting in their parent ray,
> My kindling spirit rushes to its source."

Nor does the Zoroastrian's God turn away "him that cometh unto him;" rather,

> "Who comes toward me an inch through doubtings dim,
> In blazing light I do approach a yard toward him."

The Zoroastrian would not differ from the Christian

---

[1] Here there is a difference of opinion. Rawlinson says: "The dualism professed was of the most extreme and pronounced kind. Ormuzd and Ahriman, the principles of good and evil, were expressly declared to be 'twins.' They had 'in the beginning come together to create life and death,' and to settle 'how the world was to be.' There was no priority of existence of the one over the other, and no decided superiority. The two, being coeval, had contended from all eternity, *and would, it was almost certain, continue to contend to all eternity, neither being able to vanquish the other.* Thus an eternal struggle was postulated between good and evil, and the issue was doubtful, neither side possessing any clear and manifest advantage."

in his definition of that which separates between the soul and God:

> "The dazzling beauty of the loved one shines unseen,
> And *self's* the curtain o'er the road. Away, O screen!"

Perhaps their aspirations, enkindled beneath redder stars and a warmer sun, are more sensual than ours. Watts or Wesley would scarcely have sung like this:

> "There's ne'er a spot in our bewildered world,
> Where God's exceeding glory shines so dim,
> But shapes are strung and hearts are warm,
> And lips are sweet from him."

The worshipers of Ormuzd are greatly given to prayer. God is ever near them as the sunlight, ready to listen, ready to help. No doubting Tyndall has ever arisen among them to suggest that there is no answering voice. A poor bereaved soul lay all night long crying, "God! God!" And the tempter came and whispered, "God hath not said, Here am I!" Then came the good angel Chiser, bringing to the prostrate mourner these words, full as a honeycomb of the sweetness of comfort:

> "'Go tell,' said Ormuzd, 'yonder soul, now sunken in despair,
> Each "Lord, appear," thy lips pronounce contains my "Here am I;"
> A special messenger I send beneath thine every sigh:
> Thy love is but a girdle of the love I bear to thee;
> And sleeping in thy "Come, O Lord!" there lies "Here, son!"
> from me.'"

Thus far concerning the dualism of this religion. Around this, as its central thought, we find a cluster of three distinguishing marks.

Three Characteristic Features.—Not far from the ruins of Persepolis towers aloft the famous rock of Behistun, its flinty face covered with hieroglyphics and wedge-shaped letters that have survived the storms and convulsions of twenty-four hundred years. Here one may read this proclamation: "*I, Darius, ruler of the dependent provinces, son of Hystaspis, by the grace of Ormuzd am king. It is he that hath granted me my empire. By the grace of Ormuzd my people have obeyed my laws.*" Near by is a figure, meant to represent Darius, standing before an altar whereon a fire is burning. Above the altar is a rude image of the sun. Over the king is a shadowy creature with wings. And at no great distance a struggle is represented as going on between the king and a griffin. From this picture let us derive our three characteristics of the religion of Persia—to wit:

  1st, *Fire-worship;*
  2d, *The Idea of Conflict;* and
  3d, *The Fravashis.*

1. *Fire-worship.*—The disciples of Zoroaster have, from time immemorial, been known as fire-worshipers, yet they protest against the name and avow themselves believers in the one only God. It is probably true that the wisest and most devout among them, while loyal to the old custom of worshiping with faces turned toward the sun or the fire burning on the altar, regard these simply as emblems, and look through them and beyond them to Him whose heart is infinite warmth of love and whose word is as the brightness of light. The nights in Persia are clear and beautiful. The stars

are a language which speaks to peasant and priest alike of light coming out of darkness.

> "Through the forehead of eve the Lord driveth yon star as a nail,
> And the thick-spangled darkness lets down o'er the day as a veil."

It is little wonder, therefore, if the people of that fervid and poetic land, searching for a God, should imagine they had found him hidden within those ever-present, ever-mysterious, silent yet fateful veils of light. The sun being the centre, all the orbs of heaven are as ministers that wait upon him. "We have seen his star in the east" was but another way of saying, "We have received a mandatory word from the ineffable Throne, and must needs go where it leads and do whatsoever it bids us."[1]

2. *Conflict.*—The second of the characteristics referred to is *the idea of conflict*. This naturally grows out of the dualism of light and darkness. Like gods, like people. When the gleaming of the swords of Ormuzd and Ahriman is in the air, life grows warlike

[1] The worship of the elements was no part of the original system of Zoroaster. It was borrowed from Magism, the religion of ancient Armenia and Cappadocia. When the followers of Zoroaster, in their migrations, spread over the countries lying south and west of the Caspian Sea, they came into contact with people who worshiped earth, air, fire and water, and they incorporated this religion with their own. Rawlinson says: "With their dualistic belief had been combined, at a time not much later than that of Darius Hystaspis, an entirely separate system, the worship of the elements. Fire, air, earth and water were regarded as essentially holy, and to pollute any of them was a crime. Fire was especially to be held in honor, and it became an essential part of the Persian religion to maintain perpetually upon the fire-altars the sacred flame, supposed to have been originally kindled from heaven, and to see that it never went out."

in every phase. All things are divided into twos: two gods, two marshaled hosts, two modes of living, two places of final destiny. And every man must choose. There is no fate. Will is of all things freest; it is bound to nothing save the necessity of choice. The sufis' preaching is little more than a call to enlistment: "Who is on the Lord's side? Choose ye this day whom ye will serve." There is no escaping the clash of arms. All things in heaven and earth are arrayed for battle. Ahura-Mazda summons the shining hosts of heaven; twelve companies march in the twelve signs of the Zodiac; the dog-star, Sura, stands sentinel at the bridge Chinevat, watching the abyss from which Ahriman shall come with his myriads of Dævæ. Then battle! The rolling of heaven's artillery, the swift gleaming of its electric lights, and blackness covering the field! Then light again:

> "The red dawning proclaims a victorious fight;
> From the sword of the sun flows the blood of the night."

It is thus that fervid Oriental minds set forth the conflict ever going on between right and wrong, the powers of light and darkness. The Zoroastrian entertains a profound hatred of evil; he hates it as a good soldier does the banner of his foe:

> "Beneath the tiger's jaw I heard a victim cry,
> 'Thank God that, though in pain, yet not in guilt I die.'"

Loathe sin, abhor sin, go not near it, preaches the sufi:

> "Avoid an evil-doer as you would a brand,
> Which, lighted, burns; extinguished, soils the hand."

No other religion dwells with greater emphasis on the folly of doing evil. He who pursues a vicious course of life is "as one who painfully turns up the sand with a golden plough to sow weeds; he mows a lignum-vitæ forest with a scythe of glass; he puts a jeweled vase on a sandal-wood fire to cook a dish of pebbles." The Persian hates vanity and wrong, and loves right for its own sake. His religion is, by eminence, a moral religion. Its comprehensive code is this: *Pure thoughts, pure words, pure deeds.* Ormuzd's first law is cleanliness of body and soul. The swiftness of life is a never-ending theme, and with it the vanity of earthly things:

> "I wish not for thrones and the glories of life;
> What is glory to man? An illusion; a cheat.
> What did it for Jemschid, the world at his feet?"

It was easy to ring the changes on earth's vanity when one stood among ruins. The saying of St. Paul, "We brought nothing into this world, and it is certain we can carry nothing out," is thus expressed and something more:

> "On parent's knees, a naked new-born child,
> Weeping, thou sat'st, while all around thee smiled;
> So live that, sinking in thy last long sleep,
> Calm, thou mayest smile while all around thee weep."

O. less beautifully, but with even greater force, in the story of the poet who was called to sing at Haroun al-Raschid's court. Again and again he celebrated the caliph's praise—his valor, his conquests, his princely wealth—and still Al-Raschid called for a higher strain. Then,

"Around that vast magnific hall one glance the poet threw
On courtiers, king and festival, and did the strain renew:
'And yet, and yet, shalt thou at last lie stretched on bed of death:
Then when thou drawest thick and fast thy sobs with painful breath,—
When Azrael glides through guarded gate, through hosts that camp
  around
Their lord in vain, and *will not wait*,—when thou art sadly bound
Unto thine house of dust alone—O king, when thou must die,
This pomp a shadow thou must own, this glory all a lie.'"

With such poets, preaching thoughts that breathe in words that burn, singing the battles of dawn and darkness and the praises of a virtuous life, the disciples of Zoroaster could not be otherwise than brave and earnest, a people of high thoughts and noble deeds. Their religion is the very spirit of conflict. " Endure hardness as a good soldier;" " Put on the whole armor of God, that ye may be able to withstand, and having done all to stand in the evil day."

"Wouldst thou the honey taste while afraid of the sting of the bee?
  Wouldst the victor's crown wear without knowing the terrible fight?
Could the diver get pearls that repose in the depths of the sea
  If he stood on the shore, from the crocodile shrinking in fright?
With unfaltering toil thou must seek what the Fates have decreed
May be won, and courageously pluck for thyself the glorious meed."

This might almost pass for an Oriental version of " Am I a soldier of the cross?"

The Four Laws.—At this point we note the Four Laws of Zoroastrianism, which constitute its moral code. They are piety, purity, veracity and industry.

(1) *Piety*, consisting chiefly in the worship of Ormuzd by repetition of the hymns and prayers of the Zend-

Avesta. The modes of worship are exceedingly simple: "In early morning the congregation gathers under the open sky around the altar or hearth, on which a fire is burning. The priest sits, facing the fire, on a stone platform reached by three steps. To protect the fire from the pollution of his breath, he and his assistants wear a veil reaching from below the eyes to the chin. Rising, he begins: 'I invite to this offering, and I prepare it for, Ahura-Mazda.'"[1] He then, with many invocations, offers to the fire food, flesh, milk or butter, and joins his congregation in drinking the sacred juice of the soma-plant.[2]

(2) *Purity.* This has already been referred to. The Zoroastrian's conception of purity is, indeed, far below our gospel standard, yet he professes, and his life measurably illustrates, a sincere love of "pure thoughts, pure words and pure deeds."[3]

---

[1] *Faiths of the World.*

[2] The "ceremony of the soma" consisted in the extraction of the juice of the plant while the priest was employed in prayer, after which the drink-offering was solemnly dedicated to the fire, and then quaffed by priest and worshipers.

[3] "Outward purity had to be maintained by a multiplicity of external observances, forming in their entirety a burden as heavy to bear as that imposed by the Mosaic ceremonial law on the people of Israel. But inward purity was not neglected. Not only were the Iranians required to refrain from all impure acts, but also from impure words, and even from impure thoughts. Ahura-Mazda was 'the pure, the Master of purity,' and would not tolerate less than perfect purity in his votaries."
—*Ancient Religions,* p. 73.

"The purity which was required of the Zoroastrian was of two kinds, moral and legal. Moral purity comprised all that Christianity includes under it—truth, justice, chastity and general sinlessness. It was coextensive with the whole sphere of human activity, embracing not only

(3) *Veracity.* "No Persian virtue," says Rawlinson, "is more praised by the ancients, perhaps none more astonished the cunning Greeks, than Persian truthfulness, which wins at this day the high respect of Hindus dealing with Parsees. The most shameful thing in Persian eyes was lying.[1] Debt and other faults were specially detested for the lies required to conceal them. Children were taught truth-telling as they were taught science. Ahriman is the liar of liars. The religious law reckoned severely with the breaker of an engagement. Persians were very slow to take an oath, but the pledge of a Persian hand was like the Olympian oath by the Styx."[2]

(4) *Industry.* "He who tills the ground is as good a servant of religion as he who presents a thousand holy offerings or ten thousand prayers. *Arare est orare.* 'Who is the fourth that rejoices the earth with greatest

words and acts, but even the secret thoughts of the heart. Legal purity was to be obtained only by the observance of a multitude of trifling ceremonies and the abstinence from ten thousand acts in their nature wholly indifferent. Especially, everything was to be avoided which could be thought to pollute the four elements, all of them sacred to the Zoroastrian or Sassanian times—fire, water, earth and air."—*Seven Monarchies*, iii. 586.

[1] Rawlinson says: "Druj, 'falsehood,' is held up to detestation, alike in the Zend-Avesta and in the Persian cuneiform inscriptions, as the basest, the most contemptible and the most pernicious of vices."

[2] *Faiths of the World.*

This has ceased to be true among the modern Persians. Maurice says: "Under the Mohammedan teaching, which in Turkey has certainly been favorable to veracity, the strong sense of moral right and wrong which distinguished the old Persian has deserted him. He who was celebrated by Xenophon as above all men the speaker of truth has become proverbial for lying."

joy? It is he who cultivates most corn, grass and fruit. What is the stomach of the law? It is sowing corn again and again.'"[1] The Parsees are an eminently industrious people. To this may be due the fact that they have ever been possessed of princely wealth, and that at this day no beggar can be found among them.[2]

We have spoken of two characteristic features of Zoroastrianism—viz. *fire-worship*, as indicating the leading thought in its theology and ritual; and *conflict*, as showing its conception of life's duties and responsibilities.

3. *The Fravashis.*—We now come to the *third*, which was referred to as *the Fravashis*. Under this head we consider the Persian's philosophy of the future. In the picture carved on the rock Behistun, representing Darius at the flaming altar, we saw a shadowy creature

[1] *Faiths of the World.*

[2] "The early Ormuzd worshipers were agriculturists, and viewed the cultivation of the soil as a religious duty enjoined upon them by God. Hence they connected the notion of piety with earth-culture, and it was but a step from this to make a single goddess preside over the two. It is as the angel of earth that Armaiti has most distinctly a personal character. She is regarded as wandering from spot to spot and laboring to convert deserts and wildernesses into fruitful fields and gardens. She has the agriculturist under her immediate protection, while she endeavors to persuade the shepherd, who persists in the nomadic life, to give up his old habits and commence the cultivation of the soil.

"Man was placed upon the earth to preserve the good creation; and this could only be done by careful tilling of the soil, eradication of thorns and weeds, and reclamation of the tracts over which Angra-Mainyu had spread the curse of barrenness. To cultivate the soil was thus a religious duty; the whole community was required to be agricultural; and either as proprietor, as farmer or as laboring-man each Zoroastrian must 'further the works of life' by advancing tillage."—*Seven Monarchies*, ii. 48, 56.

with wings poised above his head. This was his *Fravashi*, his "double"—his soul, if you will. The doctrine of the Zend-Avesta is that all men pre-exist in this shadowy form—that birth embodies them; and death in turn liberates the Fravashi from its fleshly bands. Here, therefore, is the great truth of immortality. The body dies and is carried out to the Tower of Silence for eagles to pluck at, but the soul, or Fravashi, lives on for ever and ever. There is to be, moreover, a resurrection, whereat the soul shall be reinvested with its earthly body, and there are to be glad reunions in the future world. A day is appointed for judgment when all must appear to render an account for the deeds done in the body. There is no probation after death ;

"Where ends wrong-doing
Begins long ruing."

The bridge that leads to the dwelling-place of the pure is stretched across the abyss Duzaht, the awful abyss where Ahriman dwells. The wicked, crossing that narrow bridge, tremble with sense of ill-desert, throw up their arms in despair, fall and are lost to view. But those who have loved pure thoughts, pure words and pure deeds reach in safety the other side. The joys of heaven are largely in the consciousness of having lived aright; for it is a true saying, outside of all bibles, that virtue is its own reward.

"In the nine heavens are eight paradises.
  Where is the ninth one? In the human breast.
Given to thee are those eight paradises
  When thou the ninth one hast within thy breast."

"What shall I Do to be Saved?"—The Zoroastrian has but a dim notion of forgiveness. He believes in it, yet for want of an atonement, having no revelation of the Lamb slain from the foundation of the world, he must needs make it purchasable for the virtue of *a threefold repetition of the divine name.*

The Patet.—Here is his "Patet," or Miserere: (*a*) "I repent, O God, of sins! All wicked thoughts, all wicked words, all wicked deeds, which I have meditated in the world, corporeal or spiritual, I repent of. Lord, forgive, for the three words' sake!" (*b*) "All sins against kindred, superiors and neighbors; the defilement with dirt and corpses; the omission of reciting the Zend-Avesta; what I ought to have thought, and did not; what I ought to have done, and did not; what I ought to have spoken, and did not,—for these, O Lord, I repent. Forgive for the three words' sake!" (*c*) "Of pride, haughtiness and anger; discontent, indolence and idol-worship; omission of the mid-day prayer; theft, robbery, unchastity; sins which I know or know not,—of these repent I. Lord, pardon, for the three words' sake!"

In the religion of the Persians there is nothing corresponding to our Christ. The light with healing in its beams never rose upon them. This is the one vital defect of the Zoroastrian system—the one joint of its harness whereat enters the arrow of death. Its saviour was but a saviour in a dream. The ancient sufis looked for one whom they called *Sosioch*, who would put down Ahriman, and, breaking all chains, usher in a golden age of righteousness and peace. Dim indeed is this, yet who shall say precisely how bright must be the image of the great personal sacrifice ere it has power to save?

It will be remembered that there was enough of light glimmering through the darkness of this false religion to lead, once upon a time, certain of its devotees to the feet of the Christ-child.

> "A comet dangling in the air
> Presaged the ruin both of death and sin,
> And told the wise men of a King,
>   The King of glory, and the Sun
>   Of Righteousness, who then begun
> To draw toward that blessed hemisphere.
>   They, from the farthest East, this new
>   And unknown light pursue
>   Till they appear
> In this blest infant King's propitious eye,
> And pay their homage to his royalty.
>   Persia might then the rising sun adore;
>   It was idolatry no more." [1]

The modern Parsees, indeed, reject all thought of forgiveness. "There is no saviour," they say; "a man must suffer the penalty of whatsoever evil he hath done. The only saviour is a virtuous life." Thus, standing at the very threshold of the truth, they enter not. Even the vague outlines of their own redeemer have vanished into air.

The writer has purposely refrained from emphasizing or enlarging upon the imperfections of the Zoroastrian system, because, whatsoever may be its faults, there is no other form of religion outside of the Bible which

[1] JEREMY TAYLOR.

in pureness of doctrine, clearness of view as to the hereafter and beneficent influence on daily life can be compared with this. Let us fondly trust that many Magi, following the dim star of their Sosioch, have come ere this, with offerings of gold and myrrh and frankincense, into the heavenly presence of the true One.

For salvation is not alone to those only who have abundance of the living Bread, but to such also as, having tasted the crumbs, are anhungered for the Bread. Perhaps in the following parable, by Saadi, there is an overweening trust in the great Father's love:

> "Once as I staggered, blind, upon the brink of hell,
> Above the everlasting fire-flood's awful roar,
> God threw his heart before my feet, and, stumbling o'er
> That obstacle divine, I into heaven fell."

But we may rest assured that if any do thus enter heaven, they are such as stumble while groping for the light.

IV.
BRAHMANISM.

Origin: The Aryan migration into India.
I. *Sacred Books:*
   (1) The Vedas.
   (2) Brahmanas.
   (3) Upanishads.
   Laws of Manu.
   Traditional Tales.
II. *Theology:*
   (1) Monotheism ⎫
   (2) Pantheism ⎬ Brahm.
   (3) Polytheism. ⎭
   The Creed; "the Six Elements."
III. *Results:*
   No Personal Responsibility.
   "Like gods, like people."
   Distinguishing Feature: Caste.
   "*What shall I do to be saved?*"   Be absorbed in Brahm.

IV. BRAHMANISM.

Its Origin.—A race of dreamers dwelt in Central Asia, on the high table-lands lying east of the Caspian Sea, so long ago that in the endeavor to trace them we lose ourselves in pre-historic mists. They called themselves *Aryans*, meaning " of noble blood." From them as the prolific mother has descended the large family of Aryan or Indo-European peoples — the Greeks and Romans, Celts, Hindus and Anglo-Saxons—dreamers all, who, mourning a lost glory and an offended Father, have built them altars and porches of philosophy, and have never ceased to grope eagerly after truth and the Unknown God.

Civilization of the Aryans.—As long as three thousand years ago these Aryans boasted a civilization scarcely inferior to that which, at the same period, prevailed among the Jews, who were just then preparing to float cedar trees from Lebanon for the pillars of their golden temple. They had a well-organized government; they dwelt in comfortable houses; they tilled the fields, ground their barley in mills, were familiar with the arts of weaving and pottery, used gold and silver currency, drove from village to village in wheeled carriages, and had weapons of bronze. They wrote epic poems in the lunar dynasty, twelve hundred years before the beginning of the Christian era.

But what concerns us most is the fact that they were worshipers of the true God. The oldest of their traditions reveal the dim outlines of One concerning whom it was said, "There is none other than He." This, however, was in their earliest years. There are traces of a slow descent into idolatry and of the struggle of the old religion for life—a vain struggle, that marked its progress with ever-multiplying fires and temples built in honor of the many who were mightier than the Unknown One. Then suddenly appeared the titanic figure of *Zoroaster the Reformer.* The old religion under him renewed its strength; the struggle deepened; there were two great parties now—one contending for the old Aryan creed, the other for the shrines of the gods.

The Migration into India.—The latter were defeated; retiring before the victorious hosts of Zoroaster, they crossed the Hindu-Kush Mountains, journeyed down the river-bed of the Indus, and from the north-west entered India. These were the progenitors of the Brahmans of to-day.

Origin of Caste.—In taking possession of the land they were brought into conflict with native tribes dwelling among the hills and tangled forests, who, after a stubborn resistance, at length yielded to their superior might. The victors set themselves at once over all as a superior order, the vanquished taking a subordinate place; and here was the beginning of that iron-banded system of CASTE which has prevailed in

India for thirty centuries, repressing the best energies of that land as did the mountain pressing on the heart of the fabulous Typhon.

The Brahmans.—No sooner had they secured the highest place by right of conquest than they proceeded to make their tenure sure by religious sanctions. A fable was invented declaring that when Brahm created the human race the Brahman sprang from his head; the Kshatriya, or soldier caste, from his breast; the Vaisya, or merchant caste, from his loins; and the Sudra, or laboring caste, from his feet.[1] This fable gave to the Brahmans a sacred pre-eminence—a right to hold themselves aloof from common mortals and to be called after the name of the unseen Brahm. They are the priests of the Hindu religion, conducting its multitudinous rites and ceremonies, and alone endowed with the privilege of reading its sacred books. They cast the horoscope at the birth of every child, whisper the *mantras* or mysterious words, preside at the betrothal and mutter incantations in the dying hour. They are mediators between heaven and earth, themselves worshiped as demigods. Cursed indeed is the man who is cursed of a Brahman, and thrice blessed if but a Brahman's shadow fall upon him.

[1] "With Purusha as victim they performed
A sacrifice. When they divided him,
How did they cut him up? What was his mouth?
What were his arms; and what his thighs and feet?
The Brahman was his mouth; the kingly soldier
Was made his arms; the husbandman his thighs;
The servile Sudra issued from his feet."
MONIER WILLIAMS'S *Hinduism*, p. 31.

It is not strange, these things being considered, that the Brahman is famed for an intense self-consciousness, walking erect with "a proud conviction of superiority depicted on every feature."[1] In the Laws of Manu it is asserted that "a Brahman, by reason of his high birth, is an object of veneration even to the gods." In the Mahâbhârata, the most beautiful of Hindu epics, occurs this passage in a vivid description of a tournament:

"With the noise of the musical instruments and the eager cries of the
    lookers-on,
A din arose like the roaring of the sea;
When, lo! wearing his white raiment and the sacrificial cord,
With snowy hair and silvery beard and the white garland around his
    brows,
Into the midst of the arena slowly walked the Brahman,
Like the sun in a cloudless sky."

These distinctions, rock-rooted by centuries of observance, are practically inviolable. Crossing the line is not so much as dreamed of.[2] To lose caste is to

[1] "Light of complexion, his forehead ample, his countenance of striking significance, his lips thin and mouth expressive, his eyes quick and sharp, his fingers long, his carriage noble and almost sublime, the true Brahman, uncontaminated by European influence and manners, with his intense self-consciousness, with the proud conviction of superiority depicted in every muscle of his face and manifest in every movement of his body, is a wonderful specimen of humanity walking on God's earth."—From SHERRING'S *Hindu Tribes and Castes*.

Rev. Narayan Sheshadrai said, in the Madison Avenue Church in New York in 1873: "I was taught as a Brahman to believe that I was a god on earth, a compound of the proudest assumptions and meanest humiliations."

[2] "In point of fact, strictness in the maintenance of caste is the only real test of Hinduism exacted by the Brahmans of the present day.

be doomed to wander, like the unburied Greeks, in darkness for ever. Imagine how repressive such a system must be on the advancement of a nation. For national life is but another name for the heart-throbbing and struggling of the lower classes to rise. But in India there is no possibility of rising. And India will always be a dependency. Ambition is dead there. To be born a Sudra is to be chained for life to treadmill duties and to the companionship of other Sudras or base ones. The water-carriers and scavengers of Bombay are the descendants of those who carried water and cleaned the streets of Bombay as far back as runneth the memory of man. Society is a ladder indeed, but there is no climbing it. What, then, remains for India, grown old in her conventional bondage? Is there no hope? *Not in Brahmanism.* The forger of chains can scarcely be expected to enact the rôle of liberator. *Caste is the strong citadel of the religion of Brahm.*

The Central Thought.—Let us emphasize that fact as indicating its most characteristic feature. It is by eminence *the religion of caste,* of priestcraft, of the elect few, and, logically, the religion of social and

> In matters of mere faith Hinduism is all-tolerant and all-receptive. No person who is not born a Brahman can become one, but any person can be admitted into the lower ranks of Hinduism who will acknowledge the supremacy of the Brahmans and obey rules of caste. So long as a man holds to his caste he is at liberty to hold any opinions he likes, even to accepting the doctrines of Christianity.
>
> > ' Perfection is alone attained by him
> > Who swerves not from the business of his caste.'"
> >
> > *Hinduism,* p. 151.

political stagnation; its genius, an unyielding pride of aristocracy, an influence as blighting as the finger of death.

In considering the character of this religion let us look first at its sacred books; second, at its theology; and third, at its morality and practical results.

I. *Sacred Books.*—The sacred literature of the Hindus consists of the Vedas, the Brahmanas and the Upanishads; in addition to which there are commentaries without number, law-books, litanies, and interminable legendary poems. These are all in Sanskrit, which is called "the perfect tongue."

(1) *The Vedas.*—The word "veda" means knowledge. It is akin to the Greek *oîda*, Latin *video*, German *wissen*, English *wit*. The Vedas are said to have issued like breath from the self-existent Deity. They are four in number, to wit:

1. The Rig-Veda, from *ric*, to praise. This is the Brahman's bible and hymn-book combined. It consists of ten hundred and twenty-eight hymns or invocations, chiefly addressed to Brahm and the lesser gods.

2. The Sama-Veda, or Book of Penitential Chants.

3. The Yagur-Veda, or Book of Sacrificial Rites.

4. The Atharva-Veda, or Book of Magical Spells and Incantations.

Not all of the poetical effusions in the Vedas are what we would call religious; the following, entitled "Every One to his Taste," will serve as an illustration:

> "Men's tastes and trades are multifarious,
> And so their ends and aims are various.

"The smith seeks something cracked to mend;
The doctor would have sick to tend;
The priest desires a devotee
From whom he may extract a fee.
Each craftsman makes and vends his ware,
And hopes the rich man's gold to share.
My sire's a doctor; I a bard;
Corn grinds my mother, toiling hard.
All craving wealth, we each pursue
By different means the end in view,
Like people running after cows
Which too far off have strayed to browse.
The draught-horse seeks an easy yoke;
The merry dearly like a joke;
Of lovers youthful belles are fond;
And thirsty frogs desire a pond."[1]

(2) *The Brahmanas* are in the form of appendices to the Vedas. They consist chiefly of ritualistic precepts and comments on the Vedic hymns. The following will serve as an illustration; it sets forth the remarkable idea that the gods were mortal until, by meritorious deeds, they extorted immortality from the Supreme Being:

"The gods lived constantly in fear of Death,
The mighty Ender; so with toilsome rites
They worshiped and repeated sacrifices
Till they became immortal. Then the Ender
Said to the gods, 'As ye have made yourselves
Imperishable, so will men endeavor
To free themselves from me; what portion then
Shall I possess in man?' The gods replied,
'Henceforth no being shall become immortal
In his own body; this his mortal frame
Shalt thou still seize; this shall remain thine own.
He who, through knowledge or religious acts,
Henceforth attains to immortality
Shall first present his body, Death, to thee.'"[2]

[1] MUIR.   [2] WILLIAMS.

(3) *The Upanishads* (meaning "beneath the surface") are also appendices to the Vedas. They consist of mystical speculations touching the Deity, the origin of the universe, the nature of the human soul and kindred themes.

In addition to the foregoing there are certain writings called *Smriti*, or Traditions, which are regarded as scarcely less sacred than the Vedas themselves. Among these must be particularly noted the Laws of Manu, consisting of twelve books of precepts having reference particularly to the maintenance of the custom of caste,[1] and the Bhakti-sastras, or Mythological Tales.

---

[1] "It will be found that, after eliminating the purely religious and philosophical precepts, the greater number of its rules fall under the four following heads:

"1. *Acara*, 'immemorial practices.' These include all the observances of caste, regarded as constituting the highest law and highest religion.

"2. *Vyavahara*, 'practices of law and government,' embracing the procedure of legal tribunals, rules of judicature and civil and criminal law.

"3. *Prayas-citta*, 'penitential exercises,' comprehending rules of expiation.

"4. *Karma-phala*, 'consequences of acts,' especially as involving repeated births through numberless existences until the attainment of final beatitude."—*Hinduism*, p. 55.

"A few specimens of Manu's moral precepts are here subjoined:

'Daily perform thine own appointed work
Unweariedly; and to obtain a friend—
A sure companion to the future world—
Collect a store of virtue like the ants,
Who garner up their treasures into heaps;

It is impossible to determine the precise date of these sacred books. If you ask a Brahman, he will gravely inform you that some of them were written more than two million years ago. Max Müller, in his *Ancient Sanskrit Literature*, places the oldest of the Vedic writings at about 1200 B. C. Professor Monier Williams says: "We may be justified in assuming that the hymns of the Veda were probably composed by a succession of poets at different dates between 1500 and 1000 years B. C." The hymns of the Rig-Veda are therefore older than the Psalms of David. They are marked by a beautiful simplicity of diction. Here is a prayer addressed to Agni, god of fire, who was known later on as Vishnu; the worshiper, rubbing together

> For neither father, mother, wife nor son,
> Nor kinsman, will remain beside thee then,
> When thou art passing to that other home:
> Thy virtue will thine only comrade be.
>
> 'Single is every living creature born;
> Single he passes to another world;
> Single he eats the fruits of evil deeds;
> Single, the fruit of good; and when he leaves
> His body like a log or heap of clay
> Upon the ground, his kinsmen walk away:
> Virtue alone stays by him at the tomb,
> And bears him through the dreary trackless gloom.
>
> 'Depend not on another, rather lean
> Upon thyself; trust to thine own exertions.
> Subjection to another's will gives pain;
> True happiness consists in self-reliance.
>
> 'Strive to complete the task thou hast commenced;
> Wearied, renew thy efforts once again;
> Again fatigued, once more the work begin;
> So shalt thou earn success and fortune win.'"—*Hinduism*, p. 69.

two pieces of wood, father and mother of the flame, until they glow, exclaims:

"O Agni, accept my service: listen to my song.
"With this wood I worship thee, Agni, son of strength and conqueror of horses!
"Let thy servants serve thee with songs, O Agni, giver of riches, who delightest in riches and lovest songs.
"O youngest of the gods and best deserving of worship, come at our praise, perform thou the sacrifice, sit down upon this sacred grass."[1]

The Rig-Veda is the most ancient and incomparably the most perfect of the sacred books. The other Vedas are more voluminous, making in all eleven huge octavos.

[1] "I would not wrest to any fanciful resemblance the points of likeness between this ancient divinity (Agni) and the later *avatars* of Indian and Christian creeds; but it is evident the god stands ready to take the part afterward given to Vishnu. And whether or no we choose to consider that the ideals which Vishnu, and still more Christ, express are implanted in human nature, it is evident that, without passing beyond his legitimate functions as a nature-god, Agni is able to realize some of the qualities of such an ideal. He is incarnate after a fashion, being born of the wood; he is, in a peculiar sense, the friend of man; he is the messenger and mediator between heaven and earth; and lastly, he is in a special manner the Holy One, the fosterer of strong emotion, of those mystic thoughts which arise when in any way the mind is violently swayed. Agni is all this without laying aside the elemental nature in which he is clothed:

'Agni is messenger of all the world.
Skyward ascends his flame, the Merciful,
With our libations watered well;
And now the red smoke seeks the heavenly way,
And men enkindle Agni here.

'We make of thee our herald, Holy One;
Bring down the gods unto our feast.
O son of might, and all who nourish man!
Pardon us when on thee we call.'"
KEARY's *Outlines of Primitive Belief,* p. 103.

The supplements are numberless and endless. There are one hundred thousand verses in the Râmayâna alone. Sir William Jones says: "Wherever we direct our attention to Hindu literature the notion of infinity is forced upon us. The longest life would not suffice for a single perusal of works that rise and swell, protuberant like the Himalayas, above the bulkiest compositions of every land."

As to the character of these writings, we may safely accept the judgment of Max Müller, who is probably more familiar with them than any other scholar except among the pundits. He says, in a word, they are "full of pedantry, shallow and insipid grandiloquence and priestly conceit." There are tales, proverbs, incantations, wise maxims, disquisitions on science, songs addressed to gods and harlots,—everything except the hopes and promises which the soul has reason to look for in religion.

"How pitying Vishnu came from heaven, and as a peasant-boy
With merry pranks filled all the cowherd lads and maids with joy;
The wondrous things he said and did while mortal men among,—
All this has saintly Shukadev in the *Brem-Sagar* sung."

In the *Laws of Manu*, the Hindu book of morals and jurisprudence, are thousands of precepts like these: "If a man desire long life, he should eat with his face turned to the east; if prosperity, to the west; if truth and its rewards, to the north;" "When a student is about to read the Vedas he must perform an ablution, compose his limbs and put on a clean vest;" "Whenever a Brahman begins or ends a lecture on the Veda he must pronounce to himself the syllable *Aum*, for unless the syllable *Aum* precede and follow, his learning will slip away from him;" "The name of a woman should be clear and soft, captivating the fancy, auspicious, ending in long vowels and sounding like a benediction." It is sad to think of two hundred millions of immortal souls walking by the light of a bible like this.

II. *Theology.*—We turn now to the theology of Brahmanism; that is, *its belief concerning God and eternal things.*

(1) *One God.*—In the original faith of the Aryans, before they crossed the mountains into India, there was *one Supreme God*, whom they called *Diaus*, from the root *diu*, "to shine"—*the Shining One.* There are invocations in the Rig-Veda addressed to *Diaus-pitar*, whom we at once identify with the Greek Ζεὺς-πάτηρ and the Latin *Jupiter;* and in all these languages it means the same—*Heaven-Father.* Our hearts are strangely moved and warmed at mention of that most sacred name occurring thus in the primeval worship of the Aryans—*Our Father which art in heaven.*

There are not a few hymns in the oldest Vedas which point clearly to the unity of God, such as the following:

> "What god shall we adore with sacrifice?
> Him let us praise, the golden Child that rose
> In the beginning, who was born the lord,
> The one sole lord of all that is—who made
> The earth and formed the sky, who giveth life,
> Who giveth strength, whose bidding gods revere,
> Whose hiding-place is immortality,
> Whose shadow death; who by his might is King
> Of all the breathing, sleeping, waking world.
> Where'er, let loose in space, the mighty waters
> Have gone, depositing a fruitful seed

> And generating fire, there He arose
> Who is the breath and life of all the gods,
> Whose mighty glance looks round the vast expanse
> Of watery vapor—source of energy,
> Cause of the sacrifice, the only God
> Above the gods."[1]

Or the following:

"He is the only master of the world; he fills heaven and earth. He gives life and strength; all the other gods seek for his blessing; death and immortality are but his shadow.

"The mountains covered with frost, the ocean with its waves, the vast regions of heaven, proclaim his power.

"Heaven and earth tremble for fear before him. He is God above all gods."[2]

But this Supreme One was conceived of as afar off—"Para-Brahm," a god too distant to be worshiped. "He is," says one of the sages, "neither the known nor the unknown. That which cannot be expressed by words, that which cannot be conceived by the mind, that which cannot be seen with the eyes,—that is Brahm;" "His spirit is divinely calm, his mind supernal;" "He is without size, quality, character or division;" "The wise man contemplates him as the Spirit who resembles space;" "He is like one asleep." So Krishna says: "The works of the universe confine me not; I am like one who sitteth aloof, taking no interest in earthly things."

(2) *Pantheism.*—Between this conception of God and Pantheism there was obviously but a single step, and

---

[1] MONIER WILLIAMS.   [2] QUACKENBOS, *Ancient Literature.*

that step was early and easily taken, as we should expect of a speculative people dwelling above the mountains in an atmosphere burdened with the spirit of dreams. The religious teachers soon came to regard *Brahm* as "the one eternal, absolute, unchangeable Being, who unfolds himself into the universe as Creator and created, becoming in turn ether, air, fire, water and earth." They represented him as saying, "I am the light in the sun and moon; I am the brilliancy in flame, the radiance in all shining things, the light in all lights, the sound in air, the fragrance in earth, the eternal seed of all things that exist, the life in all; I am the goodness of the good; I am the beginning, middle, end, the eternal in time, the birth and death of all."[1] This led to the important formula, *Ekam eva advitiyam*—"There is only One, and there is nothing beside him;" that is, nothing really exists except Brahm. All things else are *maya* or illusion.[2]

[1] DR. CAIRD.

[2] "To men conscious of sin and apprehensive of a coming retribution any system will stand commended which minifies or denies responsibility. This Hinduism does on the basis of three propositions—viz. that there is no essential distinction between the soul and God; that there is no such thing as free agency; and, consequently, no necessary and permanent distinction between sin and righteousness. Such doctrines cannot indeed heal, but they are most effectual to narcotize the conscience. They dull and ease the acuter pangs of remorse and deaden the sense of need of a Saviour. A system which, like Hinduism, is as an opiate to the pain of sin must needs stand strong in the faith of its votaries. Also, again, the doctrine of *maya*, or illusion, does much to make the Hindu position inexpugnable. To deny or doubt the affirmations of consciousness—*e. g.* as to freedom, personality, responsibility—were to render the very foundations of human knowledge more uncertain than sand. With us, here is the ultimate appeal in all argu-

The souls of men are emanations of Brahm, the universal self-existent soul; they are as "sparks from his central fire, separated for a time to be absorbed at last." The life and actions of men are "as the illusory phantoms and appearances which a conjurer calls up and the gaping crowd mistake for realities, or as the personages, scenes, events of a troubled dream."[1] One of the Brahman's proverbs is, "Our life is as a drop that trembles on the lotus-leaf, fleeting and quickly gone." The consummation of all best wishes and highest ambitions is to be thus exhaled into Brahm,

ment and end of all strife. But the Hindu, by denying the dicta of consciousness and affirming this doctrine of illusion, places himself at once beyond the reach of argument. Every missionary knows to his sorrow how, at the last, his adversary will always bring forth *maya* as a sufficient answer to any argument and an adequate solution of every difficulty. From this panoply of illusion the keenest arguments glance off like feather-shafts from a coat of mail. Still further, it is impossible that a man who has been brought to doubt the testimony of his own consciousness should be otherwise than indifferent to the truth. If the doctrine of *maya* be admitted, the distinction between truth and error vanishes into thin air. If all is error, then there is no room for truth. Truth is but a mere phantom which is not worth the chasing. All things are equally true or equally false as you please to take it. Hence, argues the Hindu always, all religions are alike true and from God. Christianity is true; so also is Hinduism, Mohammedanism and every other religion. There is only the difference of a name; and if this be so, why should a man forsake the cult of his fathers only to bring trouble and ruin on himself? It is plain that no temper of mind could well be more unfavorable to the reception of the truth than this. To a man who has come under the deadly influence of this doctrine of *maya* all argument, on whatsoever subject, becomes a mere logomachy. It is like the play of fencers, which has no other object than to display the agility and skill of the fencer."—DR. S. H. KELLOGG, in *Princeton Review*.

[1] DR. CAIRD.

to be absorbed in the Infinite One.[1] In the Rig-Veda it is written,

> "The embodied spirit has a thousand heads,
> A thousand eyes, a thousand feet, around
> On every side enveloping the earth,
> Yet filling space no longer than a span.
> He is himself this very universe;
> He is whatever is, has been and shall be;
> He is the lord of immortality.
> All creatures are one-fourth of him; three-fourths
> Are that which is immortal in the sky."[2]

Polytheism.—Philosophers may dream thus, but, manifestly, human souls burdened with toil, sorrow and guilt must have a god nearer than Brahm. The descent from Pantheism to Polytheism is by easy stages; for if God be everything, then everything is God; if Brahm be asleep, why should we utter our prayers before him? if he be afar off and invisible, here are trees, rivers, living creatures at hand; as we must worship, let us worship these. There are said to be three hundred and thirty millions of divinities in the Hindu pantheon, chiefly personifications of the forces and phenomena of nature. These are all re-

---

[1] "Their doctrine is, that the one sole, self-existing Supreme Self, the only really existing Essence, the one eternal Germ of all things, delights in infinite expansion, in infinite manifestations of itself, in infinite creation, dissolution and re-creation through infinite varieties and diversities of operation. The very name 'Brahman' (neut. from root *brih,* 'to grow') given to the eternal Essence is expressive of this growth, this expansion, this universal development and diffusion. Hence all visible form is an emanation from God."—*Hinduism,* p. 86.

[2] WILLIAMS.

garded as manifestations and representatives of the Supreme One.[1]

> "Into the bosom of the one great sea
> Flow streams that come from hills on every side:
> Their names are various as their springs."

The Trimurti.—In the catalogue of Hindu gods we must begin by naming the great *Trimurti*, or triad, consisting of Agni, Indra and Surya, personifications respectively of fire, storm and sunlight. These three in process of time came to be identified with Brahma, Siva and Vishnu.[2] The symbol of the triad thus

[1] "To account for its polytheism, idol-worship and system of caste distinctions popular Hinduism supposes that the one Supreme Being amuses himself by illusory appearances; that he manifests himself variously, as light does in the rainbow; and that all visible and material objects, good and bad, including gods, demons, demigods, good and evil spirits, human beings and animals, are emanations from him, and are ultimately to be reabsorbed into his essence."—*Hinduism*, p. 12.

[2] "The pantheon of the early Hindus was thus developed: In the beginning was *Brahma*, sole and self-existent. He willed to create various creatures out of his own substance. Accordingly, by meditation he produced the waters; into them he put a seed which developed a golden egg, and from that egg he was born. But as the people did not abandon their worship of the old gods to take up with any such abstraction, the priests, with singular tact, incorporated the most popular of these divinities with Brahma, and so the triad was formed—*Brahma* (the Creator of all things), *Vishnu* (the Preserver, who underwent ten *avataras*, or incarnations, to deliver the people from the tyranny of as many wicked princes)—and *Siva* (the Destroyer). Here was no trinity, for there was no unity, but a triad—three co-ordinate deities."—REV. S. M. JACKSON, in *Schaff-Herzog Encyclopedia*.

"It is usual to describe these three gods as Creator, Preserver and Destroyer, but this gives a very inadequate idea of their complex characters. Nor does the conception of their relationship to each other become clearer when it is ascertained that their functions are constantly interchangeable, and that each may take the place of the other,

constituted is the triangle, and it is typified by the mysterious syllable *Aum.*

according to the sentiment expressed by the greatest of Indian poets, Kalidasa:

> 'In those three persons the one God was shown—
> Each first in place, each last—not one alone;
> Of Siva, Vishnu, Brahma, each may be
> First, second, third among the blessed three.'"
>
> *Hinduism,* p. 87.

The following hymn to the Vedic Triad has a remote likeness to our Christian doxology:

> "INDRA, twin-brother of the god of fire!
> When thou wast born, thy mother Aditi
> Gave thee, her lusty child, the thrilling draught
> Of mountain-growing soma—source of life
> And never-dying vigor to thy frame.
> Thou art our guardian, advocate and friend,
> A brother, father, mother, all combined.
> Most fatherly of fathers, we are thine
> And thou art ours. Oh let thy pitying soul
> Turn to us in compassion when we praise thee,
> And slay us not for one sin or for many.
> Deliver us to-day, to-morrow, every day.
> Vainly the demon dares thy might; in vain
> Strives to deprive us of thy watery treasures.
> Earth quakes beneath the crashing of thy bolts.
> Pierced, shattered, lies the foe, his cities crushed,
> His armies overthrown, his fortresses
> Shivered to fragments; then the pent-up waters,
> Released from long imprisonment, descend
> In torrents to the earth, and swollen rivers,
> Foaming and rolling to their ocean home,
> Proclaim the triumph of the Thunderer.
>
> "AGNI, thou art a sage, a priest, a king,
> Protector, father of the sacrifice.
> Commissioned by us men, thou dost ascend
> A messenger, conveying to the sky

The first member of the triad, Brahma, is a personification of Brahm, the divine essence.

The second, "the three-eyed, thousand-named Siva," is the god who presides over the convulsions of nature. His image is adorned with a necklace of human skulls. He craves blood, the blood of children, of widows and slaves.

> Our hymns and offerings. Though thy origin
> Be threefold, now from air and now from water,
> Now from the mystic double Arani,
> Thou art thyself a mighty god, a lord,
> Giver of life and immortality,
> One in thy essence, but to mortals three;
> Displaying thine eternal triple form
> As fire on earth, as lightning in the air,
> As sun in heaven. Thou art the cherished guest
> In every household—father, brother, son,
> Friend, benefactor, guardian, all in one.
> Deliver, mighty lord, thy worshipers;
> Purge us from taint of sin, and when we die
> Deal mercifully with us on the pyre,
> Burning our bodies with their load of guilt,
> But bearing our eternal part on high
> To luminous abodes and realms of bliss,
> For ever there to dwell with righteous men.

> "Behold the rays of dawn, like heralds, lead on high
> SURYA, that men may see the great all-knowing god.
> The stars slink off like thieves in company with night
> Before the all-seeing eye, whose beams reveal his presence,
> Gleaming like brilliant flames, to nation after nation.
> Surya, with flaming locks, clear-sighted god of day!
> Thy seven ruddy mares bear on thy rushing car.
> With these, thy self-yoked steeds, seven daughters of thy chariot,
> Onward thou dost advance. To thy refulgent orb,
> Beyond this lower gloom and upward to the light,
> Would we ascend, O Sun, thou god among the gods."
> *Hinduism*, pp. 28–30.

The third, Vishnu, is the great helper. He is worshiped as the day-god. With three steps he measures the heavens—sunrise, noon and sunset. Once and again has he come upon earth to save it from the ruthless hands of Siva. These descents are known as *avatars*, or incarnations. Nine avatars are celebrated in epic verse; the tenth, still future, is to usher in the golden age.

Soma.—Next in order after the triad is the god Soma. This is a deification of the fermented juice of the moon-plant,[1] and is adored as the giver of strength. The worshiper, taking from his lips the emptied cup, sings,

> "We've quaffed the soma bright,
> And are immortal grown;
> We've entered into light,
> And all the gods have known.
> What mortal now can harm
> Or foeman vex us more?
> Through thee, beyond alarm,
> Immortal god! we soar."

Gunga.—We must not omit, moreover, the goddess Gunga, a divine personification of the river Ganges, "born on the snow-capped ranges of the Himalayas from the forehead of Brahm." To follow the Ganges on foot from its mouth to its source is regarded as an

---

[1] "*Asclepias acida* is the botanical name of this plant. From its juice can be concocted an alcoholic drink which was much cherished by the Indians and Persians (by the latter called *homa*), and which played an important part in their ritual. The soma-drink was a sacramental draught, and as such corresponded to the mystic millet-water of the Eleusinian celebrations."—KEARY'S *Outlines of Primitive Belief*, p. 102.

act of special merit. The pilgrimage requires about six years.[1]

[1] "As the Ganges was the most majestic, so it soon became the holiest and most revered, of all rivers. No sin was too heinous to be removed, no character too black to be washed clean, by its waters. Hence the countless temples with flights of steps lining its banks; hence the array of priests called 'Sons of the Ganges' sitting on the edge of its streams, ready to aid the ablutions of conscience-stricken bathers and stamp them as white-washed when they emerge from its waters. Hence also the constant traffic carried on in transporting Ganges-water in small bottles to all parts of the country."—*Hinduism*, p. 172.

THE DESCENT OF THE GANGES.
(From the Rāmāyana, by the poet Valmiki.)

"From the high heaven burst Ganges forth, first on Siva's lofty crown;
Headlong then, and prone to earth, thundering rushed the cataract down.
Swarms of bright-hued fish came dashing; turtles, dolphins, in their mirth,
Fallen or falling, glancing, flashing, to the many-gleaming earth;
And all the hosts of heaven came down, sprites and genii, in amaze,
And each forsook his heavenly throne upon that glorious scene to gaze.
On cars, like high-towered cities, seen, with elephants and couriers rode,
Or on soft-swinging palanquin lay wondering, each observant god.
As met in bright divan each god, and flashed their jeweled vestures' rays,
The coruscating ether glowed as with a hundred suns ablaze,
And in ten thousand sparkles bright and flashing up the cloudy spray,
The snowy-flocking swans less white, within its glittering mists at play.
And headlong now poured down the flood, and now in silver circlets wound;
Then lake-like spread, all bright and broad, then gently, gently flowed around;
Then 'neath the caverned earth descending, then spouted up the boiling tide;
Then stream with stream, harmonious blending, swell bubbling up or smooth subside.

Gods Many.—After these come the sacred cows, typifying the all-yielding earth, and worshiped by pouring oil upon their feet and water upon their horns.[1] Then stars, serpents, monkeys, stones, trees. There is a tree whereof the trunk is said to represent one of the great gods, and every branch and twig and leaf an inferior one. Nature is ransacked for gods, and, nature being exhausted, men with elephants' heads are conjured up, and images of all imaginable grotesque and uncouth shapes. These are India's gods.

The Creed.—The creed of Brahmanism is briefly set forth in "The Six Elements," which are as follows:

1st. The soul is sempiternal; that is, pre-existent and immortal.

2d. The substance or matter out of which the universe has been evolved is sempiternal.

3d. The soul can only act when it is invested with a bodily form and united with mind.

4th. This union of soul and body is bondage and productive only of misery.

5th. The law of consequences requires that the soul shall pass through various forms of life, wherein it receives its just apportionment of suffering and reward.

6th. This transmigration of the soul through a suc-

By that heaven-welling water's breast the genii and the sages stood;
Its sanctifying dews they blessed, and plunged within the lustral flood."
—MILMAN.

[1] "When a Brahman is dying, though he may have prayed ten hours daily, yet all his friends can do is *to clasp his hands about the tail of a cow.* The man cries in hopelessness of uncertainty, 'Where am I going?'"—*Homiletical Review*, July, 1885.

cession of bodies must continue until all personality is at length merged and absorbed in the Universal Soul.

It is plain that the Brahmans believe in immortality, but not in ever-conscious being. Death is an end of consciousness to such as are prepared for it. At the open grave they sing:

> "Approach thou now the lap of earth, thy mother,
> The wide-extending earth, the ever-kindly;
> A maiden soft as wool to him who comes with gifts,
> She shall protect thee from destruction's besom."[1]

They dream not of a resurrection. In their philosophy

---

[1] THE DIVINE SONG.

(*From the Mâhâbhârata, by the poet Vyasa.*)

The Deity addresses the warrior Bharata on the eve of battle, assuring him of the immortality of the soul:

"The soul, within its mortal frame, glides on through childhood, youth
    and age;
Then, in another form renewed, renews its stated course again.
All indestructible is He that spread the living universe;
And who is he that shall destroy the work of the Indestructible?
Corruptible these bodies are that wrap the everlasting soul—
The eternal, unimaginable soul. Whence on to battle, Bharata!
For he that thinks to slay the soul or he that thinks the soul is slain
Are fondly both alike deceived: it is not slain—it slayeth not;
It is not born—it doth not die; past, present, future, knows it not;
Ancient, eternal and unchanged, it dies not with the dying frame.
Who knows it incorruptible and everlasting and unborn,
What heeds he whether he may slay or fall himself in battle slain?
As their old garments men cast off, anon new raiment to assume,
So casts the soul its worn-out frame and takes at once another form.
The weapon cannot pierce it through, nor wastes it the consuming fire;
The liquid waters melt it not, nor dries it up the parching wind;
Impenetrable and unburned, impermeable and undried,
Perpetual, ever-wandering, firm, indissoluble, permanent,
Invisible, unspeakable."—MILMAN.

there is nothing corresponding to the Christian's heaven —no Father's house, no future recognition, no "knitting severed friendships up." Their supreme hope is to pass as rapidly as possible from one form of life into another until finally absorbed in that infinite Nothing which they call Brahm or the all-pervading Soul.

Salvation.—They believe in salvation, but from what? From sin or spiritual death? No, indeed. They look for a deliverance from life itself; that is, from self-conscious being, for being is the sum-total of evils. To escape from self, to lose personality by being merged in Brahm,—this is salvation.

"Thou that would'st find the lost One, lose thyself:
Nothing but self thyself from him divides."

They call it *apavarga*, to be swallowed up, like a particle of water exhaled by the sun's rays, floating in vapor, falling again as a raindrop into the sea.

"*What shall I Do to be Saved?*"—How is this absorption to be accomplished? In other words, What is the Brahman's "plan of salvation"?

It is twofold, theoretically.

First, *bhakti*, or "salvation by faith." This is only for the select few. The word "faith" must be understood as meaning an absolute belief in the most extravagant miracles and legendary tales, an unreasoning assent to everything in the Vedas however preposterous, and an unreserved yielding up of self to the contemplation of Brahm.

Second, *karma*, or "salvation by works." This is for the great multitude, who cannot conceive of religion except as a process of merit-making. For them deliverance is bought by pious acts of prayer, austerity and sacrifice.

In fact, however, the adherents of this religion are all believers in the efficacy of works. The "faith" of the Brahman is itself pre-eminently a meritorious work. He hopes for deliverance by bathing in the Ganges, eating clarified butter, holding the breath while reading a set portion of the Vedas, quaffing the dust raised by the hoofs of sacred cows, repeating over and over again the mystic syllable *Aum* or keeping the mind in fixed contemplation of Brahm. The most meritorious prayer in the Hindu ritual is called *Gayatri*, and is as follows:

> "Let us in silent adoration yearn
> After the Deity, the radiant Sun
> Who all illumes and who all creates,
> From whom all come, to whom all must return,
> Whom we invoke to guide our minds and feet
> In our slow progress toward his heavenly seat."

Those who aspire to great sanctity are accustomed to repeat this prayer as many as a hundred and twenty-eight times at each of the daily periods of devotion, morning, noon and sunset.

The Twice-born Yogi.—If you would discover a Hindu saint, you must search by the roadside. You will find him there, crouching upon his knees, naked, with hair uncombed these many years, the Vedas open before him. His body is smeared with ashes and dung. His countenance wears a look of utter stupidity. This is the twice-born Yogi,[1] the consummate fruit of Brahmanism. This is the answer of the sacred books to the old question, What shall I do to be saved? The twice-born Yogi is losing himself in Brahm. He has no longer any consciousness of guilt, passion or appetite, and moves not save when, with a spiritual pride which would be supremely ludicrous were it not so lamentable, he lifts his dreamy eyes and mutters, "I am God! I am God!" Thus "the highest attainment of the Brahman devotee is blasphemy," and with this blasphemy on his lips he lives uselessly and stolidly dies.[2]

[1] "The three upper castes are styled 'the twice-born,' because their sons are initiated into the study of the Veda, the management of the sacred fire and of the purifying rites by a singular ceremony—the rite of conducting a boy to a spiritual teacher—connected with which is the investiture with the sacred cord, ordinarily worn over the left shoulder and under the right arm."—*Schaff-Herzog Encyclopedia*, article "Brahmanism."

[2] "That holy man who stands immovable,
As if erect upon a pinnacle,
His appetites and organs all subdued,
Sated with knowledge secular and sacred,
To whom a lump of earth, a stone or gold,
To whom friends, relatives, acquaintances,
Neutrals and enemies, the good and bad,
Are all alike, is called 'one yoked with God.'
The man who aims at that supreme condition
Of perfect yoking with the Deity
Must first of all be moderate in all things,
In food, in sleep, in vigilance, in action,
In exercise and recreation. Then
Let him, if seeking God by deep abstraction,
Abandon his possessions and his hopes,
Betake himself to some secluded spot,
And fix his heart and thoughts on God alone.

III. *The Results.*—What, now, are the results? For this is the crucial test of all religious systems. By their fruits ye shall know them.

No Personal Responsibility.—To begin with, Brahmanism is incapable of producing morality as such, because it ignores the deep-founded and eternal distinctions between right and wrong. It has, indeed, no ground whereon to determine the moral quality of any act.[1] To hurt a Brahman or a cow is regarded as a

> There let him choose a seat, not high nor low,
> And with a cloth or skin to cover him,
> And kusa-grass beneath him, let him sit
> Firm and erect, his body, head and neck
> Straight and immovable, his eyes directed
> Toward a single point, not looking round,
> Devoid of passion, free from anxious thought,
> His heart restrained and deep in meditation.
> E'en as a tortoise draws its head and feet
> Within its shell, so must he keep his organs
> Withdrawn from sensual objects. He whose senses
> Are well controlled attains to sacred knowledge,
> And thence obtains tranquillity of thought.
> Without quiescence there can be no bliss.
> E'en as a storm-tossed ship upon the waves,
> So is the man whose heart obeys his passions,
> Which like the winds will hurry him away. Quiescence,
> Quiescence, is the state of the Supreme.
> He who, intent on meditation, joins
> His soul with the Supreme, is like a flame
> That flickers not when sheltered from the wind."
> —*Hinduism*, p. 210.

[1] "The Institutes of Manu regulated the moral and social life of the people, prescribing certain rules for the government of society and the punishment of crimes. Purity of life was enjoined on all. One of the chief duties was to honor father and mother—the mother a thousand times the most—and the Brahman more than either. Widows are forbidden to remarry, and the duties of a wife are thus described: ' *The*

mortal sin, while to lie, steal and commit all kinds of unmentionable vileness are mere peccadilloes. The independent being or personality of the soul being denied, there can be no personal responsibility or hindrance to an evil life. Tell a pundit that he is guilty of theft or lying, and his answer is, "God is everywhere—in you, in me, in everything around us. He enables me to move my lips and to extend my hands. If, therefore, I have lied or stolen, the blame must be laid on Him who lives and acts in me." Dr. Caird says: "The hidden logic of pantheism leads, by natural sequence, to a fatalistic morality—a morality which tolerates or sanctions the vices that spring from the natural desires. For moral distinctions disappear in a religion which conceives of God as no nearer to the pure heart than to that which is the haunt of selfish and sensual lusts. The lowest appetites and the loftiest

wife must always be in a cheerful temper, devoting herself to the good management of the household, taking great care of the furniture and keeping down all expenses with a frugal hand. The husband to whom her father has given her she must obsequiously honor while he lives, and never neglect him when he dies. The husband gives bliss continually to his wife here below, and he will give her happiness in the next world. He must be constantly revered as a god by a virtuous wife, even if he does not observe approved usages or is devoid of good qualities. A faithful wife, who wishes to attain heaven and dwell there with her husband, must never do anything unkind toward him, whether he be living or dead.' The following was the punishment for killing *a cow*, an animal treated with the honors due to a deity: 'All day the guilty must wait on a herd of cows, and stand quaffing the dust raised by their hoofs. Free from passion, he must stand when they stand, follow when they move, lie down near them when they lie down. By thus waiting on a herd for three months he who has killed a cow atones for his guilt.'"—QUACKENBOS'S *Ancient Literature*, p. 39.

moral aspirations, the grossest impurities and the most heroic virtues, are alike consecrated by the presence of God."

"*Like Gods, like People.*"—On the other hand, the sanctions of morality are equally impaired among the masses, who, unable to penetrate the inner sanctuary of pantheism, are content to worship the common gods. It is a true saying, "Like gods, like people." The gods of the Hindus are vile. The best of them, Vishnu the Helper, is a false and cruel monster. How can a people bowing in worship before the altars of divine thieves, liars, murderers and adulterers be otherwise than immoral? Said the Abbé du Bois, a missionary at Mysore: "I have never yet seen a religious procession in India without its presenting to me the image of hell." Add to that the testimony of Bishop Heber, also a missionary, who said: "I have never met with a race of men whose standard of morality is so low, whose ordinary conversation is so vile, who shed blood with so little repugnance." Thus in India we behold an utter divorcement of religion and morality. A large proportion of the inmates of prisons are of the Brahman caste." "The Hindu mind," says James Freeman Clarke, "is singularly pious, but also singularly immoral, capable at once of loftiest thoughts and of basest deeds." India is the land of the old-time suttee, of almost universal sensuality, of abject indolence and beggary, of false social distinctions, of thuggism and infanticide, and of woman's imprisonment in the zenana.

This is what Brahmanism, with its one transcendental

Brahm and its three hundred and thirty millions of common gods, has been able to do for the proud Aryans in a period of three thousand years. Is this religion true or false?

A Better Day Dawning.—Blessed be God! a better day is dawning for India. The flag that floats above her cities' gates is that of a Christian nation, and the name of Jesus, before which the walls and battlements of venerable usage are as spiders' webs, is being preached beneath her banyan trees. In the sacred city of Benares—where not many years ago a missionary was stoned for polluting with his feet the sacred river—a company of native Christians are wont to worship God by the river-side. Max Müller says: "Brahmanism is dead and gone." There is a tradition among the people that the old faith of the Aryans is to be supplanted in fullness of time by another coming from the distant West. That time, let us believe, is drawing nigh. It cannot be long ere Christ, assuming in fulfillment of prophecy the place of the tenth avatar of Vishnu, shall usher in the golden age.[1]

An address was delivered some years ago by Baboo

[1] "Said a Hindu to one of our missionaries: 'Reviling our gods, criticising our shastras and ridiculing our ritual will accomplish nothing. But the story you tell of Him who loved and died—that story, sir, will overthrow our temples, destroy our ritual, abolish our shastras and extinguish our gods.' In the year 1800 the first Hindu convert was baptized in the Ganges, Krishna Pal by name. He was sorely persecuted; but his reply was, 'I have been a great sinner. I heard of Christ, that he laid down his life for sinners. I thought, What love is this! Now, say, if anything like this love was ever shown by any of your gods? Did Doorga or Kale or Krishna die for sinners?' Self-prompted, he erected the first native place of worship in Bengal. In one of the

Chunder Sen—not a Christian himself, but a learned Brahman weary of his ancestral faith—in which he used these words: " Who rules India ? What power is it that sways our destinies at the present moment ? You are mistaken if you think it is Lord Lytton in the Cabinet or the military genius of Sir Frederick Haines in the field that rules India. It is not politics, it is not diplomacy, that has laid a firm hold of the Indian heart. It is not the glittering bayonet nor the fiery cannon that influences us. Armies never conquered the heart of a nation. No! If you wish to secure the allegiance of India, it must be by exercising a spiritual influence. And such, indeed, has been the case. You cannot deny that our hearts have been touched and conquered by the superior power. This power is Christ. Christ rules India. England has sent us a tremendous moral force in the life and character of that mighty Prophet to conquer and hold this empire. None but Jesus— none but Jesus—none but Jesus ever deserved this bright, this precious diadem, India; and Jesus shall have it."

hymns he wrote he, coming from dark idolatry, expresses the sentiments of all who feel themselves redeemed by propitiatory love:

> 'O thou, my soul, forget no more
> The Friend who all thy sorrows bore!
> Let every idol be forgot,
> But, O my soul, forget him not!
>
> 'Jesus for thee a body takes,
> Thy guilt assumes, thy fetters breaks,
> Discharging all thy dreadful debt;
> And canst thou e'er such love forget?'"
>
> —*Monday Club*, for 1879, p. 401.

V.
BUDDHISM.

I. *Its Founder:* Gautama, "the Buddha."

II. *Sacred Books:* Tripitaka, or "The Three Baskets."

III. *Theology:* "The Four Truths" and "The Noble Eightfold Path."

    (1) *Buddh*, or the Universal Mind.

    (2) *Karma*, or the Law of Consequences.

    (3) *Nirvana*, or Annihilation.

Central Thought: Self-culture.

"*What shall I do to be saved?*" Be sublimely indifferent to everything.

V. BUDDHISM.

The Aryans who came over the Hindu-Kush Mountains about 1200 B. C. brought with them the religion of the Rig-Veda. In course of time they pushed their way to a supreme place among the inhabitants, arrogating to themselves the title of Brahmans, or priests of Brahm. In their hands the philosophy of the Rig-Veda grew into thousands of tomes and developed into the rarest and most ethereal pantheism, and its morality degenerated at length into a system of rites and ceremonies whose end was merely the maintenance of the sacerdotal caste in a life of dreamy indolence. The people meanwhile, following their blind guides, wandered farther and farther from the true God. Their spiritual nature was cramped and crushed in the coils of a ritualism as pitiless and deadly as the serpents of Tenedos, and if they looked above the heads of their priests for relief, lo! there was the stony, smiling face of Brahm. But in the good providence of our Father there is no pain without its remedy, no night without a morning; the darkest hour is that which unfolds the surest prophecy of dawn.

I. *Birth of Gautama.*—In the year 447 B. C.[1] a child was born in the palace at Kapilavastu, the royal city

[1] James Freeman Clarke makes it 623 B. C.; Rhys Davids, 500 B. C.

of Oude, who was destined to turn and overturn the existing order of things. His family name was Gautama. If we are to form a just conception of Buddhism, it will be necessary, first of all, to know something of this wonderful child, for he was at once its founder, exemplar, preacher and god.

His birth, according to the sacred traditions, was on this wise: By the side of the river Rohini, in a grove of lofty satin trees, he first opened his eyes upon the world. Angels were there to bid him welcome; the sun stood still, casting a shadow over the sacred spot where he lay. Immediately after his birth the child walked three paces, and in a voice like thunder proclaimed a new name, *Siddartha*, "the fulfillment of wishes."[1] At that moment "a radiant light was spread over ten thousand worlds. The blind saw, the dumb spake; prisoners were loosed from their chains; refreshing winds blew gently over the earth; lotus-flowers were suddenly opened in full bloom; lilies dropped from the sky; the air was filled with perfume and with songs of angels echoing far and near." It was known thus from the beginning that he was destined to a place of unusual prominence. At five months of age

[1] "To the pious Buddhist," says Rhys Davids (p. 28 of *Buddhism*, to which the writer acknowledges special obligation for material used in the preparation of this chapter), "it seems irreverent to speak of Gautama by his mere ordinary name, and he makes use, therefore, of one of those numerous epithets which are used only of the Buddha, the Enlightened One. Such are Sakya-sina, 'the lion of the tribe of Sakya;' Sakya-muni, 'the Sakya sage;' Sugata, 'the happy one;' Sattha, 'the teacher;' Jina, 'the conqueror;' Bhagava, 'the blessed one;' Loka-natha, 'the Lord of the world;' Sarvajna, 'the omniscient one;' Dharma-raja, 'the king of righteousness,' and many others."

the infant, being left under a tree alone, meditated so deeply that he fell into a trance; when his nurse returned she saw him crowned with a halo of light, and overhead, kneeling in the clouds, were three wise men with flowing beards who chanted a prophecy: "This child shall be the teacher of a law which shall be as water to extinguish the fiery griefs of life, as light to enlighten its darkness, and as a chariot to carry us through the wilderness to the promised land."

His Early Life.—As the lad grew older he was by his friends surrounded with all the delights and allurements of a worldly life, in the hope of weaning him from his serious moods. He was married to the beautiful princess Yasodhara; three palaces were built for him,

> "Where skill had spent
> All lovely phantasies to lull the mind,
> And always breathed sweet airs, and night and day
> Delicious foods were spread, and dewy fruits,
> Sherbets new-chilled with snows of Himalay,
> And sweetmeats made of subtle daintiness.
> And night and day served there a chosen band
> Of nautch-girls, dark-browed ministers of love,
> Who fanned the sleeping eyes of the happy prince;
> And thus Siddartha lived forgetting."

Forgetting? Ah, no:

> "Still came
> The shadows of his meditation back,
> As the lake's silver dulls with driving clouds."

The prince would wander away into the deep shadows of the forest and spend days together meditating on the problems of life. He used to say, "Nothing on earth is stable, nothing is real. Life is like the spark produced by the friction of wood; it is lighted and extinguished; we know not whence it came or whither it goes. There must be some Supreme Intelligence where we may find rest. Oh that I might attain it! for I would then bring light unto men. If I were free myself, I could deliver the world."[1] At this time he beheld a threefold vision which greatly deepened his weariness of life: (1) an old man, bald, wrinkled, with chattering teeth, feebly leaning on his staff; (2) a man suffering from a loathsome disease, homeless, friendless, dying in the mire by the roadside; (3) a decomposing corpse, surrounded by mourners shrieking and tearing their hair. And, seeing these things, the prince exclaimed, "Woe to youth which hastens on to old age! Woe to health which succumbs to so many dire diseases! Woe to life which ends so miserably! I will go aside and meditate how I may bring about deliverance." This was the turning-point in Siddartha's life.

"*The Great Renunciation.*"—One night he arose from his perfumed bed, " roused into activity," says the chronicle, " like one who is told that his house is burning." All delights and luxuries invited him to stay; his wife lay buried in slumber.

> "'I will depart,' he said; 'the hour is come!
> Thy tender lips, dear sleeper, summon me
> To that which saves the earth, but sunders us.'"

Then followed the great renunciation, *Mahabhinish-*

[1] MAX MÜLLER.

Kramana. Putting aside the glittering hopes of empire and conquest, he determined to go forth " with patient, stainless feet," seeking deliverance.

> " This will I do, because the woeful cry
> Of life and all flesh living cometh up
> Into my ears, and all my soul is full
> Of pity for the sickness of this world;
> Which I will heal, if healing may be found
> By uttermost renouncing." [1]

One farewell look into the face of his sleeping wife, and he was gone out into the night alone. This was the life he had chosen—darkness, solitude henceforth, if only it might end in deliverance.[2]

[1] *Light of Asia.*

[2] " It was long years before he saw his home again. His return, in answer to the summons of his venerable father, is thus described: Gautama started for Kapilavastu, and on his arrival there stopped, according to his custom, in a grove outside the town. There his father, uncles and others came to see him, but the latter at least were by no means pleased with their mendicant clansman; and, though it was the custom on such occasions to offer to provide ascetics with their daily food, they all left without having done so. The next day, therefore, Gautama set out, accompanied by his disciples, carrying his bowl to beg for a meal. As he came near the gate of the little town he hesitated whether he should not go straight to the raja's residence, but at last he determined to adhere to a rule of the order, according to which a Buddhist mendicant should beg regularly from house to house. It soon reached the raja's ears that his son was walking through the streets begging. Startled at such news, he rose up, and, holding his outer robe together with his hands, went out quickly, and, hastening to the place where Gautama was, he said, ' Why, master, do you put us to shame? Why do you go begging for your food? Do you think it is not possible to provide food for so many mendicants?'

"' Oh, maharaja,' was the reply, ' this is the custom of all our race.'

"' But we are descended from an illustrious race of warriors, and not one of them has ever begged his bread.'

"' You and your family,' answered Gautama, ' may claim descent

He sought the Brahman priest Alara, but found no clue to the great secret. Then to the mountains of

from kings; my descent is from the prophets (buddhas) of old, and they, begging their food, have always lived on alms. But, my father, when a man has found a hidden treasure it is his duty first to present his father with the most precious of the jewels;' and he accordingly addressed his father on the cardinal tenet of his doctrine, his words being reported in the form of two verses given in the Dhammapada:

> 'Rise up, and loiter not;
> Follow after a holy life ı
> Who follows virtue rests in bliss,
> Both in this world and in the next.
> Follow after a holy life,
> Follow not after sin;
> Who follows virtue rests in bliss,
> Both in this world and in the next.

"Suddhodana made no reply to this, but, simply taking his son's bowl, led him to his house, where the members of the family and the servants of the household came to do him honor; but Yasodhara did not come. 'If I am of any value in his eyes, he will himself come,' she had said: 'I can welcome him better here.' Gautama noticed her absence, and, attended by two of his disciples, went to the place where she was, first warning his followers not to prevent her should she try to embrace him, although no member of his order might touch or be touched by a woman. When she saw him enter, a recluse in yellow robes with shaven head and shaven face, though she knew it would be so, she could not contain herself, and falling on the ground she held him by the feet and burst into tears. Then, remembering the impassable gulf between them, she rose and stood on one side. The raja thought it necessary to apologize for her, telling Gautama how entirely she had continued to love him, refusing comforts which he denied himself, taking but one meal a day, and sleeping, not on a bed, but on a mat spread on the ground. The different accounts often tell us the thoughts of the Buddha on any particular occasion; here they are silent, stating only that he then told a Jataka story, showing how great had been her virtue in a former birth. She became an earnest hearer of the new doctrines; and when, some time afterward, much against his will,

Vindyha, where, entering a hermit's cell, the fame of his holiness spread, says the chronicle, " like the sound of a great bell hung in the canopy of the skies." Here he endured a mental struggle so severe that his conflicting thoughts are represented as angels of light and darkness met on an embattled field, while sympathizing nature yielded a thousand portents: " The earth with its oceans and mountains quaked like a conscious being—like a fond bride when forcibly torn from her bridegroom—like the festoons of a vine shaking under the blasts of a whirlwind. The ocean rose under this vibration, and the rivers rolled back to their sources. Peaks of lofty mountains, where forests had grown for ages, rolled crumbling to the earth; a fierce storm howled on every side; the roar of the concussion became terrific; the very sun enveloped itself in awful darkness and a host of headless spirits filled the air." Thus for heroic days and weeks the conflict went on. At length, on a certain memorable day, as he sat meditating under a tree, to be known thenceforth as "the sacred bo tree,"[1] his face turned toward the east, it

Gautama was induced to established an order of female mendicants, his widowed wife Yasodhara became one of the first of the Buddhist nuns."—*Buddhism*, pp. 64-66.

[1] " This tree came to occupy much the same position among the Buddhists as the cross among Christians. Worship was actually paid to it, and an offshoot from it is still growing on the spot where the Buddhist pilgrims found it, and where they believed the original tree had grown, in the ancient temple at Bodh Gaya, near Rajgir, built about 500 A. D. by the celebrated Amara Sinha. A branch of it planted at Anuradhapura in Ceylon, in the middle of the third century B. C., is still growing there—*the oldest historical tree in the world.*

" Sir Emerson Tennent says of it : ' The bo tree of Anuradhapura is,

came to him in a beatific vision, it came like a sunburst—" the knowledge that can never be shaken." A throne of crystal sprang up from the earth beside him; he arose and sat upon it—no longer Siddartha, but *The Buddha*, "the Enlightened."

"*Turning the Wheel of the Law.*"—For a time he hesitated whether he should keep this knowledge to himself or reveal it; but his feeling of humanity prevailed. Burdened with the wonderful secret, he retraced his steps from the forest, saying,

> "I now desire to turn the wheel of the excellent law.
> With this intent I go to the city of Benares,
> To give light to those enshrouded in darkness
> And open the gates of immortality to men."

The watchword of his preaching was "For all! for in all probability, the oldest historical tree in the world. It was planted 288 years before Christ, and hence is now 2147 years old. Ages varying from one to four thousand years have been assigned to the baobabs of Senegal, the eucalyptus of Tasmania, the dragon tree of Orotava, the Wellingtonia of California, and the chestnut of Mount Etna. But all these estimates are matter of conjecture, and such calculations, however ingenious, must be purely inferential; whereas the age of the bo tree is matter of record, its conservancy has been an object of solicitude to successive dynasties, and the story of its vicissitudes has been preserved in a series of continuous chronicles among the most authentic that have been handed down by mankind. Compared with it the oak of Ellerslie is but a sapling, and the Conqueror's Oak in Windsor Forest barely numbers half its years. The yew trees of Fountains Abbey are believed to have flourished there twelve hundred years ago; the olives in the garden of Gethsemane were full grown when the Saracens were expelled from Jerusalem; and the cypress of Soma, in Lombardy, is said to have been a tree in the time of Julius Cæsar; yet the bo tree is older than the oldest of these by a century, and would almost seem to verify the prophecy pronounced when it was planted, that it would 'flourish and be green for ever.' "—*Buddhism*, pp. 39 and 232.

all!" No longer should the haughty priests of Brahm monopolize the path heavenward; no longer should the divisional walls of caste prevent any from seeking the great deliverance. Slaves, pariahs, sudras,—all were to be invited to embrace the rest-giving truth. On reaching Benares he called together his former friends and expounded to them the truths of his philosophy, or, to use the technical phrase, he "turned the wheel of the law." It is related that earth and heaven were moved during the delivery of this discourse: "The angels forsook their shining seats and came to hearken; the sound of their approach was like the rustling of winds in a forest, until at the blast of the archangel's trumpet they became as still as a becalmed sea. Then the everlasting hills, the foundations of the earth, leaped for joy and bowed themselves before the blessed one, while the powers of the air disposed all things appropriately and the perfumes of rare flowers was diffused around. 'The evening was like a lovely maiden; the stars were the pearls upon her neck, the dark clouds her braided hair, the deepening space her flowing robe. As a crown she had the heavens where the angels dwell; the three worlds were as her body; her eyes were the white lotus-flowers which open to the rising moon; and her voice was as it were the humming of bees. To worship the Buddha and to hear the first preaching of the word this lovely maiden came.'"

Propagation of the New Religion.—It need scarcely be said that a discourse attended by such tokens of supernatural interest was followed by many conversions. A few months later the Buddha called his disciples together and sent them forth upon a missionary journey. "Beloved mendicants," said he, "we are free from the passions which encompass men and angels. It is incumbent on us, as the most important duty, to labor on behalf of others and open to them the blessings of the great deliverance. Let us here and now part with each other and go in various directions, no two of us following the same way. Go, preach the most excellent Law." This was the beginning of the propagation of *Dharma*, the Buddhist system.

The Buddha's Death.—The great teacher was spared to gather a vast multitude of adherents. He died in peace, attended by reverent and loving friends, to whom he addressed these farewell words: "O mendicants, let me impress it upon you that the parts and powers of man must be dissolved: therefore work out your salvation with all diligence."

Buddhism is to-day one of the most prevalent religions of the earth. Its adherents are estimated at five hundred millions. Every third one of the inhabitants of the globe is a Buddhist. Beginning its sway in India, and driven thence after a struggle of a thousand years, it moved northward, building rock-cut temples as it went, over Siam, Burmah, the vast empire of Japan and considerable portions of China.

What is this religion? What was Buddha's wonderful secret? Half a century ago it would have been scarcely possible to answer that question, but of late a great light has been thrown upon this subject by the researches of Oriental scholars.

II. *The Sacred Books.*—The data for an estimate of Buddhism are to be found in the sacred books. These are three, called "Tripitaka," or *The Three Baskets.*

1. The first Pitaka or *Basket* is called *Sutra*. It contains the discourses of the Buddha.
2. The second Basket is called *Dharma*. It consists of clear presentations of doctrine and ethics for the people generally.
3. The third Basket is called *Vinaya*. It consists of rules of discipline for the priests.

These books are declared to have been written from memory by the disciples of Buddha, who met for that purpose soon after the great teacher's death and sat in council seven months. They contain an amount of literature almost bewildering, forming in all more than three hundred volumes folio and consisting of 29,368,000 letters. The market price of the Kanjur edition, printed by command of the emperor Khian-Lung of China, is seven thousand oxen, from which it is evident that the Buddhist bible is only for the select few. Its character is hardly such as to commend it to the acceptance of enlightened men. What shall we think of a book claiming to be inspired and infallible which declares the universe to consist of multitudinous worlds, circular and threefold, with an enormous mountain called Maha-Meru rising from their midst, surrounded by concentric circles of rock, of which the outer is divided into four quarters or great continents, our earth, Jambudvipa, heaven and hell, being parts of it? The doctrinal or philosophical chapters are so abstruse and tenuous as to elude the grasp of ordinary mortals.

Those portions only which have reference to the conduct of daily life are, for the most part, worthy of unqualified praise. In illustration of this statement the following precept-sentences are given:

"He who lives for pleasure only, his senses uncontrolled, idle and weak, the tempter will as certainly overcome him as the wind breaks the quivering tree."

"As the bee gathers nectar and departs without injuring the blossom, so dwelleth a wise man upon the earth."

"The fool is filled with evil, though he gather it little by little, as the water-pot is filled with the rain falling drop by drop."

"Let us live happily, calling nothing our own; not hating our enemies; free from greed among the greedy. We shall then resemble the gods, whose daily food is happiness."

Such precepts we at once perceive to be a vast improvement on those of the Rig-Veda, which, as interpreted by the Brahmans, had chiefly to do with the feeding of themselves and the sacred cows. The introduction of Buddhism was *a reformation* [1]—a reform as positive and fundamental as that which was enkindled by the intrepid zeal of Luther, and against the same

---

[1] "What, then, is Buddhism? It is certainly not Brahmanism, yet it arose out of Brahmanism, and from the first had much in common with it. Brahmanism and Buddhism are closely interwoven with each other. Brahmanism is a religion which may be described as all theology, for it makes God everything and everything God. Buddhism is no religion at all, and certainly no theology, but rather a system of duty, morality and benevolence, without real deity, prayer or priest."—MONIER WILLIAMS.

twin spirits of mysticism and cold formality. It is not without reason, therefore, that James Freeman Clarke has called this religion "the Protestantism of the East."

Central Thought: Self-culture.—The sacred books are largely devoted to the importance of self-culture [1] or the development of the intellectual as distinguished from that of the carnal life. This is indeed the central thought of the Buddhist system. Call it self-control if you please, or, better still, self-renunciation, its perfect illustration being found in "the great renunciation" of Gautama himself. The emphasis of the teaching is placed on the perfecting of the inward man

---

[1] "If we now try to sum up the evidence which we have gathered from different indications respecting Buddhism, I do not know that we can do it better than in the words of Mr. Hodgson, the Resident at Nepaul, to whom I have already referred. 'The one infallible diagnostic of Buddhism,' he says with an emphasis and decision which were the result of patient inquiries conducted during many years, 'is a belief in the infinite capacity of the human intellect.' This is the conclusion to which all our inquiries into the system have conducted us. The idea of an Adi-Buddha, or Absolute Eternal Intelligence, is there, but it is hidden; it gradually evaporates. The possibility of utter atheism is there, but the heart flies in dismay from it. The vision of a unity resulting from the reconciliation of opposites is there, but it either passes into a mere theory or seeks for images to express it, which makes it material. The conception of an intelligent soul in nature is there, but it quickly resolves itself into a recognition of all nature as symbolizing human deeds and attributes. Lastly, the idea of deified men is there, but this loses itself in another, that there is in man, in humanity, a certain Divine Intelligence which at different times and in different places manifests itself more or less completely, and which must have some one central manifestation. The human intellect is first felt to be the perfect organ of worship; finally, its one object. This is Buddhism."—F. D. MAURICE, in *Religions of the World*, p. 83.

in preference to penance, sacrifice and all outward forms of merit-making. Thus it is written in the Pitakas:

> "What is the use of platted hair, O fool?
> Or what of a garment of skins?
> Thy low passions are within thee;
> And lo! thou makest the outside clean."[1]

Never did preacher chant more dolorously "all is vanity and vexation of spirit" than does the Buddhist. Man is an infinitesimal being; his life is as a breath of wind passing over the lotus-flower.[2] The highest

[1] "That mendicant does right to whom omens, meteors, dreams and signs are things abolished; he is free from all their evils.

"That mendicant does right who is found not thinking, 'People should salute me;' who, though cursed by the world, yet cherishes no ill-will toward it.

"That mendicant does right who is tranquil and has completed his course; who sees truth as it really is, but is not partial when there are persons of different faith (to be dealt with); who with firm mind overcomes ill-will and covetousness, which injure men."—From "Rules of the Sacred Order" in the *Pitakas*.

[2] "A watchman on a lofty tower sees a charioteer urging his horse along the plain: the driver thinks he is moving rapidly, and the horse in the pride of life seems to scorn the earth from which it thinks to separate itself; but to the watchman above horse and chariot and driver seem to crawl along the ground, and to be as much a part of the earth as the horse's mane, waving in the wind, is a part of the horse itself. As a child grows up his mind reflects as in a dim mirror the occurrences of the surrounding world, and practically, though unconsciously, it regards itself as the centre round which the universe turns. Gradually its circle widens somewhat, but the grown man never escapes from the delusion of self, and spends his life in a constant round of desires and cares, longing for objects which when attained produce not happiness, but fresh desires and cares—always engaged in the pursuit of some fancied good. For the majority of men these cares are mean, petty and contemptible; but even those whose ambition urges them to

height of folly, therefore, is self-pleasing. The Buddhist who comprehends this strips himself of all except "eight possessions"—a loose robe, two undergarments, a girdle, a bowl for alms, a razor, a needle and a water-strainer. Thus reducing the gratification of the outer man to the very minimum, he sedulously devotes himself to inward culture or the sinking of self into the universal mind.

III. *Theology: The Creed.*—The creed of Buddhism is briefly set forth in the "Four Truths" and the "Noble Eightfold Path."

The Four Truths are as follows:

(1) All existence is sorrow.

(2) The cause of sorrow is thirst, or desire in whatever form.

(3) All sorrow ceases when desire is slain. This condition, the annihilation of feeling, is called *Nirvana*. "When a man overcomes his contemptible thirst, his sufferings fall from him as water from a lotus-leaf."

(4) There is only one way to reach this consummation so devoutly to be wished—to wit, by the Noble Eightfold Path.

The Noble Eightfold Path is as follows: (1) Right Belief, (2) Right Feelings, (3) Right Speech (4) Right Actions, (5) Right Means of Livelihood, (6) Right Endeavor, (7) Right Memory, and (8) Right Meditation. The pursuit of this path of self-culture is held to be the chief end of man.

<small>higher aims are equally seeking after vanity, and only laying themselves open to greater sorrows and more bitter disappointment."—*Buddhism*, p. 88.</small>

Out of this thought of self-culture radiate the three cardinal truths—namely, Buddh, Karma and Nirvana. Let us get these definitely in mind.

(1) *Buddh.*—Under this term we place theology proper; that is, the Buddhist's idea of God.

Let it be said at the outset that he has no conception of Deity as we understand it. His creed is the very refinement of atheism. Max Müller says: "Buddha admits no real cause of this unreal world. He denies the existence not only of a Creator, but of any absolute Being whatever." Draper, in his *Intellectual Development of Europe*, says: "The fundamental principle of Buddhism is that there is a supreme power, but no Supreme Being. It asserts an impelling power in the universe, a self-existent and plastic principle, but not a self-existent, an eternal, a personal God." Dr. Caird says: "It reasserts the negative element involved in pantheism, and exaggerates it till not only every finite and anthropomorphic ingredient, but every vestige of positive thought, vanishes from the idea of God, and we seem to be left in the absolute negation of atheism." Monier Williams says: "The Buddha recognized no supreme deity. The only god, he affirmed, is what man himself can become." Here is the most striking feature of this religion. All other faiths are built upon a foundation of theism—the belief in One, perchance an unknown One, to whom souls trembling or grieving can lift their cry:

"O thou eternal One, whose presence bright
All space doth occupy, all motion guide;

> Unchanged through Time's all-devastating flight;
> Thou only One! Being above all beings!
> Whom none can comprehend and none explore,
> Who fill'st existence with thyself alone;
> Embracing all, supporting, ruling o'er—
> Being whom we call *God*, and know no more."

But Buddhism has not even that—not so much as an altar to the Unknown God. What, then, does it worship?

The Universal Mind.—When Siddartha sat meditating under the sacred bo tree the thought which came to him, uplifting, illuminating, deifying, making him *Buddha*, was this: "The only real and substantial thing in the universe is INTELLECT; there is one great, all-embracing Intelligence of which the essential and constituent parts are the minds of men; of this Buddh I know nothing, but I may form a definite conception of that within me which corresponds to the aggregate or universal mind; this, therefore, will I worship— Mind, Intellect, the Buddha, my self-conscious self."[1]

In this conception of deity there seems to be a faint glimmer of the truth that was uttered by St. John: "In him was life, and the life was the light of men; and the Light shineth in darkness, and the darkness comprehended it not." Let the thought of Buddha be spiritualized, and we shall behold in it the *Wisdom* of Ecclesiastes; nay, even a suggestion of the Holy Ghost. Still, pausing where he did, a gulf infinite

---

[1] "The word Buddha, it seems to be admitted on all hands, means Intelligence. That men ought to worship pure Intelligence must have been the first proclamation of the original Buddhists."—MAURICE.

138   *THE RELIGIONS OF THE WORLD.*

and bridgeless lay between his feet and the enlightening truth.

He was a rationalist, his last appeal being to the human intellect. He was a pantheist, holding that the universal mind is everything and all. He was an atheist, practically, holding that aside from the impersonal Adi-Buddha there is no God.[1]

Idols.—It is easy to perceive how this religion, beginning as a protest against the idolatrous rites and ceremonies of Brahmanism, would itself in time surely develop into idolatry. No sooner had Buddha died than a great image was built to his memory; wonderful tales were told concerning him; ere long his name was invested with superstitious awe. The Buddha now was God: his image, designed to represent the apotheosis of Intellect, in the popular eyes was simply a deified man. But why, if Siddartha became Buddha, might not any other heroic and virtuous man do likewise? Thus buddhas were multiplied and hero-worship began. All great men had their devotees, and the craft of the image-maker was most prosperous. The Buddhist temples are pantheons.[2] There is one

---

[1] "What are we to say of a doctrine which is sometimes represented as one of almost perfect theism; sometimes as direct atheism; sometimes as having the closest analogy to what in a Greek philosopher or in a modern philosopher would be called pantheism; sometimes as the worship of human saints or heroes; sometimes as altogether symbolical; sometimes as full of the highest abstract speculations; sometimes as vulgar idolatry? Strange as it may seem, the same doctrine is, I believe, capable of assuming all these different phases; no one of them can be thoroughly understood without reference to the other."—F. D. MAURICE, in *Religions of the World*, p. 74.

[2] "As Buddhism does not recognize the idea of God, it has properly

at Canton where five hundred canonized saints sit "in a long impressive row." There is another at Ayuthia no worship or sacrifices, and originally no religious ceremonies; but as it spread a cultus arose. The image and relics of Buddha himself and the other holy personages of the legends were worshiped, and the ceremonies consisted of offerings of flowers and perfumes, with music and the recital of hymns and prayers. Formulas of prayer have also come into use, although the idea of a Being who answers prayers is utterly foreign to the system. The prayers are supposed to produce their effect by a kind of magical efficacy. Hence the praying-machines of Tibet and Mongolia are logical consequences. The religious communities assemble for prayer three times a day—*i. e.* morning, noon and evening. They publicly confess their sins on the days of the new and full moon, and the laity also attend for confession and to listen to the reading of some sacred text."—Rev. S. M. Jackson, *Schaff-Herzog Encyclopedia*, article "Buddhism."

"As the pilgrim in the story who was ordered, as a penance, to walk a long distance with peas in his shoes, took the liberty of easing his task by first boiling his peas, so the Buddhists have invented their famous contrivance of prayer-mills by which to obtain the merit of prayer without the trouble of praying. Father Huc saw many of these mills. They have a revolving wheel on which are pasted numerous prayers. Every time it is turned it is considered that as much merit is acquired as if all the prayers had been said aloud. Sometimes these wheels are put up by the side of the road, so that a traveler may acquire merit by giving them a twirl as he passes. A still more ingenious contrivance is to fill a barrel full of written prayers—say one thousand—and then arrange it by the side of a brook, so that the water shall turn it continually, night and day. In this way they can easily acquire the merit of having said several millions of prayers every day."—Clarke's *Events and Epochs in Religious History*, p. 56.

"There is no place in the Buddhist scheme for churches; the offering of flowers before the sacred tree or image of the Buddha takes the place of worship. Buddhism does not acknowledge the efficacy of prayers, and in the warm countries where Buddhists live the occasional reading of the law or preaching of the word in public can take place best in the open air, by moonlight, under a simple roof of trees or palms."—*Buddhism*, p. 168.

"This period (the rainy season), called *was* (from the Sanskrit *varsha*,

which has no less than fourteen thousand gods, beginning with a colossal image of the original Buddha. These were all designed to represent the adorableness of Intellect, but to the masses of the people they are simply gods. All day long their temples smoke with incense, and the dull dreamy eyes of the buddhas look down upon a prostrate throng of votaries. Thus there is a twofold aspect of this religion : To the enlightened few it is rationalism pure and simple, while to the mul-

---

rain), is in Ceylon the finest part of the year; and as there are no regular religious services at any other time, the peasantry celebrate the reading of *Bana* (or the Word) at *was*-time, as their great religious festival. They put up under the palm trees a platform, roofed, but quite open at the sides, and ornamented with bright cloths and flowers, and round it they sit in the moonlight on the ground, and listen through the night with great satisfaction, if not with great intelligence, to the sacred words repeated by relays of shaven monks. The greatest favorite at these readings of *Bana* is the 'Jataka' book, which contains so many of the old fables and stories so common to the Aryan peoples, sanctified now and preserved by the leading hero in each, whether man or fairy or animal, being looked upon as an incarnation of the Buddha in one of his previous births. To these wonderful stories the simple peasantry, dressed in their best and brightest, listen all the night long with unaffected delight, chatting pleasantly now and again with their neighbors, and indulging all the while in the mild narcotic of the betel-leaf, their stores of which (and of its never-failing adjuncts, chunam—that is, white lime—and the areka-nut) afford a constant occasion for acts of polite good-fellowship. The first spirit of Buddhism may have passed away as completely as the old reason for *was;* neither hearers nor preachers may have that deep sense of evil in the world and in themselves, nor that high resolve to battle with and overcome it, which animated some of the early Buddhists, and they all think themselves to be earning 'merit' by their easy service; but there is at least at these festivals a genuine feeling of human kindness, in harmony alike with the teachings of Gautama and with the gentle beauty of those moonlight scenes."— *Buddhism*, p. 57.

titude it is the worship of many gods. As to any great overruling Power, with a heart to pity and arms to help the miseries of despairing men, there is none. Buddhism in searching for a god nearer than Brahm has wrecked itself upon Charybdis. It is absolutely "without God in the world."

(2) *Karma.*—The second of the distinguishing features of Buddhism is *Karma:* that is, the Law of Consequences. Buddha said: "Karma is the most essential property of rational beings; it is like the shadow which accompanies the body." By this law of retribution the soul (or rather Intellect, for the Buddhist has no soul) is made to answer for every unjust act. As a man soweth, so also shall he reap:

> "The mills grind slow,
> But they grind woe."

There is no pardon, no escaping the doom. It is an automatic law, administering itself—eye for eye, tooth for tooth, burning for burning. It follows us after death through our various transmigrations, meting out with just scales its exact recompenses. The religion of Buddha has a thousand hells, and every one of them is more terrible than any in the Inferno of Dante. It uses abundantly the motive of fear.

> "Bite not the hook beneath the silvered bait hid well;
> The man who walked o'er treachery's road to Paradise,
> When at the journey's end found he was snug in hell."

And what is the influence of this *Karma* on the morality of the people? Fear never yet lifted a man to the highest plane of life. It feeds our worst passions—pride, hypocrisy and selfishness. A religion which overshadows all the acts and interests of daily life with a dread of what may follow in the dark labyrinths of transmigration may make slaves, but never sons of God.

The Moral Code.—The moral code of Buddhism is wellnigh perfect. "It is the singular merit of this religion, whatever view we take of the ultimate end to which it pointed as constituting the salvation of man, that the way by which it taught men to reach that end was simply that of inward purification and moral goodness. Outside of Christianity no religion which the world has ever seen has so sharply accentuated morality and duty as entering into the very essence of religion or as inseparably connected with it."[1] When the great teacher standing in the light of a jungle-fire on the opposite hillside lifted his voice against the fires of anger, ignorance and concupiscence, and against the multitude of evils, led by priestcraft, with which Brahmanism, as a flood, had covered the land,[2] he gave the keynote of the ethical system which

---

[1] Dr. Caird.

[2] "The new disciples who had been worshipers of Agni, the sacred fire, were seated with Gautama on the Elephant Rock, near Gaya, with the beautiful valley of Rajagriha stretched out before them, when a fire broke out in a jungle on the opposite hill. Taking the fire as his text, the teacher declared that so long as men remained in ignorance they were, as it were, consumed by a fire—by the excitement produced within them by the action of external things. These things acted upon them through the five senses and the heart (which Gautama regarded as a sixth organ of sense). The eye, for instance, perceives objects; from this perception arises an inward sensation producing pleasure or

is contained in the Tripitakas. "It is difficult," said Laboulaye in the French Academy, "to comprehend how men not assisted by revelation could have soared so high and approached so near the truth." Knighton also says: "In Buddhism we have a code of morality and a list of precepts which for pureness, excellence and wisdom are only second to that of the divine Lawgiver himself." Its five great commandments are not to kill, not to steal, not to commit adultery, not to lie, not to use intoxicating drink. It forbids also pride, anger, greediness, gossiping and every kind of vice. It enjoins reverence for parents, kindness toward the poor, meekness, rendering good for evil, and, above all, charity, which is the crown of virtues.

The Brief Formula.—There is a celebrated formula, called *Patimakka*, which is supposed to embrace the sum and substance of the moral code, as follows:

pain. Sensations produce this misery and joy, because they supply fuel, as it were, to the inward fires, concupiscence, anger and ignorance, and the anxieties of birth, decay and death. The same was declared to be the case with the sensations produced by each of the other senses. But those who follow the Buddha's scheme of inward self-control—the four stages of the path whose gate is purity and whose goal is love—have become wise; the sensations from without no longer give fuel to the inward fire, since the fires of concupiscence, etc. have ceased to burn; true disciples are thus free from that craving thirst which is the origin of evil; the wisdom they have acquired will lead them on, sooner or later, to perfection; they are delivered from the miseries which would result from another birth; and even in this birth they no longer need the guidance of such laws as those of caste and ceremonies and sacrifice, for they have already reached far beyond them."—*Buddhism*, p. 59.

> "To cease from sin;
> To get virtue;
> To cleanse one's heart,—
> This is the Buddhist Law."

The Beatitudes.—An elaboration of this formula is found in the beatitudes of Gautama, which are thus given:

> "Not to serve the foolish,
> But to serve the wise;
> And to honor the honorable,—
> This is the greatest blessing.

> "To enjoy, in a pleasant land,
> Good works done in a former life,
> With right desires in the heart,—
> This is the greatest blessing.

> "Deep insight and education,
> Self-control and pleasant speech,
> And words thoughtfully spoken,—
> This is the greatest blessing.

> "To support father and mother;
> To cherish wife and child;
> To follow a peaceful calling,—
> This is the greatest blessing.

> "To bestow alms and live righteously;
> To give help to one's kindred;
> To perform blameless deeds,—
> This is the greatest blessing.

> "To abhor and cease from sin;
> To abstain from strong drink;
> Not to be weary in well-doing,—
> This is the greatest blessing.

> "Reverence and lowliness,
> Contentment and gratitude,
> Hearing the Law at due seasons,—
> This is the greatest blessing.

"To be long-suffering and meek;
To associate with the pious;
To speak of religion at due seasons,—
This is the greatest blessing.

" Self-restraint and purity,
The knowledge of the Noble Truths,
The realization of Nirvana,—
This is the greatest blessing.

" Beneath the stroke of life's vicissitudes
To keep the mind unshaken,
Without grief or passion, and secure,—
This is the greatest blessing.

" On every side they are invincible
Who perform such acts as these;
On every side they walk in safety,
And theirs is the greatest blessing." [1]

[1] The *Ten Commandments* of the Buddhist religion consist of the five prohibitions against—(1) killing, (2) stealing, (3) adultery, (4) falsehood, and (5) drunkenness; together with five others less binding— namely, against (6) eating at improper times, (7) wearing garlands and using perfumes, (8) sleeping on an easy bed, (9) singing, dancing and the drama, and (10) gold and silver.

The *Ten Sins* are as follows: Three of the body: (1) murder, (2) theft, and (3) uncleanness; four of speech: (4) falsehood, (5) gossip, (6) swearing, (7) vain conversation; and three of the mind: (8) covetousness, (9) malice, (10) unbelief.

The *Duties of Men* are classified under six relations, as follows:

I. *The Relation of Parent and Child.*—(I.) Parents should (1) restrain their children from vice, (2) train them in virtue, (3) teach them the arts and sciences, (4) provide them with good wives or husbands, and (5) leave them an inheritance. (II.) Children should (1) support their parents in old age, (2) perform all filial duties, (3) guard the family possessions, (4) study to be worthy of the inheritance, and (5) honor their parents' memory.

II. *Pupil and Teacher.*—(I.) Pupils should honor their teachers (1) by rising in their presence, (2) by ministering to them, (3) by obeying them, (4) by supplying their wants, (5) by heeding their instructions. (II.) Teachers should show their affection for their pupils (1) by train-

The Morality of the Buddhists.—But the moral code of the sacred books must not be taken as a true index of the morality of the people. Little enough do they know of the Tripitaka; still less do they regulate their lives by the maxims written therein. If we would know the practical results of the doctrine of *Karma*,

ing them in the right way, (2) by teaching them to hold fast what they learn, (3) by instructing them in the wisdom of the ancients, (4) by speaking well of them, and (5) by protecting them from danger.

III. *Husband and Wife.*—(I.) Husbands should (1) treat their wives with respect, (2) be kind to them, (3) be faithful to them, (4) defend their reputation, and (5) provide them suitable clothes and ornaments. (II.) Wives should show their love toward their husbands (1) by properly training their children, (2) by suitably entertaining guests, (3) by preserving their chastity, (4) by being good housekeepers, and (5) by showing skill and industry in all things.

IV. *Friend and Friend.*—(I.) An honorable man will minister to his friends (1) by giving them presents, (2) by addressing them respectfully, (3) by promoting their interests, (4) by treating them as his equals, and (5) by giving them a share of his prosperity. (II.) His friends should reciprocate (1) by watching over him when unguarded, (2) by protecting his property when he neglects it, (3) by affording him a refuge in danger, (4) by proving faithful to him in adversity, and (5) by befriending his loved ones.

V. *Master and Servant.*—(I.) The master should (1) apportion the task according to his servant's strength, (2) pay him properly, (3) care for him in sickness, (4) sometimes give him delicacies, and (5) grant him a holiday on occasion. (II.) The servant must (1) rise up before his master, (2) retire later to rest, (3) be content with what he receives from him, (4) do his work cheerfully and well, and (5) always speak well of him.

VI. *Priest and Layman.*—(I.) The priest should (1) dissuade the layman from vice, (2) exhort him to virtue, (3) entertain a sincere regard for him, (4) instruct him in religion, (5) clear up his doubts, and (6) point him to heaven. (II.) The layman must minister to his religious superior (1) by affectionate deeds, (2) by affectionate words, (3) by affectionate thoughts, (4) by a hearty welcome, and (5) by generously supplying all his temporal wants.

we must close the sacred books of Buddhism and enter its chambers of imagery—see woman degraded and crushed, held as an inferior being, her womanhood regarded as the penalty of sins committed in a preexistent state, her only hope the possibility of being one day delivered from the curse by being born a man; or go out upon the highways and question the multitude of pilgrims who drag their slow length toward the sacred rivers. They have no more conception of true virtue, seemingly, than the irrational things that crawl beside them. They are driven on by *Karma* as by a whip of scorpions. Or " visit the cities of the dead, as at Canton, where tens of thousands lie unburied, waiting for a lucky day. Listen to the midnight din of the superstitious masses who are ringing gongs and discharging fireworks to keep away the evil spirits. Watch the incantations over the sick, and honors paid to dead beggars to propitiate their ghosts, and the pampering of monkeys and doves and sacred pigs as a work of merit, while men and women die of starvation in the streets." This is Buddhism—not as it is in the Tripitaka, but as it appears in common life. In spite of its theoretical cleanness, it is practically vile. Says the Abbé Huc: " The leprosy of vice has spread so completely through this skeptical society that the garment of modesty with which it covers itself is continually falling off and exposing hideous wounds which are eating away the vitals of this unbelieving people."[1]

[1] " It is a melancholy fact that, in China, Buddhism has led the entire nation not only into indifferentism, but into absolute godlessness. They have come to regard religion as merely a fashion, to be followed accord-

III. *Nirvana.*—The third distinguishing feature of Buddhism is *Nirvana*. This is the name of the Buddhist's only heaven. It is defined in glowing terms as "the happy seat,—the excellent, eternal place; the other side of the ocean of existence; the harbor of never-ending rest,—the transcendental formless state, the truth, the infinite, the unspeakable." But under all these euphemisms lies the cold undoubted fact that *Nirvana* means total annihilation. This is the Buddhist's supreme wish.

ing to one's own taste; that as professed by the state it is a civil institution, necessary for the holding of office and demanded by society, but not to be regarded as of the smallest philosophical importance; that a man is entitled to indulge his views on these matters just as he is entitled to indulge his taste in the color and fashion of his garments; that he has no more right, however, to live without some religious profession than he has a right to go naked. The Chinese cannot comprehend how there should be animosities arising on matters of such doubtful nature and trivial concern. The formula under which they live is: 'Religions are many, reason is one; we are brothers.' They smile at the credulity of the good-natured Tartars, who believe in the wonders of miracle-workers, for they have miracle-workers who can perform the most supernatural cures, who can lick red-hot iron, who can cut open their bowels, and, by passing their hand over the wound, make themselves whole again,—who can raise the dead. In China, these miracles, with all their authentications, have descended to the conjurer and are performed for the amusement of children. The common expressions of that country betray the materialism and indifferentism of the people, and their consequent immorality. 'The prisons,' they say, 'are locked night and day, but they are always full; the temples are always open, and yet there is nobody in them.' Of the dead they say, with an exquisite refinement of euphemism, 'He has saluted the world.' The Lazarist Huc, on whose authority many of these statements are made, testifies that they die, indeed, with incomparable tranquillity, just as animals die; and adds, with a bitter, and yet profoundly true, sarcasm, 'they are what many in Europe are wanting to be.'"—DRAPER'S *Intellectual Development of Europe*, i. 74.

> "Count o'er the joys thine hours have seen,
> Count o'er thy days from anguish free,
> And know, whatever thou hast been,
> 'Tis something better—not to be." [1]

The Japanese followers of Buddha have this proverb: "The worst thing you can wish a man is that he may live again." There is, indeed, no acknowledgment of the existence of the soul as a thing distinct from the parts and properties which dissolve at death.[2] "Our

---

[1] Contrast with this the Christian sentiment:

> "Whatever crazy sorrow saith,
> No life that breathes with human breath
> Has ever truly longed for death.
> 'Tis life, whereof our nerves are scant,
> Oh life, not death, for which we pant;
> More life, and fuller, that we want."

[2] "Man consists of an assemblage of different properties or qualities, none of which corresponds to the Hindu or modern notion of the soul. These are material qualities, sensations, abstract ideas, tendencies of mind and mental powers; and as the point is a matter of great importance for a right appreciation of Buddhist teaching, and the enumeration is not without interest for its own sake, a few words may be devoted to the details of each of these Skandhas or Aggregates:

"[1.] The Material Properties or Attributes are twenty-eight in number:

Four elements—earth, water, fire, air.
Five organs of sense—eye, ear, nose, tongue, body.
Five attributes of matter—form, sound, smell, taste, substance.
Two distinctions of sex—male, female.
Three essential conditions—thought, vitality, space.
Two means of communication—gesture, speech.
Seven qualities of living bodies—buoyancy, elasticity, power of adaptation, power of aggregation, duration, decay, change.

"[2.] The Sensations are divided into six classes, according as they are received immediately by each of the five senses, or, sixthly, by the mind (through memory); and further, into eighteen classes, as each of these six classes may be either agreeable, disagreeable or indifferent.

life, to use a constantly recurring Buddhist simile or parable, is like the flame of an Indian lamp, a metal

"[3.] The Abstract Ideas are divided into six classes of sensations; for instance, the ideas blue, a tree, are classed under sight; the idea sweetness under taste, and so on.

"[4.] The Tendencies or Potentialities (literally confections) are in fifty-two divisions, which are not, however, mutually exclusive. Some of these include, or are identical with, items in the previous classes; but whereas the previous groups are arranged as it were from an objective, this group is arranged as it were from a subjective, point of view:

1. Contact.
2. The resulting sensation.
3. Abstract ideas, formed on sensation.
4. Thought, the regrouping of ideas.
5. Reflection, turning these groups over and over.
6. Memory.
7. Vitality.
8. Individuality.
9. Attention.
10. Investigation.
11. Effort.
12. Steadfastness.
13. Joy.
14. Impulse.
15. Indifference.
16, 17. Sleep and torpor.
18, 19. Stupidity and intelligence.
20, 21. Covetousness and content.
22, 23. Fear and rashness.
24, 25. Shame and shamelessness.
26, 27. Hatred and affection.
28–30. Doubt, faith and delusion.
31, 32. Repose of body or mind.
33, 34. Lightness, activity, of body or mind.
35, 36. Softness, elasticity, of body or mind.
37, 38. Adaptability, pliancy, of body or mind.
39, 40. Dexterity, of body or mind.
41, 42. Straightness, of body or mind.
43–45. Propriety, of speech, action or life.

or earthenware saucer in which a cotton wick is laid
in oil. One life is derived from another, as one flame
is lit at another; it is not the same flame, but without
the other it would not have been." In other words,
there is continuity, but no identity.[1] Thus the Buddhists

    46. Pity, sorrow for the sorrow of others.
    47. Gladness, rejoicing in the joy of others.
    48. Envy, sorrow at the joys of others.
    49. Selfishness, dislike to share one's joys with others.
    50. Moroseness.
    51. Vanity.
    52. Pride.

"[5.] Thought, reason, is the last Skandha, and is really an amplification from another point of view of the fourth of the last group, which is inherent in all the others. It is divided from the point of view of the merit or demerit resulting from different thoughts into eighty-nine classes—a division which throws no light on the Buddhist scheme of the constituent elements of being, and does not, therefore, concern us here."—*Buddhism*, p. 90, abbreviated.

[1] An apt illustration of this continuity without identity is given by Maurice, as follows: "In Tibet, which must be regarded as the centre and proper home of the religion, the priests are called lamas; it is they who decide who *the* Lama, the true high priest of the universe at any given time, is. I say they decide who he is, for they could never allow that the faculty of *choosing* the chief Lama resides in them. In some person or other the spirit of Buddha dwells; he is meant to be the head of the universe; to him all owe homage. This Lama, therefore, never dies; he is lost sight of in one form, reappears in another. The body of some old man who has had this honor loses its breath, is laid in the tomb. The Lama has passed into some infant, who is brought up in a convent with special care, preserved from sensual influences, taught from the cradle to look upon himself as the shrine of the divinity, and to receive the homage of rajahs, nations, even of the Celestial Empire; nay, even of European monarchs. Some of you may remember to have read of a solemn embassy sent by the English government at Calcutta, in the days of Warren Hastings, to the court of the Lama. A very affecting letter had been addressed by him to the English authorities in India, asking their help in checking quarrels between cer-

speak of "the heresy of individuality;" and Buddha himself pronounced it heresy to speak of the eternity of the soul. It is obvious, therefore, that *Nirvana* means merely extinction or annihilation. This, indeed, is the necessary sequence of the philosophy of Buddha. He said: "There is nothing in life but sorrow; all is perishable; all is void; to be is pain; not to be is everlasting rest." The most desirable of all things, therefore, is non-existence—" to break through the prison-walls, not of life only, but of being." To this end transmigration—that is, the passage of life through an endless cycle of existence,[1] which continues so long as there is conscious thirst or desire of any kind—must be prevented.

"*What shall I Do to be Saved?*"—How shall this transmigration be prevented? By the killing of desire. The intellect must conquer the heart; feeling must give way to meditation. The senses must be dulled. Nirvana is gained by the victory of sublime indifference to everything in life.

"The heart, scrupulously avoiding all idle dissipation,
Diligently applying itself to the Holy Law of Buddha,

tain native sovereigns—an object, he said, which he sought diligently in prayers by day and night. An old man was the author of this letter; before Mr. Turner, the English envoy, arrived he had left the world, and a child of eighteen months was acknowledged as his successor. It reigned by no hereditary right, but the other lamas presented him with unquestioning faith as the representative of the Perfect Intelligence, through whom it would most surely utter itself."

[1] "Transmigration is constantly called the *ocean:* its ever-tossing waves are births; the foam at the crest of the waves is this perishable body; the other shore is Nirvana; having reached which, one does not again enter the great ocean of Sag-sara."—*Buddhism*, p. 136.

Letting go all lust and consequent disappointment,
Fixed and unchangeable, enters on *Nirvana*."[1]—DAVIDS.

Struggling to release itself from all passion, life journeys on from home to home, from one mode of existence to another, until its heart is numbed, eyes blinded, feeling dead, and the dreamer, inhaling the perfume of the lotus-flower, ere the dream ceases murmurs his farewell:

> "Thy rafters crushed, thy ridge-pole too,
> Thy work, O Builder, now is o'er.
> My spirit feels Nirvana true,
> And I shall transmigrate no more."

Sadness.—Is it to be wondered at that Buddhism is a religion of sadness? that "a night of hopelessness" has passed over all the peoples who profess it?[2]

[1] "He whose senses have become tranquil, like a horse well broken in by the driver; who is free from pride and the lust of the flesh and the lust of existence and the defilement of ignorance,—him even the gods envy. Such a one, whose conduct is right, remains like the broad earth, unvexed; like the pillar of the city-gate, unmoved; like a pellucid lake, unruffled. For such there are no more births. Tranquil is the mind, tranquil are the words and deeds, of him who is thus tranquillized and made free by wisdom."—*Buddhism*, pp. 110, 111.

[2] "A lamentable instance of the failure of Buddhism seems to be afforded by the present condition of Japan. Travelers picture the Japanese as people without religion and without hope. A current and favorite proverb is that 'the worst thing you can wish a man is to live again.' As the old faith has died out, there is nothing left but its unconscious effects and the habits taught by it to stem the tide of selfishness; and the people seem given up, say very candid observers, to 'licentiousness and untruthfulness,' while a deep shade of melancholy settles over all. The great doctrine of Sakya-Muni, that the 'end of righteousness is rest,' has degenerated into the dogma that the 'end of righteousness is nothingness,' and a night of unbelief and hopelessness has fallen over a whole race."—BRACE's *Gesta Christi*, p. 456.

Selfishness.—It must be obvious to the most careless observer that the philosophy of Buddha is the very consummation of selfishness. "Since its object," as Draper says, "was altogether of a personal kind, the attainment of individual happiness, it was not possible that it should do otherwise than engender an extreme selfishness. It enjoined on each man to secure his own salvation (or deliverance), no matter what became of all others. Of what concern to him were parents, wife, children, friends, country, so long as he attained Nirvana?" The very benevolence which the Buddhist boasts is nothing more than a means toward the securing of an utterly selfish end. His piety is pure self-worship, for beyond his own intellect he cannot conceive of God.[1]

---

[1] "This grand moral system," says Dr. Eitel, "starting with the idea of the entire renunciation of self, ends in that downright selfishness which abhors crime, not because of its sinfulness, but because it is a *personal* injury; which sees no moral pollution in sin, but merely a calamity to be deprecated or a misfortune to be shunned."

The following, to the same point, is from a conversation with a Buddhist priest in the temple at Kioto (*The Century* magazine, July, 1886):

"'What do you mean by *wrong?*' I asked.

"'That which is not for the best.'

"'Well, when my watch goes too fast or too slow, I say it is wrong: does it commit sin?'

"'I do not understand.'

"'When a tiger comes into the village and eats a man, it is not for the best, is it?'

"'No.'

"'Does the tiger do right or wrong?'

"'He does right for the tiger and wrong for the man. It is best for the tiger to eat the man—for the man to kill the tiger.'

"'Is it wrong for one man to kill another?'

No Help from Above.—We observe a most striking difference between the system of Buddha and that of Jesus Christ in this: that, while the former bids its votaries work out alone and unaided their deliverance from the sorrows of life,[1] the latter says, "Work out

"'Yes.'
"'And to lie and steal?'
"'Yes.'
"'Why?'
"'Because it destroys the harmony of the social relations. You must not hurt me, for then I would want to hurt you; and if all men lived in that way, there could be no peace. You must not lie to me, for then I should not know whether to do one thing or another, for I could not trust you.'
"'So, then, I must not hurt you, for fear you might hurt me?'
"'Yes.'
"'Is there no other reason?'
"'I do not know any.'
"'Is there no *rule* of right which all men must follow?'
"'No; if there were all men would think the same things bad. They do not. You think it is bad to have more than one wife; some other nations do not. They think it is bad to drink anything which you drink. There can be no rule, but each nation finds out what is best for itself.'
"'We, too,' said I, ' think that things may be expedient for one nation which are not so for another, but deeds are right or wrong as they conform or do not conform to a rule, which is the will of our God; and those things of which we have spoken—lying, stealing, murder and such like—we agree with you in thinking wrong and hurtful to society, and we have commandments forbidding them. This we call our duty to man; but besides that is there no other duty?'
"'I do not understand.'
"'*Do you owe nothing to Amida-Buddha?*'
"'*Oh, no.*'"

[1] The cold comfort which the Buddhist gets from his religion in time of trouble is well illustrated in the "Parable of the Mustard-seed:" "Kisagotami is the name of a young girl whose marriage with the only son of a wealthy man was brought about in true fairy-tale fashion. She

your own salvation, for it is God that worketh in you both to will and to do." The Buddhist stands with arms reached vainly out, the very prayer hushed upon his lips, his cold eyes fixed on Nirvana, the end of all. The Christian feels the overshadowing of divine love and the strength of everlasting arms beneath him; he knows a present God.

<small>had one child, but when the beautiful boy could run alone he died. The young girl in her love for it carried the dead child clasped to her bosom, and went from house to house of her pitying friends asking them to give her medicine for it. But a Buddhist mendicant, thinking, 'She does not understand,' said to her, 'My good girl, I myself have no such medicine as you ask for, but I think I know of one who has.'—'Oh tell me who that is,' said Kisagotami.—'The Buddha can give you medicine; go to him,' was the answer. She went to Gautama, and, doing homage to him, said, 'Lord and master, do you know any medicine that will be good for my child?'—'Yes, I know of some,' said the Teacher. Now, it was the custom for patients or their friends to provide the herbs which the doctors required, so she asked what herbs he would want. 'I want some mustard-seed,' he said; and when the poor girl eagerly promised to bring some of so common a drug, he added, 'You must get it from some house where no son or husband or parent or slave has died.'—'Very good,' she said; and went to ask for it, still carrying her dead child with her. The people said, 'Here is mustard-seed, take it;' but when she asked, 'In my friend's house has any son died or a husband or a parent or slave?' they answered, 'Lady, what is that you say? The living are few, but the dead are many.' Then she went to other houses, but one said, 'I have lost a son;' another, 'We have lost our parents;' another, 'I have lost my slave.' At last, not being able to find a single house where no one had died, her mind began to clear, and, summoning up resolution, she left the dead body of her child in a forest, and returning to the Buddha paid him homage. He said to her, 'Have you the mustard-seed?'—'My lord,' she replied, 'I have not; the people tell me that the living are few, but the dead are many.' Then he talked to her on that essential part of his system—the impermanency of all things, till her doubts were cleared away, and, accepting her lot, she became a disciple and entered the first path."—*Buddhism*, p. 133.</small>

> "O heart! weak follower of the weak,
>   That thou shouldst traverse land and sea,
> In this far place that God to seek
>   Who long ago had come to thee!"

Ay, God is come down to us in the person of Him who is the fullness of the Godhead bodily. Buddhism has no Christ. Its spectre of a God is blind and heartless. Man, guilty, penitent, despairing, reaches up, but there are no hands reaching down.

> "An immense solitary Spectre waits!
> It hath no shape, it hath no sound,
> It hath no place, it hath no time;
> It is, and was, and will be;
> It is never more nor less, nor glad nor sad;
> Its name is *Nothingness*.
> Power walketh high, and Misery doth crawl,
> And the clepsydron drips,
> And the sands fall down in the hour-glass;
> Men live and strive, regret, forget,
> And love and hate, and know it.
> The Spectre saith, '*I wait!*'
> And at the last it beckons, and they pass;
> And still the red sands fall within the glass,
> And still the water-clock doth drip and weep;
> And that is all!"

A writer in the Presbyterian *Foreign Missionary* for June, 1886, thus marks the leading contrasts between Christianity and Buddhism:

"Christ taught the existence and the glory of God as supreme over all, the Creator, Upholder and Father; Buddhism knows nothing of God or of anything like divine sympathy or help.

"Christ claimed to be divine, God with us; Gautama

made no such claim to a divine nature or to divine power.

"Christ is represented as having been an equal sharer in the ineffable purity and glory of heaven; Buddha is said to have been once a hare and once a rat, and Mr. Arnold adorns the contest in which Siddartha strove with other princes for a beautiful bride with the legend that he once in like manner fought with his fellow-brutes of the jungle for a female tiger.

"Christ by his atonement wrought a real and general salvation; Buddha wrought nothing except for himself, and bade all others do the same. 'Be ye clothed and be ye fed' was the only gospel he had to preach.

"Christ held up the hopes of an immediate and eternal state of blessedness after death; Buddha consigned his followers to an almost endless career of strivings, with no real and positive happiness even at the goal.

"Christ taught that life, though attended with fearful alternatives, is a glorious birthright, with promise of endless progress in all virtue and felicity; Buddhism makes life an evil which it is the supreme end of man to conquer and virtually extinguish."

"It is the misfortune of our time," says Saint-Hilaire, "that the same doctrines which form the foundation of Buddhism meet at the hands of some of our philosophers with a favor which they ill deserve. It is well that they should learn from this religion what becomes of man if he depends on himself alone, and if his meditations, misled by a pride of which he is hardly conscious, lead him to the precipice where Buddha was lost."

The London *Times* not long ago observed that "the teaching of Buddha is second only to the teaching of Christ." This was but an echo of a sentiment which of late has prevailed among so-called liberal thinkers. But let us be first just, then generous, toward this religion. The simple truth is, that between the teachings of Christ and those of Buddha there is a gulf as wide and bridgeless as that which separates between God's holy of holies and the midnight region of despair. Let Sir Monier Williams, professor of Sanskrit at Oxford University, England, speak:

"Let us, then, take Buddhism, which is so popularly described as next to Christianity. Let us for a moment, with all reverence, place Buddhism and Christianity in the crucible together. It is often said that Buddha's discourses abound in moral precepts almost identical with those of Christ. Be it so, but in fairness let us take a portion of Buddha's first sermon, which contains the cream of his doctrine. I should like to read it from the translation which has just come out at Oxford. The Buddha, who is said to be second only to Christ, made use of these words: 'Birth is suffering. Decay is suffering. Illness is suffering. Death is suffering. The presence of objects we hate is suffering. Separation from objects we love is suffering. Not to obtain what we desire is suffering. Clinging to existence is suffering. Complete cessation of craving for existence is cessation of suffering; and the Eightfold Path which leads to cessation of suffering is right belief, right aspiration, right speech, right conduct, right means of livelihood, right endeavor, right memory, right meditation. This is the noble truth about suffering.'

"And now, with all reverence, I turn on the other hand to the first gracious words which proceeded from the mouth of the founder of Christianity as given by St. Luke: 'The Spirit of the Lord is upon me, because he hath anointed me to preach good tidings to the poor; he hath sent me to heal the broken-hearted, to preach deliverance to the captives, and recovery of sight to the blind; to set at liberty them that are bruised; to preach the acceptable year of the Lord.' In contrasting these first utterances of two Eastern teachers, one of whom we Christians believe to be divine, I ask what is there of hope for poor suffering humanity in the first utterance of Buddha? Is it not more like a death-knell than a voice proclaiming good tidings of great joy to suffering sinners?

"I feel that I am compelled to speak out on this occasion, even as I spoke out recently at Oxford in contrasting the Veda of the Brahmans with our own Holy Bible, for a kind of doctrine called Neo-Buddhism is spreading, I am sorry to say, in many places both in Europe and America, and also in India, where we hoped that Buddhism had been long extinct.

"This new doctrine magnifies Buddhism, as if, forsooth! it were a very rational sort of creed for an intelligent man to hold in the nineteenth century. Yes, monstrous as it may seem, the gospel of our Saviour—the gospel of peace—is in some quarters giving place to the gospel of misery—the gospel of Buddha—and the former seems to be becoming a little out of fashion here and there. The Buddhist gospel of misery is, I fear, in some places—certainly in India, where we hoped it was extinct—coming into vogue. But mark two or three more contrasts which I should like to place before you. In the gospel of the Buddha we are told that the whole world lieth in suffering, as you have just heard. In the gospel of Christ the whole world lieth in wickedness. 'Glory in your sufferings ; rejoice in them ; make them steps toward heaven,' says the gospel of Christ. 'Away with all suffering! stamp it out, for it is the plague of humanity,' says the gospel of Buddha. 'The whole world is enslaved by sin,' says the Christian gospel; 'The whole world is enslaved by illusion,' says the gospel of Buddha. 'Sanctify your affections,' says the one; 'Suppress them utterly,' says the other. 'Cherish your body, and present it as a living sacrifice to God,' says the Christian gospel; 'Get rid of your body as the greatest of all curses,' says the Buddhist. 'We are God's workmanship,' says the Christian gospel, 'and God works in us, and by us, and through us;' 'We are our own workmanship,' says the gospel of Buddha, 'and no one works in us but ourselves.'

"Lastly, the Christian gospel teaches us to prize the gift of personal life as the most sacred, the most precious, of all God's gifts. 'Life is real, life is earnest,' it seems to say, and it bids us thirst not for death, not for extinction, but for the living God; whereas the Buddhist doctrine stigmatizes all thirst for life as an ignorant blunder, and sets forth, as the highest of all aims, utter extinction of personal existence."

VI.
THE RELIGION OF GREECE.

Sacred Books: None.
Poets and Philosophers.
I. *The Gods:* Mythology.
   (1) Twelve Supreme or Olympic Gods.
   (2) The Superior Gods.
   (3) The Servile Gods.
   (4) Shadows.
   (5) Monsters.

Central Thought: Nature.

II. *Philosophy:* Founder, Thales,
   (1) The Academy; Plato.
   (2) Sophists.
   (3) Epicureans.
   (4) Stoics; Zeno.
   (5) Cynics.
   (6) Skeptics.
   (7) Peripatetics.

"*What shall I do to be saved?*" No answer.

VI. THE RELIGION OF GREECE.

A TRAVELER of the olden time, sailing up through the Saronic Gulf, would be charmed while yet a great way off by the shining splendors of Athens, "the Eye of Greece,"[1] and, drawing nearer, he would mark with ever-increasing wonder and admiration the beauty of its homes and temples lifting their white columns with golden adornments against the green and purple of the Hymettian range of mountains. In the foreground, though five miles inland, stood the Acropolis, crowned with the citadel for an helmet, from whose high summit a statue of Athene caught the morning light and scattered it far and wide from her uplifted shield.

In like manner, as we approach our theme, The Religion of the Greeks, we find ourselves encompassed and dazzled by the most perfect civilization the world has ever known. Art and science and literature enjoyed at once a golden age of a thousand years. The illustrious names of history seem massed together here. Of poets, Homer the godlike; Hesiod, wearing the wreath of the Heliconian Nine; Sappho, "spotless,

[1] "On the Ægean shore a city stands—
Built nobly, pure the air and light the soil—
Athens, the eye of Greece, mother of arts
And eloquence, native to famous wits,
Or hospitable in her sweet recess,
City or suburban, studious walks and shades."

sweetly-smiling, violet-wreathed;" Sophocles, "the bee;" Anacreon, whose lips dropped honey; Æschylus, the poet of wine; and Euripides, of whom the famous epigram was written,

> "If it be true that in the grave the dead
> Have sense and knowledge, as some men have said,
> I'd hang myself to see Euripides."

Of historians, Herodotus, the great father, and Thucydides and Xenophon. Of philosophers, the immortal three—Socrates, Plato and Aristotle, of whom more anon. Of mathematicians, Euclid, Archimedes, the inventor of the lever, and Eratosthenes, who was surnamed "measurer of the universe." Of artists, an endless roster, beginning with Phidias and Praxiteles. Of orators, Gorgias, Æschines and his great rival Demosthenes,

> "Whose resistless eloquence
> Wielded at will the fierce democracie,
> And fulmined over Greece to Artaxerxes' throne."

What a roll-call! Around such names for thousands of years have gathered the glories of Greece. We may not turn aside here into the broad field of general culture which opens before us. We have to do only with the religion of Greece, her gods and her godlike men who sang and reasoned about them. On this let us attempt to converge our gaze as the traveler on that golden ægis of Athene, the symbol of an overruling and protecting—what?

The Greeks a Religious People.—The Greeks were constitutionally religious. St. Paul began his sermon on Mars' Hill by saying, "Ye men of Athens, I perceive that in all things ye are exceedingly devout." Their habits of thought were devotional. Their language, clear, stately and flexible, was peculiarly adapted to the expression of theological ideas. It was not a mere accident that the New Testament was written in Greek.

Our theme falls naturally into a twofold division—namely, The Gods and The Philosophers. These cannot be treated separately, because the latter both logically and chronologically succeeded the former, coming upon the boards just in time to save a melodrama from degenerating into a farce.

I. *The Gods, or Mythology.*—Far back in legendary times there came from the plains of Bactria in Mid-Asia, the motherland of religions, a wandering tribe, who, pursuing their journey northward, paddling from island to island, found their way at length across the Ægean into Greece. In course of time they forgot their birthland, and, wearing a golden grasshopper in their hair, called themselves *Autochthones;* that is, children of the soil. They had brought along with them a religion of nature akin to that of the Rig-Veda.

Central Thought: Nature.—At this point we mark the leading characteristics of their mythology—viz. the *deification of nature.* Let us enter their Pantheon, the temple of their gods. Here we shall find Nature enthroned, the four elements deified, and sacrifices laid upon the altars of Storm and Season and Fruitfulness. "The Greek moved," says Dr. Milligan,[1] "amidst

[1] In *Faiths of the World.*

the objects that nature presented to him, like a child or a young animal, to which everything with which it comes in contact is as full of life as itself. He listened to and endeavored to interpret her meaning as he would have listened to or interpreted a companion at play. He saw her act, he heard her speak, in every one of her departments. There was a rippling sound in the stream: it did not proceed from drops of water only; it came from a living spirit in the stream, fair and sweet, singing with the waters as they tripped along. There was a rustling or a hollow sound in the wood: it was not simply produced by the movement of leaves or of branches; it came from living spirits inhabiting the wood, who the one moment played in the breeze, the next moment sighed as the breeze freshened or groaned as it deepened into a gale. A rainbow glistened in the sky: it was not there by chance or inexorable law; it was

> ‘A midway station given
> For happy spirits to alight
> Betwixt the earth and heaven.’ ”

The source of supply for the Pantheon was thus inexhaustible. Nature is the polytheist's treasure-trove. “Not only had each mountain-chain and mountain-top a separate presiding god or goddess, but troops of oreads inhabited the mountain-regions and disported themselves among them; not only was there a river-god to each river, a Simois and a Scamander, an Enipeus and an Acheloüs, but every nameless stream and brooklet had its water-nymph, every spring and fountain its naiad; wood-nymphs peopled the glades and dells of the forest regions; air-gods moved in the zephyrs and the breezes; each individual oak had its dryad. To the gods proper were added the heroes, gods of a lower grade, and these are spoken of as 'thirty thousand in number, guardian demons, spirits of departed heroes, who are continually walking over earth, veiled in darkness, watching the deeds of men and dispensing weal or woe.'"[1]

It is customary to divide the Greek Pantheon into five groups—namely:

(1) *The Supreme or Olympic Gods.*—These were twelve in number—six male (Zeus, Poseidon, Apollo, Ares, Hephæstus and Hermes) and six female (Hera, Athene, Artemis, Aphrodite, Hestia and Demeter).

(2) *The Superior Ones.*—The vast multitude of superior gods, such as Æolus, Hyperion, Hades; the Graces, Muses, Furies, Fates; the Nymphs, Naiads, Nereids, and the like.

(3) *The Dependent Ones.*—The servile gods, such as Hebe the heavenly cup-bearer, Iris the messenger, and all the servants and handmaids of the superior gods.

(4) *The Shadowy Ones.*—These played their part chiefly in the fabrications of the poets. They were such as Day and Night, Sleep and Darkness, Death and Retribution.

(5) *The Monsters.*—These were marvelous or grotesque beings resulting from mismarriages among gods and men; for example, the Cyclopes, the Harpies

[1] RAWLINSON'S *Ancient Religions.*

and Centaurs, Cerberus with his fifty heads, and innumerable "gorgons, hydras and chimeras dire."

Zeus.—The father of the gods was Zeus, or Zeus-pater, a deification of æther. Behold him reigning among the high crags of Olympus! Do clouds and darkness gather around its summit? They are visible tokens of the anger of Zeus. The lightning is the flash of his eye: with his javelin, the thunderbolt, he hurls his enemy down the mountain-side. This is the great ruler of the upper heavens, the Primal Principle. As one of the early poets wrote:

> "Zeus, the mighty thunderer, is first, is last,
> Is head, is middle of all.
> He is the breadth of the earth, the height of the starry heavens,
> The depth of the sea, the force of untamed fire,
> The origin of all things,—
> One power, one god, the Supreme One."

The expression "For we are also his offspring," used by St. Paul in his address to the philosophers (Acts 17:28), and referred by him to certain of the Greek poets, is found in the following passage from Aratus, wherein the author pays eloquent tribute to this father of the gods:

> "With Zeus begin we—let no mortal voice
> Leave Zeus unpraised. Zeus fills the haunts of men,
> The streets, the marts; Zeus fills the sea, the shores,
> The harbors. Everywhere we live in Zeus.
> *We are his offspring too;* friendly to man,
> He gives prognostics; sets men to their toil
> By need of daily bread; tells when the land
> Must be upturned by ploughshare or by spade,
> What time to plant the olive or the vine,
> What time to fling on earth the golden grain.

> For he it was who scattered o'er the sky
> The shining stars and fixed them where they are,
> Provided constellations through the year
> To mark the seasons in their changeless course.
> Wherefore men worship him, the First, the Last.
> Their Father, Wonderful, their Help and Shield."

Poseidon.—Next to the great All-Father was Poseidon, ruler of the sea. He was represented with locks flowing in the wind, and in his right hand a trident with which he stirred the ocean into billows. He was the sailors' god, invoked with hymns at the hoisting of the anchor and placated with prayers and sacrifices at the approach of the storm.

Apollo.—Next was reckoned Apollo, a very terrestrial god, patron of the healing art and of eloquence, poetry and music. He was a ruler among men, curbing in their behalf " the fierce, flame-breathing steeds of day." His statue in the palace of the Vatican at Rome, known familiarly as the Apollo Belvedere, is remarkable not only for its artistic pre-eminence, but as an exposition of the early religious thought of Greece:

> "All, all divine! no struggling muscle glows;
> Through heaving vein no mantling life-blood flows,
> But, animate with deity alone,
> In deathless glory lives the breathing stone."[1]

These three—Zeus, Apollo and Poseidon, represent-

---

[1] "But if we ask for the moral import of Apollo and his worship, we are speedily at a loss. Beyond the obvious truth that happiness is better than sadness, it is difficult to find any precept directly bearing on the moral welfare of man in his religion. He is the embodiment of a glorious natural power, not of a moral influence."—*St. Paul in Greece*, by Rev. G. S. Davies, M. A.

ing Nature in her three provinces of heaven, earth and sea—formed the great triad of the Pantheon. By these were begotten the multitude of lesser gods.

Hera.—Of the female divinities, the most important were Hera, Athene and Aphrodite. The first was the companion of Zeus and queen of the Olympian court, proud, haughty and passionate—a poor pattern for earthly dames.[1]

Athene.—In Athene we find "the purest and highest creation of the Greek religious spirit."[2] She was the patron of home industry and of the quiet graces of

[1] "She does not present to us an elevated idea of female perfection, since, despite her exalted rank, she is subject to numerous female infirmities. Mr. Grote notes that she is 'proud, jealous and bitter.' Mr. Gladstone observes that she is passionate, wanting in moral elevation, cruel, vindictive and unscrupulous. Her mythological presentation was certainly not of a nature to improve the character of those women who might take her for their model, since, although she was possessed of certain great qualities—passion, fervor, strong affection, self-command, courage, acuteness—yet she was, on the whole, wanting in the main elements of female excellence—gentleness, softness, tenderness, patience, submission to wrong, self-renunciation, reticence. She was a proud, grand, haughty, powerful queen, not a kind, helpful, persuasive, loving woman. The mythology of Greece is in few points less satisfactory than in the type of female character which it exhibits at the head of its pantheon."—RAWLINSON.

[2] "In the ideal of Athene we have perhaps the purest creation of the Greek religion, and one in which, in spite of its imperfectness, the good probably greatly outweighed the bad in its effects upon the moral destinies of the people, offering to them at least the highest ideal of divine wisdom which was within the reach of a nation merely self-taught, and preparing the mind of the people for their reception thereafter of the greatest and purest when it should be placed before them. It is impossible, however, even while we admit the great beauty of that myth by which the Greeks accounted for the creation (not simultaneous with, but subsequent to, other creation) of their divine wisdom, not to compare it with the picture drawn for us of the Divine Wisdom in the book of

wifehood. She was reputed to have sprung full armed from the forehead of Zeus, and was intended originally to represent the dawn appearing in the east, rising, as it were, from the brow of the sky.

Aphrodite.—Aphrodite, goddess of beauty and love, was appropriately called the daughter of heaven and ocean. " The lights and shadows of the heavens, the tints of dawn, the tenderness of clouds, unite with the toss and curving of the wave in creating beauty—outline of the sea, with light and color of the sky." Tennyson has written,

> " Aphrodite beautiful,
> Fresh as the foam, new-bathed in Paphian wells,
> With rosy slender fingers backward drew
> From her warm brow and bosom her deep hair
> Ambrosial, golden round her lucid throat
> And shoulder: from the violets her light foot
> Shone rosy white, and o'er her rounded form,
> Between the shadows of the vine-branches,
> Floated the golden sunlight as she moved."

The Pantheon.—It would be vain, however, to at-

Proverbs (written probably 1015 B. C.) when the Greeks were struggling with the darkness that surrounded even their clearest visions. In the words of the king of Israel, it is the Divine Wisdom which precedes all creation, and is itself the spring and fount of creation : ' I was set up from everlasting, from the beginning, or ever the earth was. When there were no depths, I was brought forth ; when there were no fountains abounding with water. Before the mountains were settled, before the hills, was I brought forth : while as yet he had not made the earth, nor the fields, nor the highest part of the dust of the world. When he prepared the heavens, I was there : when he set a compass upon the face of the depth: when he established the clouds above : when he strengthened the fountains of the deep: when he gave to the sea his decree, that the waters should not pass his commandment : when he appointed the foundations of the earth.' "—*St. Paul in Greece*, REV. G. S. DAVIES, M. A.

tempt to enumerate the gods. There were many thousands of them. It was a trite saying that in Athens it was easier to find a god than a man. All Nature was populous with deities: in them, indeed, she made herself known. "The Greek," says James Freeman Clarke, "went nowhere without finding some spot over which hung the charm of romantic or tender association. Within every brook was hidden a naiad; by the side of every tree lurked a dryad; if you listen you may hear the oreads calling among the mountains, or if you come cautiously around the bending hill you may catch a glimpse of great Pan himself. When the moonlight showers filled the forests one might see the untouched Artemis gliding rapidly among the mossy trunks, while beneath, in the deep abysses, reigned the gloomy Pluto, with the sad Persephone homesick for the upper air. By the seashore Proteus wound his horn, the Sirens sang their fatal song among the rocks, the Nereids and Oceanides gleamed beneath the green waters; and vast Amphitrite stretched her all-embracing arms." There were gods everywhere. All nature was animated with divine life.

The Gods Humanized.—As time passed on, however, the thought of nature was so enlarged as to take in human nature; and at this point began the humanization of the gods. They were brought down from the clouds and forth from the shadowy dells and grottos, and made to take upon themselves the form and fashion of humanity. The Olympian gods were now simply men and women made after a large pattern and endowed with extraordinary gifts and graces. They ate and drank, labored and slept, made love and war. "They lived and laughed, and quarreled and strove and sinned in the Olympian commonwealth as if they had belonged to the *Agora* or to the purlieus of a Greek city. No doubt they were stronger and more beautiful than the inhabitants of earth; a finer blood coursed in their veins, and they were nourished by more heavenly food; but they made merry like revelers of earth upon their mountain-top, and when they descended from it to the world below they were often mistaken for mortal men."[1] They were, indeed, simply men "projected on the skies."

Thus, in process of time the Greek mythology came down to the levels of common life. And herein lies the explanation of its swift decay and death. If a false

[1] Rev. William Milligan, D. D., in *Faiths of the World*. The same writer says: "The Greek had an inborn sense at once of the greatness and the beauty of man. During the earlier stages of his history he had been nursed amidst the active politics of the little state to which he belonged and which maintained a proud independence of every other. At a later stage, when the different states of the same Hellenic blood felt the necessity of union, he cultivated the feeling of a common brotherhood at the Olympic or the Isthmian games, which were the very apotheosis of muscular strength and physical energy. A happy climate and a fruitful soil had developed into its most perfect form the frame which is often relaxed beneath the heat of a southern or cramped by the cold of a northern clime. The noblest productions, too, of the merely human intellect had appeared in Greece; and it would be absurd to suppose that those whose poetry and art have delighted all other ages of the world should themselves have failed to perceive their sublimity and their gracefulness. Man, in short, considered merely as a being of this world, was to the Greek the expression of all that was best and brightest in his thoughts. What could he do but humanize his gods? This, accordingly, was what he did."

god is to inspire confidence, he must keep his distance. Let him come too near and he will show the leather and prunella. The people began to suspect that their gods were but a trifle better than themselves, and they smiled in each other's faces even as they laid their gifts upon the altar. This was the beginning of the end. One of the poets wrote:

> "Homer and Hesiod, whom we own great doctors of theology,
> Said many things of blissful gods that cry for large apology—
> That they may cheat and rail and lie, and give the rein to passion;
> Which were a crime in men who tread the dust in mortal fashion."

The Gods Immoral.—It was true. The gods of Olympus were a company of revelers. Hermes was a thief; Aphrodite, a drab; Athene, an adept at billingsgate; Hera, no better than she ought to be; and Zeus, their worthy sire, a base deceiver, who oftentimes drank too deeply of the mirth-inspiring nectar, quarreled with his guests, and was faithless to his wife, whom he "hung up in mid-heaven with anvils tied to her heels."[1]

"*Like Gods, like People.*"—These being the gods, what should the people be? Away from the solemn rites of nature-worship they were led by these humanized deities into vanity of imagination and darkness of heart. The gods themselves were the great corrupters.

[1] "The gods of antiquity, particularly those of Greece, were of infamous character. Whilst they were represented by their votaries as excelling in beauty and activity, strength and intelligence, they were also described as envious and gluttonous, base, lustful and revengeful. Jupiter, the king of the gods, was deceitful and licentious; Juno, the queen of heaven, was cruel and tyrannical. What could be expected from those who honored such deities?"—*The Ancient Church*, W. D. KILLEN, D. D.

> " Wandering o'er the earth,
> By falsities and lies the greatest part
> Of mankind they corrupted to forsake
> God their Creator, and th' invisible
> Glory of Him that made them to transform
> Oft to the image of a brute, adorn'd
> With gay religions full of pomp and gold,
> And devils to adore for deities."

Nor was this all. Not only were the altars defiled, but the lives of the worshipers were also debased and sensualized.

> " Like gods they lived, with happy, careless souls,
> From toil and care exempt. Nor on them crept
> Wretched old age; but all their life was passed
> In feasting; and when they died,
> 'Twas but as if they were o'ercome by sleep."

Happy, sensual Greeks! They lived, indeed, "like gods;" and what better could be expected of them? They had no longer a serious ideal of manhood.[1] There

---

[1] "One may, I think, fairly say that Homer means Achilles to be *the* hero of the *Iliad*, at any rate on the Greek side. He is, in every sense, the most heroic of the Greeks, and may perhaps be quoted as Homer's ideal of what a hero should be. He lacks, therefore, many of the littlenesses which deface Agamemnon and others of the Greeks. Yet even at the moment of his highest achievement, his conquest of Hector in the single combat beneath the walls of Troy, he is represented to us in a light which makes us forget all other traits in him except the unspeakable want of generosity toward a noble but fallen enemy. Nor is it possible that Homer should have so painted the choicest of his heroes if it was likely to have marred him so completely in the eyes of his then readers (or rather hearers) as it does in ours. Hector, failing fast, thus begs his conqueror to grant him the one favor that his dead body shall not be cast in dishonor to the dogs and vultures, but sent back to Troy to be buried by his relations. The Greek replies—addressing the dying man as ' hound!'—that nothing would induce him to forego the pleasure

was a theatre in Athens provided with thirty thousand seats, and it is said to have been filled every day. Life was valued only for the pleasure that could be crowded into it. Mimnermus said: "When the flower of youth is past it were better to die. Life without the golden-haired goddess is not worth living."

Forms of Worship.—The worship of the Greeks was offered in sacrifices and prayers and festivals. The sacrifices were only for great emergencies. The prayers were genuine and instinctive breathings of desire. "They threw kisses to the gods upon their hands." But if we would see their religion at its best, and at its worst also, we must visit the festivals.[1] These were held in the open air, with magnificent processions, dances, athletic sports, tournaments of poets and musicians, chariot-races and whatever else a pleasure-loving people could devise. The so-called "mysteries" were

---

of leaving his hated enemy to the dogs, and that he only regrets that he cannot eat his flesh raw."—*St. Paul in Greece*, DAVIES, pp. 38, 39.

[1] "The Greek looked forward to his holy days as true holidays, and was pleased to combine duty with pleasure by taking his place in the procession or the temple or the theatre, to which inclination and religion alike called him. Thousands and tens of thousands flocked to each of the great Pan-Hellenic gatherings, delighting in the splendor and excitement of the scene, in the gay dresses, the magnificent equipages, the races, the games, the choric and other contests. 'These festivals,' as has been well observed, 'were considered as the very cream of the Greek life, their periodical recurrence being expected with eagerness and greeted with joy.' Similarly, though to a minor extent, each national or even tribal gathering was an occasion of enjoyment; cheerfulness, hilarity, sometimes an excessive exhilaration, prevailed; and the religion of the Greeks, in these its most striking and obvious manifestations, was altogether bright, festive and pleasurable."—*Ancient Religions*, RAWLINSON, p. 153.

closely connected with these diversions, and consisted mainly of striking representations, dramatic and otherwise, of the adventures of the gods.[1] All this was worship. The poet sang the praises of Apollo; the wrestler called on Hercules; and the lewd dancers, flushed with wine, mingled the names of Bacchus and Aphrodite.

This was the last chapter. Religion had become low comedy; the gods wore the buskins. Lucian began to write satires against them; he was called "blasphemer:" it mattered not; he went on with the unmasking of the tricksters. Some one asks of Heraclitus: "What do you hold human life to be?" He answers, "A child at play, handling its toys and changing them with every changing whim."

"And what are men?"
"Gods, but mortal."

[1] "The mysteries were certain secret rites practiced by voluntary associations of individuals, who pledged themselves not to reveal to the uninitiated anything which they saw or heard at the secret meetings. They were usually connected with the worship of some particular god, and consisted mainly in symbolical representations of the adventures and circumstances connected with the god in the mythology. They contained nothing that was contradictory to the popular religion, and little that was explanatory of it. The various mysteries had each its own apparatus of symbols and formularies, by which the *mystæ* knew each other, as Freemasons do; but they only vaguely hinted at any theological dogmas or opinions. The Greek greatly affected these secret rites; and it is said that but few Greeks were not initiated in some mystery or other. Their attraction lay in their veil of secrecy, transparent though it was; in the variety of feelings brought into play by lively dramatic representations; in the rapid transition from anxiety and suspense to serenity and joy, and the combination of all arts and artistic enjoyments, of music and song, the mimic dance, the brilliant lighting up and effective decoration."—*Ancient Religions*, RAWLINSON, pp. 154, 155.

"And the gods?"
"The gods? They are men, but immortal."

III. *Philosophy.*—We come now to consider the philosophies. In time the degeneracy of the gods brought on an age of doubt and inquiry. The shrines were abandoned; the fires slowly died out upon the altars; and from the deep recesses of the forest the winds came wailing, "Great Pan is dead!" By the river-banks were planted groves and gardens; on the hillsides porches were built, and among them walked thoughtful men wearing a new name—*Philosophoi*, or "lovers of wisdom." These were the protestants of that day, who fearlessly approached the stalking ghosts and spectres of the popular religion and laughed them out of countenance. They summoned the gods before the bar of reason and subjected the myths to critical analysis. Then came the inevitable: Anaxagoras was condemned to death for blasphemy, and a noble troop followed in his train; Pericles was branded as a heretic for lifting his eyebrows at the Olympian fables; and Socrates was doomed to drink the cup of hemlock. This is the universal law: the darkness begets death, and out of death comes newness of life. No falsehood is immortal.

> "The outworn rite, the old abuse,
>   The pious fraud transparent grown,
> The good held captive in the use
>   Of wrong alone,—
> These wait their doom, from that great law
>   Which makes the past time serve to-day;
> And fresher life the world shall draw
>   From their decay."

No age of reform is without its martyrs, but out of their dust arise armies that grasp the standard and go marching on.

The mythology of Greece had been intended to meet the soul's demand for an object of worship; but the philosophers, their eyes pained with looking upward into a voiceless and unwritten sky, turned their gaze away toward the origin of things. This was the question they sought to explain: "Whence came the universe and I?" The starting-point of philosophy was doubt; its first step was into illimitable paths of fearless inquiry; its hoped-for destination was truth. Once, and only once, the Greeks approached the realization of that hope when from the stone steps of the Areopagus they looked up into the face of Christ's apostle, half ready to believe the words that were falling from his fire-touched lips.

It will not be unprofitable to note some of the more illustrious names of those who were identified with this philosophic movement, this grander quest than of San Greal or the Golden Fleece.

The Founder, Thales.—The founder of philosophy was Thales, about 600 B. C. He devoted his attention to physical science, beginning with the assumption that water is the First Principle. His intention, probably, was to establish an alliance between philosophic research and the popular faith in Oceanus as one of the parent gods. An advance was made when Pythagoras asserted that the First Principle of all things is number. He was the inventor of the multiplication table. One of his cardinal precepts was, "All comes from one," or, in other words, "God embraces all, inspires all, and is only One." Here is an example of this teacher's golden verses, and the gold is lustrous still:

> "Ne'er suffer thine eyes to close
> Before thy mind hath run
> O'er every act and thought and word
> From dawn to set of sun."[1]

Out of the researches and speculations of such pioneers came the Seven Schools of Philosophy—namely:

(1) *The Academy.*—Socrates was the discoverer of conscience among the Greeks and the founder of ethical science. He denounced the gods, asserted that virtue is the most desirable thing, and was an enthusiast in the pursuit of truth. He said: "I have uttered some things of which I am not altogether confident; but I am ready to contend to the utmost of my ability, in word and deed, to prove that we shall be better and braver and less helpless if we think that we ought to inquire than we can possibly be in the indulgence of the idle fancy that there is no knowing and no use in searching after what we know not." He

[1] "With such perfect confidence did his disciples regard their master, who usually gave his instructions from behind a thick curtain, that when any one called their doctrines in question they deemed it sufficient to reply, 'He said so' (*ipse dixit*). Indeed, they invested him with supernatural powers, nor, according to his early biographies, did he deny the soft impeachment. On one occasion, we are told, to convince his pupils that he was a god he showed them his thigh, which was of gold, and declared that he had assumed the form of humanity only the more readily to impart his letters to mankind."—QUACKENBOS'S *Ancient Literature.*

had also vague dreams of immortality. In prison he said: "A man that hath arrayed his soul in its own proper jewels—which are wisdom, temperance, courage and justice—is prepared to go at the appointed hour on his journey to the other world." And with the hemlock at his lips he said to his weeping friends, " I take comfort in the hope that something remains of man after death."

But Socrates himself founded no school; it was left for his disciple Plato to establish the Academy, where he was accustomed to walk among the plane trees discoursing on the four cardinal virtues[1] and on the problems of immortality and a personal God. He was a loyal follower of Socrates, but his life was purer and his eyes were clearer to see within the veil. Over the doorway of his lecture-room was written, " Let no one enter here who is a stranger to the symmetry of a virtuous life."

(2) *The Sophists*, a favorite school in Athens. These were the " word-snapping quibblers " who denied that there was any radical difference between right and wrong, and who devoted themselves to the task of " making the worse appear the better reason." With

---

[1] " Plato was an enthusiast in the pursuit of truth. He believed in a personal God, rational, immutable, eternal. He realized that man could never attain absolute wisdom, possible to God alone, and looked upon philosophy as ' a longing after heavenly wisdom.' He sought to correct abuses, to elevate humanity, and made man's highest duty consist in searching out God and imitating the perfection of the Almighty as his rule of conduct. The four cardinal virtues were wisdom, temperance, courage and justice; but none could be virtuous without aid from on high."—QUACKENBOS'S *Ancient Literature*, p. 243.

them originated the saying, "Might makes right." They undertook to prove "that knowing one thing is knowing everything, and there is no such thing as knowing anything at all; that as the beautiful exists by the presence of beauty, so a man becomes an ass by the presence of an ass; and so on, ringing myriads of changes, like the fools in Shakespeare, upon these quirks of jugglery." A satirist, pointing to their grove, said:

> "That's the great thinking-school of the new philosophy;
> There live the men who teach that heaven around us
> Is a vast oven, and we the charcoal in it.
> And they teach also—for a consideration, mind you—
> To plead a cause and win it, right or wrong."[1]

(3) *The Epicureans*, or school of Epicurus. They were materialists, holding that matter is the sum and substance of all, and that the apparent order of the universe is the result of a fortuitous concourse of atoms. This obviously rules out God, immortality and moral responsibility. The philosophy of Epicurus finds its monograph in the maxim, "Let us eat and

[1] "What shall we say of such a system and such a state of things? Simply this: that it indicated a complete mental and social demoralization—mental demoralization, for the principles of knowledge were sapped, and man was persuaded that his reason was no guide; social demoralization, for he was taught that right and wrong, virtue and vice, conscience and law and God, are imaginary fictions; that there is no harm in the commission of sin, though there may be harm, as assuredly there is folly, in being detected therein; that it is excellent for a man to sell his country to the Persian king, provided that the sum of money he receives is large enough, and that the transaction is so darkly conducted that the public, and particularly his enemies, can never find it out."— DRAPER's *Intellectual Development of Europe*, i. p. 136.

drink, for to-morrow we die." He made expediency the test of action; he said, "We are governed by chance; pleasure is the highest good; death ends all."[1]

(4) *The Stoics.*—This school was founded by Zeno, who taught the precise opposite of the Epicurean system. The latter made expediency the supreme purpose; in the philosophy of Zeno the chief end of man was to adjust his life to the order of nature.[2] There is nothing higher than duty, nothing more heroic than mastery of self. The Stoics were sublime egotists. They were also predestinarians of the straitest sect. Zeno's slave, detected in stealing, cried out, "O master, I am a Stoic; it was fated that I should steal."— "Yes," retorted his master, "and it was also fated that

[1] "In its best shape Epicureanism was little better than a prudent selfishness; in its worst it degenerated into vice. In St. Paul's day the Epicureans were like the Sadducees, the pleasure-loving men of the world, who adopted the principle, but repudiated the example, of their master. The physical philosophy of Epicurus produced the sublime poem of Lucretius, but in the spirit and tone of his morality, in his austere and intense moral earnestness, Lucretius was far more of a Stoic than an Epicurean. The genial and pleasant Horace was an Epicurean, but the type of life which Horace preaches is lower than that of his teacher. Or take as the representative of the better class of Epicureans in Roman times, of men who understood how to seek pleasure in a refined, gentlemanly way, declining every public duty and living a life of lettered ease, Atticus, the friend of Cicero. Him Sir James Mackintosh has called in language not one whit too severe, ' the accomplished, prudent, friendly, good-natured time-server, Atticus, the pliant slave of every tyrant, who could kiss the hand of Antony, imbrued as it was in the blood of Cicero.'"—*St. Paul at Athens*, SHAKESPEARE, pp. 120, 121.

[2] "The ethical theory of the Stoics may be summed up as consisting in the subordination of our instinctive love of pleasure and instinctive shrinking from pain to obedience to the moral order revealed in the world."—*Ibid.*, p. 132.

you should be flogged for it." Taken for all in all, the *Stoa*, or "Painted Porch," was the most admirable of the schools. Its spirit finds expression in the soliloquy of Archilochus:

> "My soul, my soul! by cares past all relief
> Distracted sore, bear up, with manly breast
> And dauntless mien, each fresh assault of grief
> Encountering. By hostile weapons pressed,
> Stand firm. Let no unlooked-for triumph move
> To empty exultation, no defeat
> Cast down. But still let moderation prove
> Of life's uncertain cup the bitter and the sweet."[1]

(5) *The Cynics.*—These were misanthropes. Their greatest name was Diogenes, who affected the manners of a lazy vagrant.[2] They professed to entertain a pro-

---

[1] "Zeno brought into use the method of refuting error by the *reductio ad absurdum*. His compositions were in prose, and not in poetry as were those of his predecessors. As it had been the object of Parmenides to establish the existence of 'the One,' it was the object of Zeno to establish the non-existence of 'the many.' Agreeably to such principles, he started from the position that only one thing really exists, and that all others are mere modifications or appearances of it." . . . "He furnishes us with an illustration of the fallibility of the indications of sense in his argument against Protagoras. It may be here introduced as a specimen of his method: 'He asked if a grain of corn or the ten-thousandth part of a grain would, when it fell to the ground, make a noise. Being answered in the negative, he further asked whether, then, would a measure of corn. This being necessarily affirmed, he then demanded whether the measure was not in some determinate ratio to the single grain; as this could not be denied, he was able to conclude either, then, the bushel of corn makes no noise on falling, or else the very smallest portion of a grain does the same."—DRAPER'S *Intellectual Development of Europe*, i. pp. 122, 123.

[2] "He may be considered as the prototype of the hermits of a later period in his attempts at the subjugation of the natural appetites by means of starvation. Looking upon the body as a mere clog to the soul, he

found contempt for the affairs of the world and the opinions of men. Their philosophy is aptly said to have been "steeped in gall."

(6) *The Skeptics*, or *Agnostics*, founded by Pyrro. They glorified doubt. "All things are uncertain; there is no standard of truth." "We assert nothing," said they, "no, not even that we assert nothing." "Sense is limited, intellect is weak, life is short." This is the philosophy of despair.

(7) *The Peripatetics*, founded by Aristotle. He originated the inductive method of reasoning—*i. e.* from particulars to universals [1]—which is the opposite of the

mortified it in every possible manner, feeding it on raw meat and leaves and making it dwell in a tub. He professed that the nearer a man approaches to suicide the nearer he approaches to virtue. He wore no other dress than a scanty cloak; a wallet, a stick and a drinking-cup completed his equipment: the cup he threw away as useless on seeing a boy take water in the hollow of his hand. It was his delight to offend every idea of social decency by performing all the acts of life publicly, asserting that whatever is not improper in itself ought to be done openly. It is said that his death, which occurred in his ninetieth year, was in consequence of devouring a neat's foot raw. From his carrying the Socratic notions to an extreme he merits the designation applied to him, 'the mad Socrates.' His contempt for the opinions of others and his religious disbelief are illustrated by an incident related of him, that, having in a moment of weakness made a promise to some friends that he would offer a sacrifice to Diana, he repaired the next day to her temple, and, taking a louse from his head, cracked it upon her altar."—DRAPER'S *Intellectual Development of Europe*, i. p. 150.

[1] "The philosophical method of Aristotle is the inverse of that of Plato, whose starting-point was universals, the very existence of which was a matter of faith, and from these he descended to particulars or details. Aristotle, on the contrary, rose from particulars to universals, advancing to them by inductions; and his system, thus an inductive philosophy, was in reality the true beginning of science."—*Ibid.*, i. p. 176.

method of Plato. The latter was an idealist; Aristotle was a materialist, holding nothing true which could not be demonstrated, and therefore rejecting as unsubstantial all the great verities of the eternal world.

We have thus hastily glanced at the various systems of philosophy that arose and flourished in Greece at one time or another during her thousand golden years. Here was a great step onward from the Bacchanalia and the Olympic games. The Greeks were beginning to feel after God, if haply they might find him. Yet how dim were their eyes! One of the philosophers said God was fire; another, water; another, air; another said,

"All eyes, all ears, all thought is God, the Omnipresent Soul."[1]

It was demanded of Simonides by the king of Syracuse that he should define God. After weeks of meditation he answered, " The more I think of him, the more he is unknown." To this inglorious result had their philosophy come in its ten centuries: its best summary at the beginning of the Christian era was an interrogation-mark. And Paul said, " As I passed by and be-

[1] "The idea of one Supreme God, combining all the attributes of divinity—omniscience, omnipotence, wisdom, love—was, by the very nature of the case, excluded from the range of Greek religious comprehension; and although some of those great searchers after truth, such as Socrates, obtained a very feeble and far-off glimpse of such an existence, it was confined to but a few whose vision by the honest search for truth may be said to have been purified. The higher view of divine agencies which was thus called into existence by a few of the greater minds of Greece became the property of those who followed philosophy, rather than of the orthodox followers of the national creed."—*St. Paul in Greece*, DAVIES, p. 67.

held your devotions, I found an altar with this inscription: *To the Unknown God."*

We may search never so closely into these various systems, and we shall nowhere find a definite creed as to the great truths of the eternal world, not even an answer to the question, "If a man die, shall he live again?" The fact of personal responsibility, which lies at the base of all political and social order, is predicated with an *if.* And when a poor sinner comes pleading, "Who shall deliver me?" the oracles are dumb.

The Maxims of the Seven Wise Men.—This, therefore, was no *religion* in any proper sense, for there was no uplifting of the soul to God. Let us observe the maxims of the Seven Wise Men:

That of Solon was " Know thyself;"
 Chilo, " Consider the end;"
 Thales, " Who hateth suretyship is sure;"
 Bias, " Most men are bad;"
 Cleobulus, " Avoid extremes;"
 Pittacus, " Seize time by the forelock;"
 Periander, " Nothing is impossible to industry."

In these seven epigrams was supposed to reside the concentrated wit and wisdom of the various schools; but, however much of worldly sagacity or shrewdness we may discover in them, of religion there is none.

The Morality of the Greeks.—And there was little or no morality in Greece. Can a man gather grapes of thorns or figs of thistles? The two ages of mythology and philosophy were equally barren as to right methods of life. Athens in the day of her greatest prosperity and culture was a city of magnificent vices. Society was polluted through and through. Demetrius says: "There was not in Athens, in my time, one great or noble mind." The women were divided into two classes, courtesans and drudges. Divorces were so frequent as to be counted boastfully by rings on the fingers. Infanticide was also of common occurrence, and was formally approved by Aristotle and Plato. Indeed, the philosophers themselves, with scarcely an exception, are, out of their own mouths, convicted of beastly vices and uncleannesses.[1] The crime of Lesbos was theirs, insomuch that Plutarch, in his treatise on the education of boys, declares that parents wishing their children to be pure must not allow them to form the acquaintance of philosophers. The establishment of an Athenian gentleman must be furnished with cooks, jesters and a *harem*. "I suppose it to be literally true," says Professor Seelye, "that no vice nor crime nor cruelty can be named which did not show itself at home in the highest circles of this most blooming society of the ancient world."[2]

[1] "'We despise,' says an early Christian writer, 'the supercilious looks of philosophers, whom we have known to be the corrupters of innocence, adulterers and tyrants, and eloquent declaimers against vices of which they themselves are guilty.'"—DR. KILLEN, from Minucius Felix.

[2] "And what shall we say of Socrates and Plato? There have been many who have ventured to place Socrates by the side of Christ; and Socrates was great and noble and wise, and his death is one of the most moving scenes of ancient history. Let us not breathe one word against that holy and high-souled sage, but the truth is dearer to us even than Socrates; and when we think of Socrates conversing with Theodota

And why not? What shall we look for in a society where right and wrong, duty and expediency, virtue and vice, are regarded as mere conventional terms? or feasting with Agathon,—when we remember the mingled leniency and coarseness with which he spoke of the sins of Critias,—when we recall his cold and almost impatient dismissal of his wife and children at his hour of approaching death; and then, with bowed head, think of Him who talked by the well-side with the woman of Samaria or stood alone by that guilty adulteress as she sobbed upon the temple floor,—or who, as he hung upon the cross between the thieves, chose out the tenderest-hearted of his disciples and in the midst of his anguish said to his mother, '*Woman, behold thy son,*'—then, indeed, if our spiritual sense be not utterly blunt and dead, we may see how infinite is the gulf which separates the teacher of Athens from the Son of God.

"And Plato—the '*divinus ille Plato*' of Arnobius—the Plato of whom Clement said that he touched the very gates of truth—the Plato whom Jerome carried with him under his hermit mantle and Augustine under his bishop's robe—the Plato whom our own Coleridge called 'a plank from the wreck of Paradise cast upon the shores of idolatrous Greece'—we all know the depth of his insight, the subtlety of his reasoning, the splendor of his imagination, the magic of his style; and yet when we think how overwhelming would have been the shock to our moral sense, how fatal the overthrow of our distinctions between right and wrong, had he been accepted as the world's teacher; when we place the *Phædrus* or the *Symposium*, with all their poetic eloquence and all the subtly dangerous poison of their perfumed but unwholesome air, beside the sweet, pure, simple books of the humble fishermen of Galilee,—when we compare his ideal republic with its community of women, its destruction of the family, its degradation of the multitude, its exposition of children, its tolerated and worse than tolerated crimes, with the kingdom of heaven as preached by Christ,—then must we not see in such a comparison, unless made by way of contrast, I will not say a gross injustice, but I will say, for so it is, an unwarrantable blasphemy against the simple truth? Ay, my brethren, the most golden idol of pagan excellence stands but on feet of clay. There is flagrant intellectual error in their very wisest; there is fearful moral aberration in their very best. Over their graves, as in the sigh of the wailing wind, we hear the words, '*The world by wisdom knew not God.*'"—FARRAR'S *Witness*, 139-141.

In process of time Greece with her gods and reasoners was brought into contact with the higher faith. Look at this picture of Paul preaching to the newsmongers and philosophers! Little did they dream that this man of unimposing presence, whom they thought to be a setter-forth of two strange gods, Jesus and Anastasis, was preparing the way for the ultimate rending asunder of their whole religious fabric.[1] For hundreds of years thereafter the two systems existed side by side, but at length the thunders of Zeus were hushed and the colossal figures of the philosophers grew dim before the brighter presence of the Man of Nazareth, until, as Goldwin Smith has said, " Greece arose from the dead with the New Testament in her hand." It is a notable fact that the Greeks received the gospel more readily than any other people. It was, perhaps, because they needed it more. To the wise among them it seemed foolishness, but to those who were weary of reaching forth the hand of Tantalus and of performing the futile

[1] " From the day that his foot first touched their shores, and that his voice was first heard in their cities, the religion that had once held some of the greatest minds of ancient Greece under its influence was doomed to pass away from the minds of men for ever except as a harmless memory. It was no mean task to sweep away even the ruins of a faith which was so connected with the glories of the past. It was to be still the work of centuries to remove them from the soil where they had so long been venerated. In so doing there was far more to be got rid of than the fallen masses of the building itself: there was a close and complicated growth of philosophy, mythology, national tradition, national associations, which clung together in a thick, impenetrable mass of ivy and creeper, bindweed and brier, wild flower, thicket and shrub, amongst which appeared, half hidden and deep sunk into the soil, the timeworn ruins of the old Greek religion."—*St. Paul in Greece*, DAVIES, p. 57.

task of Sisyphus it was the very wisdom and power of God.

These people had fed upon husks so long that they came to the Father's table as to a feast of fat things and wine upon the lees. No Bible, even, had been theirs, for theirs was the only great nation that had no sacred books. Think of the wretchedness of being without a word from God! And when they prayed, it was as if they cast their longings to the winds. For their gods took no interest in their welfare, cared naught for their troubles, but dwelt afar off on the Olympian heights,

> "haunting
> The lucid interspace of world and world,
> Where never creeps a cloud or moves a wind,
> Nor ever falls the least white star of snow,
> Nor ever lowest roll of thunder moans,
> Nor sound of human sorrow mounts to mar
> Their sacred everlasting calm."

"*What shall I Do to be Saved?*"—This was a religion that could not satisfy the cravings of the heart. It knew no duty nor self-denial. It put upon the passions no effectual curb. It uttered no warning as to the future, and, with all the gladness of its festivals, it left the doorway of the tomb shrouded in unbroken night. And, above and beyond all, it gave no answer to the cry, "What shall I do to be saved—saved from sin and shame and eternal death?"

It was indeed a preparation for better things in that it awakened a sense of utter guilt and helplessness. The moral poverty and wretchedness of the whole nation found a voice on the lips of those Greeks who went up to Jerusalem at the time of the Passover saying, "We would see Jesus."

What, then, is our lesson? *Philosophy cannot save.* The world by wisdom knew not God. And *culture cannot save.* At the very moment when Zeuxis was painting the walls of Athens with a beauty which modern art has sought in vain to imitate—when Socrates was theorizing about virtue—the social life of Greece stank with rottenness. And the gods went on feasting. How weird is the lament of Io!—

> "Eleleu! Eleleu!
> How the spasm and the pain,
> And the fire on my brain
>   Strike burning through!—
> How my heart in its terror is spurning my breast!
> And my words beat in vain, in wild storms of unrest,
>   On the sea of desolate fate!"

It was Prometheus chained to the rock; it was Ixion on the wheel; it was Tantalus in hell.

We hear it asserted in some quarters that natural religion is enough for the soul. It were a sufficient answer to point backward to the bewildered and despairing Greeks. They had all that nature could suggest or the human intellect devise, and yet they were without God and without hope. They searched for truth as blind men groping for the wall. Verily, the world by its own wisdom knoweth not God. A recent writer (Dr. Milligan of the University of Aberdeen) says: "Never had the thought of the natural dignity of man and the sacredness of human feelings a better opportunity to show what they can do for humanity than they had in Greece. The result was disastrous, humiliating, melancholy failure. A corruption was nourished in the Greek world which gradually sapped the foundations of its life. . . . It has been said by an eloquent writer of the day that what concerns us at the present time is to learn how to face the problems of the world with Greek serenity. If we have nothing more to face them with, we shall sink before them as Greece did. The great question is, Where is that divine life to be found which faces all problems without sinking? Is it to be found in nature or in Christ? Greece answers that question. She sought it and found it in nature; and she perished. The search for the divine in nature alone led to self-abasement, and

'Self-abasement paved the way
To villain bonds and despot sway.'"

We turn from the coldness and barrenness of nature-worship on the one hand and philosophy on the other —from dumb, sightless gods and impotent dreamers all—to the gospel of our Lord and Saviour Jesus Christ. Here is a God whose eyes run to and fro through all the earth, and whose ears are attentive to the cry of the least of his little ones. His name is Love. God-love was never dreamed of in Greek philosophy, but here it glows as tender and beautiful as that of a mother bending over her sleeping child. "God *so* loved the world." Blessed be his name! And there is a sunlit path leading into his very presence—the royal way of the cross, the path for you and me.[1]

[1] "Yes, it was of God, and they could not overthrow it; the catacomb triumphed over the Grecian temple; the cross of shame over the wine-cup and the Salian banquet, the song of the siren and the wreath of rose.

"These obscure sectaries—barbarians, Orientals, Jews as they were—fought against the indignant world and won. 'Not by power, nor by might, but by my Spirit, saith the Lord of hosts'—by heroic endurance, by stainless innocence, by burning zeal, by inviolable truthfulness, by boundless love. The world's seductive ideals and intoxicating joys, the world's enchanting mythologies and dissolute religions—young Dionysus,

'As he burst upon the East
A jocund and a welcome conqueror,
And Aphrodite, sweet as from the sea
She rose and floated in her pearly shell,
A laughing girl,'

all fled before a cross of wood! Yes, my brethren, because that cross was held by the bleeding hands of the world's true King, who perfected the strength of his followers in weakness, and, having been lifted up, drew all men unto him."—FARRAR'S *Witness*, pp. 106-108.

VII.
THE RELIGION OF THE NORSEMEN.

I. *Sacred Books:* The Two Eddas.
II. *Theology:*
    (1) The Gods;
        Odin, the All-Father.
        The Twelve Æsir:

Thor,	Heimdall,
Baldur,	Hödur,
Njord,	Vidar,
Frey,	Vali,
Tyr,	Ullur,
Bragi,	Forseti.

        Loki.
        Minor Powers.
    (2) The Creation.
    (3) The Future:
        Ragnarok.
        Heaven and Hell.
III. *Forms of Worship.*
IV. *Morals.*
    Central Thought: Courage.
"What shall I do to be saved?" Fight a good fight.

VII. NORSE MYTHOLOGY.

The Norsemen.—The fair-haired Norsemen came originally from Bactria in Central Asia, the prolific motherland of nations. The memory of the warm suns and blooming hills of that country must have been to them, dwelling among the rigors of Scandinavia, like the thought of a lost heaven. The time came at length when, weary of interminable winter and twilight, they sent forth their vikings, fearless sea-rovers, in search of a more propitious home. These vikings found their way to Britain, conquered and possessed it, and became the forefathers of our Anglo-Saxon race.

I. *Sacred Literature.*—Our knowledge of the Norse mythology is chiefly derived from the Eddas. For the survival of these sacred books we are indebted, strange to tell, not to Scandinavia, but to the people of another and far-distant land. On the introduction of Christianity into Northern Europe pains were taken to obliterate, as far as possible, all traces of the primitive faith: not only were temples and altars destroyed, but the people were required to disuse their sacred traditions. In the mean time, however, a hardy company of Norsemen had sailed away to Iceland, taking their religion with them, and amid the frozen fields and geysers and volcanoes of that desolate corner of the earth—a land not unfitted to be the final refuge of a religion of warring gods and giants—it was preserved for the coming ages.

In Longfellow's *Tales of a Wayside Inn* a blue-eyed Saxon refers to the Eddas as

> " a wondrous book
> Of legends, in the old Norse tongue,
> Of the dead kings of Norroway—
> Legends that once were told or sung,
> In many a smoky fireside nook
> Of Iceland in the ancient day,
> By wandering Saga-man."

The name *Edda* means "great-grandmother," the reference being, probably, to the manner in which these tales were transmitted, unwritten, from lip to lip by the dames of the olden time. The book is in two volumes. The *Elder Edda* consists of thirty-seven ancient poems, mythical and legendary, collected and put forth in their present form by Sæmund, a Christian priest of the eleventh century. It opens with the "Voluspa, or Wisdom of Vala," which purports to be a description of the universe before the inauguration of the present order of things. It begins thus:

> " I claim the devout attention of all noble ones,
> The lofty and lowly of the Heimdall race;
> I tell the works of *the All-Father*
> As related in the most ancient sagas.

> " I tell of the age of Ymer,
> When there was neither sea, nor shore, nor briny wave,
> No earth below nor heaven above,
> Nor yawning chasm, nor verdant plain."

One of the poems of the Elder Edda, called "The Havamal," consists of a hundred and ten quatrains of proverbial philosophy. The following will serve as illustrations:

> "Carefully consider the end
> Before you undertake anything;
> For all is uncertain when the foe
> Lies in wait in the house.
>
> "The guest on entering
> Needs water, a towel and entertainment;
> A kind reception secures a return
> In word and deed.
>
> "A man cannot journey with a worse friend
> Than drunkenness;
> Not so beneficent as many believe
> Is beer to the children of men;
> The more one drinks, the less he knows,
> And the less power he has over himself.
>
> "A man's own house, though small, is best;
> At home thou art master;
> Two goats and a thatched roof
> Are better than beggary.
>
> "Is there one whom you distrust,
> And who yet can help you?
> Be smooth in words and false in thought,
> And pay back his deceit with cunning.
>
> "I hung my clothes on two scarecrows,
> And when dressed they seemed
> Ready for battle;
> Unclothed, they were derided by all.
>
> "It is well to be wise, not well
> To be too wise;
> He has the happiest life
> Who knows well what he knows." [1]

Another of the poems of the Elder Edda is "The

[1] CLARKE.

Song of Runes." The Norsemen believed that certain combinations of the letters of the alphabet possessed a magical virtue; such combinations were called *runes*. It was customary for warriors to write runic rhymes on their sword-blades; lovers carved them on their drinking-horns, sailors on the masts and rudders of their ships, leeches on the bark of sacred trees.

The remainder of the Elder Edda is made up of wonderful tales of the adventures of heroes. In these the Norsemen found inspiration for their audacious deeds by land and sea.

The Younger Edda is a prose compendium of mythology. It was arranged and put forth in the early part of the twelfth century by Snorro Thurleson of Iceland. The sources of his information were old songs and ballads and "ancient family registers containing the pedigrees of kings." It is from this Younger Edda that we chiefly derive our knowledge of the Norse religion.

II. *Theology.*—(1) *The Gods.*—There is good reason to believe that the faith of the Norsemen was originally monotheistic. They bowed in worship before One whom they believed to be "the Author of everything that exists, the Eternal, the Ancient, the living and awful Being, the Searcher who concealeth things, the Being that never changes;" One who, as Dr. Burns says, "possessed infinite power, boundless knowledge and inflexible justice—who was not to be worshiped in temples reared by human hands, but in consecrated groves and in the solitudes of the forest. It was forbidden to represent him by any image. He was the great, invisible Spirit who pervaded the universe, too awful even to be named—who was to be served with sacrifices and prayers, and who delighted in seeing men lead pure and brave lives."

We find among the wonderful tales of the Younger Edda the adventures of Gylfi, who visited Asgard, the home of the Æsir or Norse gods. He is said to have seen there a triple throne whereon sat Har "the high one," Jafnhar "the high one's fellow," and Thridi "the third one." To these the doughty explorer was allowed to propound certain questions.

"Who," he asked, "is the first and eldest of the gods?"

And Har answered: "In our language he is called Al-Fadir;" that is, the Father of all.

"Where," asked Gylfi again, "is the dwelling-place of this Supreme One, and what is his power, and what hath he done to display his glory?"

Har answered, "He liveth from all ages, governeth all realms and swayeth all things great and small."

To which Jafnhar added, "He formed heaven and earth and the air, and all things belonging thereto."

Thridi continued: "He also made man, and gave him a soul that shall never perish, though his body moulder away or be reduced to dust."

Polytheism.—Thus it appears that the Norsemen were not without some sort of belief in an infinite One. But, however this One may have stood forth in the foreground of their original faith, it is certain that as time passed on he was practically lost sight of in a multiplicity of gods. The writer from whom we have already quoted[1] says: "Monotheism could not long satisfy a rude and fierce people, many of them living in countries remarkable for wild grandeur of scenery and subject to sudden and extreme climatic changes, involving great and striking elemental disturbances—most of them in a state of almost perpetual war. Nature by her changeful moods suggested the presence of more gods than one; their own experience, sometimes as victors, sometimes as vanquished, did the same. Rude minds never discover the unity of nature, and are quite unable to trace the endless variety of phenomena which meets them to the action of never-varying law."[2]

Nature-worship.—So it came about that while the dim image of the true God was at the centre of this religion, its form to the casual glance and in popular practice was distinctly polytheistic. Its gods were the personified powers and phenomena of nature.[3] Let us

---

[1] DR. BURNS, in *Faiths of the World.*

[2] I doubt if this can be laid down *as a general proposition.* The opposite seems to be taught in Rom. 1 : 19, 20. There is always a possibility of finding the One, though the natural tendency of the mind is away from him.

[3] James Freeman Clarke takes a different view. He says: "The gods are idealizations of human will set over against the powers of nature. The battle of the gods and giants represents the struggle of the soul against the inexorable laws of nature, freedom against fate, the spirit with the flesh, mind with matter, human hope with change, disappointment, loss; 'the emergency of the case with the despotism of the ruler.'"

In the opinion of others the Norse gods are deified heroes. Odin is said to have been an adventurer from a town called Asgard, who, serving in the army of Mithridates, in defeat fled to the forests of Scythia, where he collected a band of desperadoes and with them invaded

be mindful of the rugged birthplace of this religion, where sun and frost and tempest and subterranean fire were engaged in a perpetual struggle for mastery. Left to themselves, was it not inevitable that the inhabitants of that land should deify these titanic forces? They dwelt in gloomy solitudes and along the edge of mountain-heights that overlooked an icy and tempestuous ocean. " The Eddas tell us of a marriage between a god of the sea and a daughter of the hills. Each uttered a complaint of the other's home:

> 'Of mountains I weary,' said he:
> 'Not long was I there—
> Nine nights only—
> But the howl of the wolf
> To my ears sounded ill
> By the song of the sea-bird.'

The hill-goddess answers :

> 'I could not sleep
> In my bed by the shore;
> For the scream of the wild birds,
> The sea-mews, who came
> From the woods flying,
> Awoke me each morning.'

The child of this union between the mountain and the sea was the religion of the Teutonic race; beside the howl of the wolf and the scream of the sea-mew it struggled into life."[1]

Here we have, therefore, as we should expect, the most romantic of the great religions, sending forth its

Northern Europe: he placed his sons upon the thrones of the conquered, and died in Sweden, B. C. 40.

[1] KEARY, *Outlines of Primitive Belief.*

stalwart gods to traverse the earth in ten-league boots, to shake the hills with thunderous voice and wither the verdant forests with a glance; abounding also in wonder-tales of the adventures of supernatural vikings, and in milder folk-lore which has furnished half the world with its nursery-rhymes. To the Norseman all mysterious things were supernatural, and the easy way to solve all questions in the supernatural realm was to conjure up a giant or a god. As has been well said by an eloquent writer: "The thunder was the rattle of Thor's chariot, the lightning the flash of his hammer swiftly hurled from his strong hand; the wind was Sleipnir, the fleet steed of Odin; the dew was foam from the bit of the horse of Night. When the hard winter-crust of earth began to thaw it was Rind yielding to the rough wooing of her persistent lover. When in spring the early flowers bloomed and the first braird was seen, it was Gerd cajoled by Skernia to listen to the addresses of Frey. As the yearly wave of verdure washed up the hillside, and the herdsman drove his cattle from the lowland meadows to the green uplands, Sif was beside him with her yellow hair. As the farmer looked at his fields covered with rich grain, he blessed the nuptials of Odin and Frigg. The fisherman rowing his boat through the dancing waves saw in each of them a daughter of Œger, and, listening on shore to the loud tumult of the angry sea, he heard the wrathful clamor of these fickle maidens. The huntsman was haunted by a divine presence in the silent deeps of the forest; the child as he looked upon the rainbow was told by his mother that that was the trembling bridge by which the gods crossed from heaven to earth. When the long days of summer were over and winter with its darkness and cold had come, the sad tale of the bright and good Baldur was doubtless told at many a fireside, and many a tear shed over the unhappy fate of that best beloved of the gods."[1]

The Twelve Æsir.—There were twelve Æsir, or great gods, who dwelt in Asgard in palaces of gold.

Odin, the All-Father.—The father of the twelve was Odin, the Al-Fadir, of whom it is written in the Younger Edda, " He governs all things, and, although the other deities are powerful, they all serve and obey him as children do their father." On account of this relation it is customary to speak of the Norse deities as " the Odinic gods." Odin is, in fact, a deification of the overarching canopy of heaven. He is represented as a venerable, one-eyed man, wearing a blue mantle and a broad-brimmed hat.

> " Then into the Volsung dwelling a mighty man there strode,
> One-eyed and seeming ancient, yet bright his visage glowed;
> Cloud-blue was the hood upon him, and his kirtle gleaming gray
> As the latter-morning sun-dog when the storm is on the way."

His arm is encircled with a ring from which other rings are ever uncoiling themselves and dropping earthward. On his shoulders are perched two ravens, and at his feet crouch two ravening wolves. In his right hand he carries an all-conquering spear. The mantle is symbolical of cloud and tempest. The broad hat—the *tarnkappe* of the Niebelungen lay—signifies twilight or

[1] *The Faiths of the World.*

concealment. The prolific ring means fruitfulness. The two ravens are Reflection and Memory, who, flying to and fro, keep the god mindful of all things in heaven and earth. The one eye denotes the gift of prophecy, which belongs to Odin alone. It is related that he was compelled to throw his other eye into the water in order to secure the right of access to the well of wisdom; which is only a poetic way of saying that the sun, the eye of heaven, sinks into the ocean at close of day. Odin, as his name *Al-Fadir* indicates, was regarded as the universal benefactor, the giver of every good and perfect gift:

> "He gives and grants
> Gold to the deserving;
> He gave Hermond
> A helm and corslet,
> And from him Sigmund
> A sword received.
> Victory to his sons he gives;
> But to some riches,
> Eloquence to the great,
> And to men wit.
> Fair winds he gives to traders,
> But visions to skalds.
> Valor he gives
> To many a warrior."

(1) *Thor.*—The mightiest of the twelve Æsir was Thor, the god of thunder, of whom it was said, "He is the strongest of gods and men." He dwelt in a splendid mansion called Bilskirnir.

> "Five hundred halls
> And forty more,

Methinketh, hath
Bowed Bilskirnir.
'I am the god Thor;
I am the war-god,
I am the Thunderer!
Here in my Northland,
My fastness and fortress,
Reign I for ever.'"

This god was possessed of three precious things: the hammer Mjolnir, with which he wrought many wonderful deeds;[1] the belt Mejingjardir, which, girded

[1] "The giant Thrymr once stole this hammer, and Loki was sent to find where he had hidden it. It had been buried deep in the ground, and Thrymr would restore it only on condition that the Æsir should give him the beautiful Freyja to wife. But at such a proposal the goddess waxed wroth, and would in no wise consent to it. So the gods took counsel, and by the advice of Heimdall, one of the Æsir, they devised a plan by which the giant could be cheated. The thunder-god dressed himself in Freyja's weeds: he adorned himself with her necklace—the famed Brisinga necklace; he let from his side keys rattle, and set a comely coif upon his head. Then he went to Jotunheim as though he were the bride; Loki went with him as his serving-maid. The god could scarcely avoid raising some suspicions by his unwomanly behavior; he alone devoured an ox, eight salmon and all the sweetmeats women love, and he drank three *salds* of mead. Thrymr exclaimed with wonder,

'Who ever a bride saw sup so greedily?
Never a bride saw I sup so greedily,
Nor a maid drink such measures of mead.'

Sat the all-cunning servant-maid by,
Ready her answer to the giant to give:
'Naught has Freyja eaten for eight nights,
So eager was she for Jotunheim.'

'Neath the linen hood he looked, a kiss craving
But sprang back in terror across the hall:

about his loins, redoubled his strength; and a pair of iron gauntlets, without which it was impossible for him to grasp his hammer or tighten his belt.

He was represented as a young man with a luxuriant red beard. When it thundered the Norsemen were accustomed to say, "Thor is blowing through his beard." He was a benignant god, whose special office was to bring the opposing forces of nature under subjection to men. There is no end of the

> 'How fearfully flaming are Freyja's eyes!
> Their glance burneth like a brand.'
>
> There sat the all-cunning servant-maid by,
> Ready with words the giant to answer:
> 'For eight nights she did naught of sleep enjoy,
> So eager was she for Jotunheim.'
>
> In stepped the giant's fearful sister;
> For a bride's gift she dared to ask :
> 'Give me from thy hand red rings
> If thou wilt gain my love,
> My love and favor.'
>
> Then spake Thrymr, the giants' prince:
> 'The hammer bear in, the bride to consecrate;
> Lay Mjolnir on the maiden's knee
> And unite us mutually in marriage-bonds.'
>
> Laughed Thor's heart in his breast
> When the fierce-hearted his hammer knew.
> Thrymr first slew he, the thursar's lord,
> And the race of jotuns all destroyed.
>
> He slew the ancient jotun sister,
> Who for a bride's gift had dared to ask;
> Hard blows she got instead of skillings,
> And the hammer's weight in place of rings."
>
> —*Outlines of Primitive Belief*, p. 355.

wonderful tales of his feats of strength.[1] "His hammer broke the skull of the frost-giant, and freed earth

[1] The following, by way of illustration, is a history of the journeyings of Thor to Jotunheim:

"The god set out with the intention of discovering a certain giant, Utgardloki, who was especially powerful and especially the enemy of the gods. In truth, he was a sort of king of the under world, and Thor's journey to his hall is comparable to the descent of Heracles to the realm of Hades. After some travel the god arrived at the shore of a wide and deep sea. On the sea stood the bark of the ferryman, the Northern Charon, Harbard by name:

> 'Steer hitherward thy bark;
> I will show thee the strand.
> But who owns the skiff
> That by the shore thou rowest?'

"Thor was on this occasion travelling with Loki and two mortals, his servants, called Thialfi and Roska. They crossed the wide, deep sea and entered a boundless forest. No sooner had Thor and his comrades thus got well into Jotunheim than they began to fall victims to its spells and enchantments; and the glamour increased the farther they went, till at last their adventure ended only in a disastrous defeat. They came to what they took for a hall with wide entrance, having one small chamber at the side; and while resting they were disturbed by a noise like an earthquake, which made all but Thor run into the chamber to hide themselves. In the morning an immense man, who had been sleeping on the ground hard by, and whose snoring it was that had so frightened all, arose, and presently lifted up that which they had fancied was a hall, and which now proved to be his glove. Then Thor and his companions and the giant, who was named Skrymir, continued their journey together. But in the night Thor, thinking to kill Skrymir, hurled against the giant's head his death-dealing hammer, Mjolnir, the force of which none, it was thought, could resist. Yet, behold! Skrymir only asked if a leaf had fallen upon him as he slept. A second time the god raised his hammer and smote the giant with such force that he could see the weapon sticking in his forehead. Thereupon Skrymir awoke and said, 'What is it? Did an acorn fall upon my head? How is it with you, Thor?' Thor stept quickly back and answered that he had just awakened, and that it was midnight and

from the bondage of winter, ground rocks and stones into powder and turned them into fruitful earth. He there were still many hours for sleep. Presently he struck a third time, with such force that the hammer sank into the giant's cheek up to the handle. Then Skrymir rose up and stroked his cheek, saying, 'Are there birds in this tree? It seems to me as if one of them had sent some moss down on my face.'

"Anon Thor and his companions came to the city of the giant Utgardloki, in whose hall and among the company of giants feats of strength were performed to match the newcomers against the men of that place. First, Loki vaunted his skill in eating, and was matched against Logi (Fire). A trough was placed between them, and after each had seemed to eat voraciously they met just in the middle. But it was found that Loki had eaten the flesh only, whereas Logi had devoured the bones and the wood of the trough as well. Then, again, Thialfi stood to run a race with any one, and was set to try his speed against Hug (Thought), who in three courses vanquished him utterly. And now the turn came to Thor. First, he was challenged to drain a horn, 'which,' said Utgardloki, 'a strong man can finish in a draught, but the weakest can empty in three.' Thor made three pulls at the beaker, but at the end of the third had scarce laid bare more than the brim. The next trial was to raise a cat from the ground. 'We have a very trifling game here,' said the giant, 'in which we exercise none but children. It consists in merely lifting my cat from the ground; nor should I have dared to mention it to thee, Thor, but that I have already seen thou art not the man we took thee for.' As he finished speaking a large gray cat leapt upon the floor. Thor advanced and laid his hand beneath the cat's belly and did his best to lift him from the ground; but he bent his back, and, despite all Thor's exertions, had but one foot raised up; and when Thor saw this he made no further trial.

"'The trial,' said the giant, 'has turned out as I expected. The cat is biggish and Thor is short and small beside our men.' Then spake Thor, 'Small as ye call me, let any one come near and wrestle with me, now I am in wrath.' Utgardloki looked round at the benches and answered, 'I see no man in here who would not esteem it child's play to wrestle with thee. But I bethink me,' he continued: 'there is the old woman now calling me, my nurse Elli (Age). With her let Thor wrestle if he will.' Thereupon came an old dame into the hall, and to her Utgardloki signified that she was to match herself against Thor.

drove past in his chariot, and sent the pleasant showers which refreshed the parched field and made the

We will not lengthen out the tale. The result of the contest was that the harder Thor strove the firmer she stood. And now the old crone began to make her set at Thor. He had one foot loosened, and a still harder struggle followed; but it did not last long, for Thor was brought down on one knee. . . .

"The next morning, at daybreak, Thor arose with his following; they dressed and prepared to go their ways. Then came Utgardloki, and had a meal set before them in which was no lack of good fare to eat and to drink. And when they had done their meal they took their road homeward. Utgardloki accompanied them to the outside of the town, and at parting he asked Thor whether he was satisfied with his journey, and if he had found any one more mighty than himself. Thor could not deny that the event had been little to his honor. 'And well I know,' he said, 'that you will hold me for a very insignificant fellow, at which I am ill pleased.' Then spoke Utgardloki: 'I will tell thee the truth, now that I have got thee again outside our city, to which, so long as I live and hear rule there, thou shalt never enter again; and I trow that thou never shouldst have entered it had I known thee to be possessed of such great strength. I deceived thee by my illusions; for the first time I saw thee was in the wood; me it was thou mettest there. Three blows thou struckest with thy hammer; the first, the lightest, would have been enough to bring death had it reached me. Thou sawest by my hall a rocky mountain, and in it three square valleys, of which one was the deepest. These were the marks of thy hammer. It was the mountain which I placed in the way of thy blow, but thou didst not discover it. And it was the same in the contests in which ye measured yourselves against my people. The first was that in which Loki had a share. He was right hungry and ate well. But he whom we call Logi was the fire itself, and he devoured the flesh and bowl alike. When Thialfi ran a race with another, that was my *thought*, and it was not to be looked for that Thialfi should match him in speed. When thou drankest out of the horn, and it seemed so difficult to empty, a wonder was seen which I should not have deemed possible. The other end of the horn stretched out to the sea: that thou didst not perceive, but when thou comest to the shore thou mayest see what a drain thou hast made from it. And that shall men call the ebb.' He continued: 'Not less wonderful and mighty a feat didst thou when

grass green far up the hillside. In his strife with the hostile forces of nature he was man's firm friend; and when with the poor serfs the strife was over, he took them to himself. They could not 'fare to Odin,' but they fared to Thor. We are told that the newly-converted Germans had under the name of Christ the lord of thunder and giver of rain in view, and confounded the sign of the cross with the sign of the hammer. It was not an unnatural mistake."[1]

(2) *Baldur, the Summer God.*—" He is the best, and all mankind are loud in his praise. So fair and dazzling is he in form and features that rays of light seem to issue from him; and thou mayest have some idea of the beauty of his hair when I tell thee that the whitest of all plants is called 'Baldur's brow.'" He dwells in a heavenly mansion called Breidablik, meaning that bright upper air which is the home of the sun.

thou wast at lifting of the cat; and, to speak sooth, we were all in a fright when we saw thou hadst raised one paw from the ground. For a cat it was not, as it seemed to thee. It was the Midgard worm, who lies encircling all lands; and when thou didst this he had scarce length enough left to keep head and tail together on the earth, for thou stretchedst him up so high that almost thou reachedst heaven. A great wonder it was at the wrestling-bout which thou hadst with Elli; but no one was nor shall be whom, how long soever he live, Elli will not reach and *Age* bring to earth. Now that we are at parting thou hast the truth; and for both of us it were better that thou come not here again. For again I shall defend my castle with my deceptions, and thy might will avail nothing against me.' When Thor heard these words he seized his hammer and raised it on high, but when he would have struck he could see Utgardloki nowhere. He turned toward the city, and was for destroying it, but he saw a wide and beautiful plain before him, and no city."—*Outlines of Primitive Belief,* p. 349.

[1] *The Faiths of the World.*

> " 'Tis Breidablik called,
> Where Baldur the fair
> Hath built him a bower,
> In that land where I know
> The least loathliness lieth."

In all the mythologies of the nations there is no more fascinating or affecting tale than that of Baldur's death.[1]

[1] "The death of Baldur the good is thus related: Having been tormented with bad dreams, indicating that his life was in danger, he told them to the assembled gods, who made all creatures and things, living or dead, take an oath to do him no harm. This oath was taken by fire and water, iron and all other metals, stones, earths, diseases, poisons, birds and creeping things. After this they amused themselves at their meeting in setting Baldur up as a mark, some hurling darts or shooting arrows at him, and some cutting at him with swords and axes; and, as nothing hurt him, it was accounted a great honor done to Baldur. But wicked Loki (or Loke) was envious at this, and, assuming the form of a woman, he inquired of the goddess who administered the oath whether all things had taken it. She said everything except one little shrub called mistletoe, which she thought too young and feeble to do any harm. Therefore Loki got the mistletoe, and, bringing it to one of the gods, persuaded him to throw it at Baldur, who, pierced to the heart, fell dead. The grief was immense. A special messenger was despatched to Queen Hela, in hell, to inquire if on any terms Baldur might be ransomed. For nine days and nights he rode through dark chasms till he crossed the river of Death, and, entering the kingdom of Hela, made known his request. Hela replied that it should now be discovered whether Baldur was so universally loved as was represented, for that she would permit him to return to Asgard if all creatures and all things, without exception, would weep for him. The gods then despatched messengers through the world to beg all things to weep for Baldur, which they immediately did. Then you might have seen not only crocodiles, but the most ferocious beasts, dissolved in tears. Fishes wept in the water, and birds in the air. Stones and trees were covered with pellucid dewdrops, and, for all we know, this general grief may have been the occasion of some of the deluges reported by geology. The messengers returned, thinking the work done, when they found an old hag sitting in a cavern, and begged her to weep Baldur out of hell.

He was slain by his brother, who unwittingly threw at him a sprig of mistletoe. All nature mourned to bring him back—" all living things and trees and stones and metals "—but in vain. His body was placed upon the ship Ringhorni, whereon a funeral-pyre was lighted, and thus it drifted out upon the boundless sea. How could pen or pencil more splendidly set forth the funeral-fires of summer—a dead glory sinking in the red conflagration of a sunset sea?

(3) *Njord, the Sailors' God.*—" He rules over the winds and checks the fury of the sea and of fire, and is therefore invoked by seafarers and fishermen." He has his dwelling close by the shore, where he may hear the voices of the wrecked and bewildered. The scream of the sea-bird makes music in his ears.

(4) *Frey*, the patron of agriculture. " He presides over rain and sunshine and all the fruits of the earth, and should be invoked to obtain good harvests, and also for peace. He, moreover, dispenses wealth among men."[1]

But she declared that she could gain nothing by so doing, and that Baldur might stay where he was, like other people as good as he, planting herself, apparently, on the great but somewhat selfish principle of non-intervention. So Baldur remains in the halls of Hela. But this old woman did not go unpunished, She was shrewdly suspected to be Loki himself in disguise, and on inquiry so it turned out. Whereupon a hot pursuit of Loki took place, who, after changing himself into many forms, was caught and chained under sharp-pointed rocks below the earth."—CLARKE's *Ten Great Religions*, p. 373.

[1] "THE MARRIAGE OF FREY.

" Once Frey mounted the seat of Odin, which was called Air-Throne, and, looking northward into far Giant-Land, he saw a light flash forth. Looking again, he saw that the light was made by the maiden Gerd,

(5) *Tyr, the One-handed God*, the most daring and intrepid of all. He is the dispenser of courage, and must be invoked by all who would deport themselves well in life's conflict. It is he who enables men to win their way to Walhalla, the paradise of the brave.

(6) *Bragi, the Master Skald or Singer.*—He is the divine patron of eloquence, poetry and the painter's art.

(7) *Heimdall, the White God*, the reputed son of seven virgins:

> "Son am I of maidens nine;
> Born am I of sisters nine."

He is the sentinel of heaven, ever on guard to prevent the giants from forcing their way into it. " He requires less sleep than a bird, and sees, by night as by day, a hundred miles around him. So acute is his ear that

who had just opened her father's door, and that it was her beauty which thus shone over the snow. Then Freyr was smitten with love-sadness, and determined to woo the fair one to be his wife; and so he sent his messenger, Skirnir, to whom he gave his horse and magic sword. Skirnir went to Gerd, and he told her how great Freyr was among the Æsir, and how noble and happy a place was Asgard, the home of the gods; but, for all his pleading, Gerd would give no ear to his suit. At last the messenger drew his sword and threatened to take her life unless she would grant to Freyr his desire. So Gerd promised to visit the god nine nights thence in Barri's wood.

" Here a very simple nature-myth is told us. The earth will not respond to the wooing of the sun unless he draw his sharp sword, the rays. In very northern lands we know that the sun himself does actually disappear in the cold north, the death-region. When he is there the earth consents to meet him again with love nine nights hence —that is to say, after the nine winter months are over. They meet in Barri's wood, which is the wood in its first greenness."—*Outlines of Primitive Belief*, p. 372.

no sound escapes him; for he can even hear the grass growing on the earth and the wool on a sheep's back."

(8) *Hödur, the Blind, the God of Darkness.*—It was he who pierced to the heart his brother, the summer god, with the sprig of mistletoe. His name is held in abhorrence; therefore gods and men alike never mention it.

(9) *Vidar, the Silent.*—He wore shoes of thick wool. His counsel was sought by lovers of artifice in peace or war.

(10) *Vali, the Archer,* invoked by warriors when facing the foe.

(11) *Ullur, God of the Skees or Snow-skates.*—He was famed for athletic beauty, as well as for the incomparable speed with which he traversed the fields of ice.

(12) *Forseti, the God of Even-handed Justice,* consulted especially by disputants at law.

These were the twelve Æsir, or Odinic gods.

Loki.—There was yet another, a luckless thirteenth, who must by no means be overlooked: this was Loki, the calumniator of the gods. He was at the bottom of all fraud and mischief; handsome and graceful, cunning and treacherous, woe to god or giant who fell under his evil eye! He was the Norseman's devil. He had three children—the wolf Fenrir, the serpent Jormungand, and Hel, or Death.

Minor Powers.—In addition to the deities already mentioned, there were others, minor gods and goddesses, without number. Moreover, "the earth and air were filled with unseen but most active agents—with dwarfs, busy in the bowels of the mountains among metals and stones; with elves, watching and pervading the life of plants and trees and beasts and men. War-maidens—the Valkyries[1]—went with Odin to battle, and chose the combatants who were to fall, and waited on the slain heroes in bright Walhalla. Fulgiur and Hamingiur, as guardian angels, accompanied every man from the cradle to the grave. The fate of all was in the hands of the Norns,[2] who, spinning the threads of destiny, determined everything that should be."[3]

(2) *The Creation.*—The Eddas relate that in the beginning there was chaos,

> "When all was not;
> Nor sound, nor sea,
> Nor cooling wave;
> Nor earth there was
> Nor sky above;
> Naught save a void
> And yawning gulf."

The name given to this void and yawning gulf was

---

[1] "These cloudy beings, the Valkyries, remote as they may seem from the things of nature and from the experience of life, filled a considerable space in Teutonic thought. They represented the ideal of womanhood to the rude chivalry of the North. Their functions were twofold: they presided over battles and foretold future events. Tacitus and Cæsar have described how the German wives used to urge their husbands forward in the day of the fight, and how, on more than one occasion, an army which had actually turned to fly had been driven back against the spears of their opponents by the exhortations or the jibes of their womankind. The same writers have told us of the prophetic powers ascribed to women by the Teutons. These Valkyri had some influence upon the Middle-Age conceptions of angels, and a greater influence upon the conception of witches."—*Outlines of Primitive Belief*, p. 345.

[2] The names of the Norns were Urd, Verdandi and Skuld, meaning past, present and future.

[3] *The Faiths of the World.*

Ginnungagap, or "the gaping gap."[1] On the north side of it was a cold, dark region called Niflheim; on the south, a warm, bright region called Mispelheim. From the former there flowed into the gulf a stream of frigid venom, which, being melted by benignant fires from Mispelheim, took the form of a giant, the terrible Ymir. This giant was nourished by a cow. The cow licked the hoar-frost from the rocks, and from this hoar-frost sprang a full-grown man, whose son, Boë, became the father of the illustrious trio Odin, Vili and Vi; that is, Spirit, Will and Holiness. These three slew the giant Ymir, and of his flesh they made the earth; of his blood, the seas, lakes and rivers; of his bones, the mountain-ranges; of his teeth, jaws and broken bones, the stones and pebbles. They fastened the earth together, and bound the ocean round it like a ring. Of the giant's skull they made the sky, and raised it over the earth. At its four corners were stationed the watchful dwarfs Austre, Vestre, Nordre and Sudre; that is, East, West, North and South. In the mean time, sparks flying from Mispelheim were caught and fixed in heaven to illuminate the heavens and earth. The earth was surrounded by a wall made from the giant's shaggy eyebrows, that so its inhabitants might be prevented from falling off. His brains also, scattered through the air, became the flying clouds. The giant at length being quite used up, the work of creation was perforce regarded as finished, and all very good.

---

[1] The exact equivalent of *chaos*, from the Greek χάω, to gape.

Observe, there is no suggestion here of the production of anything *ex nihilo*. The Norsemen were strict evolutionists. They must have something to begin with, even though it were necessary to get back of everything in order to find it.

As the three sons of Boë were passing along the sea-strand they found two wonderful trees, an ash and an elm, out of which they produced the first human pair, calling them Ask and Embla. Odin breathed into them the breath of life, Vili gave them reason, and Vi gave them a fair complexion and the senses; as it is written:

> "Spirit they owned not,
> Sense they had not,
> Blood nor vigor.
> Spirit gave Odin,
> Thought gave Vili,
> Blood gave Vi
> And color fair."

It was thus that the Norsemen accounted for the origin of things.

(3) *The Future.*—They believed in a future life. Death was called *heimgang*, or home-going—"a thought always beautiful and tender, but still more so as coming from these wild rovers of the homeless sea." They placed coins under the tongues of their dead to pay their fare to the other world. But while they believed in a future life, they rejected immortality. The present order, however far extended, will ultimately come to rack and ruin. Gods and men together will perish when the cycle ends.

> "Between divine and human life what is the odds?
> A human life is but a watch-tick to the gods.
> Their hour has many ticks, their day has many an hour,
> And many days fill up their years' enormous dower;
> But when threescore and ten of those large years a god
> Has told, he is touched by death's appropriating rod."

Ragnarok.—The crisis of the universal struggle depicted in the Norse religion is reached at Ragnarok, or *gods' doom*. By this is meant the awful and universal catastrophe which is to terminate the existing order and make room for a new heaven and a new earth. It is to be preceded by three successive winters without a summer, during which war and tumult are to prevail universally:

> "Brothers will fight together
> And become each other's bane;
> Sisters' children
> Shall foully wrong each other.
> Hard is the world;
> Sensual sins grow huge.
> There are axe-ages, sword-ages;
> Shields are cleft in twain.
> There are wind-ages, wolf-ages,
> E'er the world falls dead."

In the mean time, Odin has been recruiting his army of heroes from all earth's battlefields in anticipation of the final struggle with the giants of the lower world. The last day is at length ushered in by the shrill crowing of three cocks—the gold-bright, the bright-red and the sooty-red. From above the gateway of the infernal regions Egdir, the storm-eagle, screams his defiant response.

> "Loud howls Garm from the Gnupa cave;
> The fetter breaks and the wolf runs free."

From the east a ship comes sailing, bringing the frost-giants, and another, made of dead men's nails, comes laden with a troop of ghosts. In front are the wolves that sat at Odin's feet, the sea-monster, and Garm the hell-hound. One of the wolves devours the sun, the other, the moon. The stars fall and the earth is convulsed. The Midgard serpent seeks the land, and the sea rushes over all. In the midst of this universal wrack a blast from the trumpet of Heimdall awakes the gods, who prepare for the fray. Now the heavens are rent, and from the five hundred and forty gates of Walhalla they issue forth, leading the four hundred and thirty-two thousand heroes of Odin. In the midst of Vigrid's plain they meet the Fenris wolf, the serpent, the giants, Loki himself, and all the hosts of Hel. Odin is swallowed by the Fenris wolf; the Fenris wolf is pierced by the sword of Vidar. Thor slays the Midgard serpent, but, suffocated by its poisonous breath, recoils nine paces and falls dead. Frey is overcome by Surt. Tyr is killed by the dog Gurt. Heimdall measures weapons with the fierce Loki, and both fall. Then Surt flings a handful of fire on the earth, and there is universal conflagration.

> "The sun grows dark;
> The earth sinks into the sea;
> The bright stars
> From heaven vanish;
> Fire rages,
> Heat blazes,
> And high flames play
> 'Gainst heaven itself." [1]

[1] For most of the translations in this article the author is indebted to ANDERSON's *Norse Mythology*.

Restoration.—But this general catastrophe is to be followed by a renewal or "regeneration." The earth is to rise again, green and fair, from the sea. The fields are to produce spontaneous harvests. The two surviving gods—Vidar the silent and Vadi the archer—are to dwell upon the former site of Asgard, and thither shall come the sons of Thor and other mighty ones. Two mortals, Lif and Lifthraser, who also have escaped the conflagration, are to repeople the earth. The sun's daughter is to take her mother's place in mid-heaven, giving light to all. " And if you ask any more questions," said Har to Ganglere, " I have never heard any one tell further of the world's fate. Make now the best of what I have told you."

Heaven.—The heaven of the Norsemen was a place of two apartments. The first, Walhalla, was for heroes only. It was a vast hall " shining with pure gold, its ceiling formed of spears, its walls of shields, its benches glittering with coats of mail." The distinguished warriors who were admitted here regaled themselves on the flesh of the wild boar Sahrimner—

> " 'Tis the best of flesh;
> There are few who know
> What the Einherjes eat "—

and luscious beer from the goat Heidrun. Every morning, as soon as dressed, they went forth into the court and fought and slew one another; then came in to breakfast.

> " All the Einherjes
> In Odin's court
> Hew daily each other.
> They choose the slain,

And ride from the battlefield;
Then sit they in peace together."

The other apartment of heaven is called Gimli. It is for all the virtuous and brave. "Plenty is there of good drink for those who deem this a joy."

Hell.—The Norsemen's hell also consists of two apartments. The first, Niflheim, is a kind of purgatory, to be used only until Ragnarok is passed. The other, Nastrand, is to be, through all successive cycles, a place of unmitigated torment. It is represented as a great hall opening toward the stormy north, built of serpents wattled together, their heads inward, vomiting venom that flows in streams along the floor, wherein all perjurers and murderers are doomed to wade. The dwelling of the goddess Hel is thus described: "Her palace is anguish, her table is famine, her knife is starvation, her waiters are slowness and delay, her door is a precipice, her bed is care, and its curtains are splendid misery."

III. *Forms of Worship.*—The rites and ceremonies of the Norsemen were of the simplest. They had three annual festivals. The first, called Yul (whence our Yule-tide), occurred at the winter solstice, on the longest night of the year. The second was in the spring-time, in honor of the goddess Ostara, whence our Easter. The third was the great festival of Odin, at which sacrifices and prayers were offered, though at no time would the Norsemen confess an utter dependence on their gods. They seem to have believed, as James Freeman Clarke says, "in nothing but their own might and main."

Their sacred rites were most frequently celebrated in the forests, the worshipers full armed and uplifting jovial cups. From them we have our custom of drinking toasts. They drank to Odin, then to the lesser gods, and then to dead heroes, at which period of the sacred ceremonies the martial worshiper was usually *hors du combat*—*i. e.* under the table. This was reckoned the height of religious fervor.

The trees of the forest were regarded with special reverence: the oak, with the mistletoe springing out of its bosom, the ash and the elm were looked upon as sentient things. A tree was thought to be growing somewhere with branches overshadowing the earth and top reaching into heaven.

> "I know an ash that stands, Yggdrasil named,
> Towering aloft with limpid water laved:
> Thence come the dews that fall into the dales;
> Over Fate's fountain stands it ever green."

From these ancient beliefs and customs we have derived our May pole[1] and Christmas tree.[2]

[1] The author of the *Anatomie of Abuses* (sixteenth century) thus refers to the customs of May Day: "They goe some to the woods and groves, some to the hills and mountaines, where they spend the night in pleasaunt pastime, and in the morning they return, bringing with them birche boughes and branches of trees to deck their assemblies withal. But their chiefest jewel they bring thence is *the Maypoale*, which they bring home with great veneration, as thus: they have twentie or fourtie yoake of oxen, and everie oxe has a sweet nosegaie of flowers tied to the top of his hornes, and these oxen drawe the Maypoale, the stinking idol rather."

[2] "The *village tree* of the German races was originally a tribal tree, with whose existence the life of the village was involved; and when we read of Christian saints and confessors that they made a point of

IV. *Morals.—Central Thought: Courage.*—The central thought of the Norse religion was courage. The business of these people was war. They saw perpetual strife in nature—sea against land, winter against summer, light against darkness; personifying the forces of nature, they made a pantheon of warlike gods and giants, typifying the endless antagonisms of good and evil; and—as the proverb holds good, "Like gods, like people "—they themselves conceived that to be the manliest life which in utter fearlessness was most nearly like that of their gods.

"*What shall I Do to be Saved?*"—Their answer to the question, "What shall I do to be saved?" was, Fight a good fight; against what, it scarcely matters; whether the cause be good or bad, quit yourself like a man, and the gates of Walhalla will open to receive you.

Not that these people had no true moral conceptions. They condemned, in particular, blasphemy, perfidy and unchastity; not so much, however, because these were morally wrong as because they unmanned men. They held that the sin of all sins was cowardice. No braver souls, let it be said, ever lived than these Norsemen. They encountered the tempests of their northern seas in rude, fragile boats, and, wielding the simplest weapons, were unconquerable in battle. They were so jealous of their personal independence, so determined on having elbow-room, that they dwelt in homes apart,

cutting down these half-idols, we cannot wonder at the rage they called forth, nor that they often paid the penalty of their courage."—*Outlines of Primitive Belief*, p. 65.

contemning the restraints of village-life. They loved freedom with all their heart and soul and strength, and they left as a heritage to the nations a broad spirit of individual sovereignty which has expressed itself, in these last days, in the manifesto, "All men are created free and equal, and with certain inalienable rights."[1]

The old Norse king, Ragnor Lodbrok, when about to die, refusing to complain, said, "We are cut to pieces with swords, but it fills me with joy to think of the feast prepared for me in Odin's palace. Quickly, quickly, seated in the splendid habitation of the gods, I shall be drinking beer out of a curved horn. A brave man fears not to die."

The conversion of the Teutons to Christianity was a matter of brief time and little difficulty. Their independent spirit had fully prepared them for acquiescence in a gospel whose prime virtue is manliness and whose highest aspiration is the glorious liberty of the children of God; and, moreover, they perceived that the new religion offered as a gratuity what the old had not even suggested to them—namely, a complete deliverance from the bondage and shame of sin.

> "King Olaf raised the hilt
> Of iron, cross-shaped and gilt,
> And said, 'Do not refuse;
> Count well the cost and loss—
> Thor's hammer or Christ's cross:
> Choose!'

[1] Montesquieu says: "The Goth Jornandes calls the North of Europe 'the forge of mankind.' I would rather call it the forge of those instruments which broke the fetters manufactured in the South."

"And Halfred the scald said, 'This
  Is the name of the Lord I kiss,
    Who on it was crucified.'
  And a shout went round the board:
  'In the name of Christ the Lord
    Who died!'

"Then over the waste of snows
  The noonday sun uprose,
    Through the driving mists revealed,
  Like the lifting of the Host,
  By incense clouds almost
    Concealed.

"On the shining wall a vast
  And shadowy cross was cast
    From the hilt of the lifted sword;
  And in foaming cups of ale
  The Berserks drank, 'Was hael!
    To the Lord!'"[1]

It was in the eighth century that St. Boniface hewed down the sacred oak of Thor. While his axe rang against the gnarled trunk the worshipers of the thunder-god stood by, expecting momentarily to see him struck with Heaven's wrath. When, at length, he knelt unharmed by the side of the fallen oak, they recognized him as a hero after their own heart, and were ready to kneel beside him in reverence to Thor's conqueror, the Christ. The proclamation of the gospel, as Frederick Maurice says, "did not find the Goths watching the embers of an expiring civilization, but, full of boyish vigor and life and rudeness, eager to break and subdue the earth; possessed by the wildest dreams of powers in earth and sea which wrestled for

[1] LONGFELLOW, *King Olaf's Christmas.*

victory; doing homage to a champion of strong hand and seeing eye, the leader of their host and their prophet. With much joy, though amidst much confusion, these barbarians welcomed the tidings of a Redeemer in whom men could recognize at once their Lord and their brother."

To these worshipers of Odin and his twelve mighties we are largely indebted for the free, broad, hearty Protestantism which now so largely prevails among the more advanced peoples of the earth. It was a Saxon monk who nailed to the royal chapel door in 1517 the ninety theses of the Reformation, and his countrymen are to-day in the van of the great struggle for spiritual freedom. The battle goes bravely on—a grander than that of Æsir against giants—and "the White Christ" must win. He, being lifted up, will draw all men unto him.

> "Cross against corslet,
> Love against hatred,
> Peace-cry for war-cry!

> "Stronger than steel
> Is the sword of the Spirit;
> Swifter than arrows
> The light of the truth is;
> Greater than anger
> Is love, and subdueth.

> "The dawn is not distant,
> Nor is the night starless;
> Love is eternal!
> God is still God, and
> His faith shall not fail us;
> Christ is eternal!"

VIII.
CONFUCIANISM.

A. *Its Central Thought:* The Kingdom.
B. *Its Characteristic Features:*
    I. Filial Piety.
        " What shall I Do to be Saved ?"
    II. Veneration for Learning.
    Sacred Books:
        (I.) The Five King:
            1. Shu-King; Ancient Chronicles.
            2. Shi-King; Ancient Poems.
            3. Li-King; Book of Etiquette,
            4. Yih-King; Book of Divination.
            5. Chun-tsiu; or, Spring and Autumn.
        (II.) The Four Shoo:
            1. Lun-Yu; or Table-talk of Confucius.
            2. Ta-Hio; or Great Learning.
            3. Chung-Yung; or Doctrine of the Mean.
            4. The Works of Mencius.
    III. Conservatism.
C. *Its Fruits:*
    1. No intellectual vigor.
    2. No ambition.
    3. No good cheer.
    4. No common morality.

VIII. CONFUCIANISM.

Its Founder.—In the sixth century B. C. there was an old officer in the province of Lu named Shuh-liang-heih, who was the last living scion of the proudest lineage in China. At seventy years of age he sought an alliance with a family wherein there were three fair daughters. The two oldest gave an adverse answer to his suit; the youngest married him from a sense of duty, in the hope of perpetuating his honorable line. In the year 551 she became the mother of a son who was named K'ung-foo-Tse, the "Master Kung," or, as the world knows him, Confucius.

The chronicles say that not long before this a curious stone had been found in his father's garden bearing this inscription: "A child is about to be born pure as the crystal wave; he shall be *a king without a kingdom.*"[1]

This occurred at about the time when the Jews were beginning to return from Babylon, when Pythagoras was teaching his disciples under the palm trees, and when the Tarquins were governing Rome.

The boy K'ung-foo-Tse was early left fatherless. His youth was passed in poverty. Tradition says that when six years old he developed a taste for playing at

---

[1] This prediction has been fulfilled. The subjects of the uncrowned king have been hundreds of millions. No other teacher has ever spoken to so many souls.

sacrifices, and at fifteen he conceived an insatiable thirst for learning. On coming of age he married and was appointed superintendent of parks in his native place.

At this time the government of China was in dire confusion. "It had fallen into decay," writes his disciple Mencius, "and sound principles had disappeared." The people cherished dim traditions of an age of innocence in the far-away past, "when the whole creation enjoyed a state of happiness, when everything was beautiful and everything good, when all beings were perfect of their kind." How sad the change! Now "perverse disputings and oppressive deeds were waxen rife. Ministers murdered their rulers, and sons their fathers." Mencius adds significantly, "Confucius was frightened at what he saw."

The popular ballad of that day, which still survives in the Book Shi-King, was this:

> "Cold blows the north wind,
> Thickly falls the snow;
> Oh come, all ye that love me,
> Let us join hands and go.
> Can we any longer stay,
> Victims of this dire dismay?"

Thus did the people lament the disorders of the times. Confucius took advantage of his official position to inquire into the origin of these disorders; and he found it, as he supposed, in the abandonment of the practical precepts of the fathers. It was an age of speculation; the people went stumbling along the paths of duty because their eyes were dreamily fixed on the things of the invisible world. Dr. Matheson says: "Men were forgetting the light of the common day in their search for that transcendental light which never shone on sea or land. On such a world the message of Confucius fell like a thunderbolt fraught with sanitary influences. To an age immersed in transcendentalism there was health in the message, 'Do the will, and ye shall know of the doctrine.' There was health in the recall to the practical duties of life of men who had forgotten that life had any duties or that practice had any sphere."[1]

[1] "He professed to answer the question by what means a man was qualified to become a citizen of that heavenly kingdom which had been established in the Chinese empire. When he came upon the scene he found his countrymen already engaged in endeavoring to solve that problem. He found them inquiring into the nature of that mysterious life which they believed to be diffused throughout the empire. Some held it to be the manifestation of a personal God, some looked upon it as the emanation of an impersonal force of nature, and some saw in it a stream of beneficent life poured down by the immortal spirits of their ancestors. Accordingly, there was everywhere observed a form of religious worship. There were public sacrifices; there were private prayers addressed either to the Supreme Being or to the ancestral dead; there were rituals and rules for their performance. Confucius stood forth in the midst of this old world and cried, 'I show you a more excellent way!' He did not, indeed, tell his countrymen that theirs was a bad way; he was far too wise and politic for that. He did not tell them that their worship of a supramundane God was a delusion, their belief in immortality a dream, and their observance of a sacrifice a waste of time. What he did say was this: 'There are things above the power of human comprehension, beyond the grasp of human intelligence; follow those things which are within the reach of that intelligence. You cannot figure to yourself the nature of God; you cannot certainly know that there is any point of contact between His nature and yours; and in the absence of such knowledge the efficacy of your prayers and of your sacrifices must ever be an open question. But there is a region lying at the door which he who will may enter, and

In pursuance of his purpose to revive the practical wisdom of the past he devoted himself to the study of neglected books and parchments, and, as opportunity was afforded, he applied in the discharge of his own official functions the moral and political maxims of the sages. "A transforming power," says Mencius, "went abroad. Dishonesty and dissoluteness hid their heads. Loyalty and good faith became the characteristics of the men, and chastity and teachableness of the women." The one object of Confucius's life now was to reform society and the government, and to do this by a restoration of old customs. He opened a school. It was not long before three thousand students were sitting at his feet, and among them many of the most learned and illustrious youths of the land.

His pupils reverenced him as the wisest and best of men; insomuch that they have left on record his most commonplace doings—his table-talk, how he ate his food, lay on his bed and sat in his carriage; how he changed countenance when it thundered, how he "rose up before the old man and the mourner." These chronicles, together with a voluminous setting forth of the

which is itself the entrance into the heavenly kingdom—a region within the reach of the most humble intellectual powers and capable of being trodden by the simplest minds. That region is the world of duty: this is the door by which a man must enter the kingdom of heaven. What you have called in the past the observance of religion is in reality but an exercise of imagination: it may represent a truth or it may not—we cannot tell. But morality, the doing of that which is right, the performance of the plain and practical duties of the day and hour,—this is the road which is open to every man, and which will lead every man that follows it to the highest goal.'"—GEORGE MATHESON, D. D., in *Faiths of the World*, p. 66.

precepts of ancient wise men, form the sacred books of China.

The purpose of Confucius, be it remembered, was not to originate a religious system, but to quicken the neglected wisdom of the past and reinstate the spirit of the forefathers as the presiding genius of the empire. The objective point of all his teachings was sound government. On one of his journeys he saw a woman weeping before a tomb, and sent his disciple Tze-loo to inquire the cause of her sorrow. She informed him that here her father-in-law, her husband and her son had successively been killed by a tiger. "Why, then," said Tze-loo, "do you not remove from this place?"—"Because," she answered, "there is no oppressive government here." On hearing this Confucius observed to his disciples, "Remember, oppressive government is fiercer than a tiger."

His method of instruction was dogmatic. Unlike Socrates, he would have no questioning. "When I have presented," he said, "one corner of my lesson, and the pupil cannot of himself make out the other three, I do not repeat it."

As to the personal appearance of the philosopher, we may learn something from an incident which occurred in connection with his visit to the capital of Ching. "There is a man," said one of the townspeople, "standing at the east gate with a forehead like Yaou, a neck like Kaou Yaou, his shoulders on a level with those of Tsze-chan, but wanting below the waist three inches of the height of Yu, and altogether having the appearance of a stray dog." This description was recognized by Tze-Kung, one of Confucius's disciples, who, hastening to his master, repeated what he had heard. "Capital!" exclaimed Confucius. "Personal appearance is a matter of slight consequence, but it is something, indeed, to resemble a stray dog."

He traveled to and fro among the provinces, his disciples at his back sharing his toil and hardships, and visited many courts in the hope of persuading their rulers and dignitaries to respect the maxims of just government. The land was full of recluses, who, tired of the monotonous sight of oppression and wrong, had betaken themselves to the wildernesses in stoical despair; but Confucius held himself aloof from them. Born to sympathize with men and be one among them, he preferred to "struggle on against the tide, hoping against hope." Once in his journeying, having come to an impassable river, he sent his disciple Tze-loo to inquire for the ford. The man whom Tze-loo happened to meet was a hermit. "Go tell thy master," said he, "that the disorders of our kingdom are a flood without a ford. Bid him cease his endeavor to repress the wrongs that are surging and spreading on every hand, and retire from the world." Tze-loo went back and reported what had been said, whereupon Confucius made this noble and philosophic reply: "We must not withdraw from the world to associate with birds and beasts that have no affinity with us. With whom shall I mingle but with suffering men? It is my vocation to see that abuses shall cease by the prevalence of right principles throughout the state." We cannot but respect the true spirit of a reformer wherever it may be found—one who knows the possibility of failure and defeat, yet keeps a brave heart, and, having done all, stands in his appointed place.

Thus engaged in rekindling the old lights of wisdom and virtue, K'ung-foo-Tse, "unconsciously," as he tells us, "grew old." The pains and weaknesses of age came rapidly upon him; he leaned heavily upon his staff. One morning in the fourth month of the year 478 he was found moving about his door, his hands behind him, crooning over and over,

> "The great mountain must crumble,
> The strong beam must break,
> The wise man must wither like a plant."[1]

His disciples led him gently in and spake comforting words; but the pitcher was broken at the fountain. "No," he answered, "comfort is vain. No king has

[1] "These words came as a presage of evil to the faithful Tszekung. 'If the great mountain crumble,' said he, 'to what shall I look up? If the strong beam break and the wise man wither away, on whom shall I lean? The master, I fear, is going to be ill.' So saying, he hastened after Confucius into the house. 'What makes you so late?' said Confucius when the disciple presented himself before him; and then he added, 'According to the statutes of Hea, the corpse was dressed and coffined at the top of the eastern steps, treating the dead as if he were still the host. Under the Yin the ceremony was performed between the two pillars, as if the dead were both host and guest. The rule of Chow is to perform it at the top of the western steps, treating the dead as if he were a guest. I am a man of Yin, and last night I dreamt that I was sitting, with offerings before me, between the two pillars. No intelligent monarch arises; there is not one in the empire who will make me his master. My time is come to die.' It is eminently characteristic of Confucius that in his last recorded speech and dream his thoughts should so have dwelt on the ceremonies of bygone ages."—PROFESSOR R. K. DOUGLAS, in *Confucianism*, pp. 62, 63.

received me as his counselor,[1] nor is any willing to adopt the wisdom of the sages; my time has come to die."

Outside the city of K'uih-fow, approached by an avenue of cypress trees, stands an image on a lofty mound kept ever green, and a memorial tablet bearing

[1] "According to his theory, his official administration should have effected the reform not only of his sovereign and the people, but of those of the neighboring states. But what was the practical result? The contentment which reigned among the people of Loo, instead of instigating the duke of Ts'e to institute a similar system, only served to rouse his jealousy. 'With Confucius at the head of its government,' said he, 'Loo will become supreme among the states, and Ts'e, which is nearest to it, will be swallowed up. Let us propitiate it by a surrender of territory.' But a more provident statesman suggested that they should try to bring about the disgrace of the sage.

"With this object he sent eighty beautiful girls, well skilled in the arts of music and dancing, and a hundred and twenty of the finest horses which could be procured, as a present to the duke Ting. The result fully realized the anticipation of the minister. The girls were taken into the duke's harem, the horses were removed to the ducal stables, and Confucius was left to meditate on the folly of men who preferred listening to the songs of the maidens of Ts'e to the wisdom of Yaou and Shun. Day after day passed, and the duke showed no signs of returning to his proper mind. The affairs of state were neglected, and for three days the duke refused to receive his ministers in audience.

"'Master,' said Tze-loo, 'it is time you went.' But Confucius, who had more at stake than his disciple, was disinclined to give up the experiment on which his heart was set. Besides, the time was approaching when the great sacrifice to Heaven at the solstice, about which he had so many conversations with the duke, should be offered up, and he hoped that the recollection of his weighty words would recall the duke to a sense of his duties. But his gay rivals in the affections of the duke still held their sway, and the recurrence of the great festival failed to awaken his conscience even for the moment. Reluctantly, therefore, Confucius resigned his post and left the capital."—*Confucianism*, pp. 38, 39.

this inscription: "The most sagely ancient teacher, the all-accomplished, all-informed king, K'ung-foo-Tse—king without a kingdom, yet reigning in hearts innumerable." Hither the people come from all parts of the vast empire to honor his grave with votive offerings.[1]

[1] "To the great temple adjoining the philosopher's tomb the emperor goes in state twice a year, and, having twice knelt and six times bowed his head to the earth, invokes the presence of the sage in these words: 'Great art thou, O perfect sage. Thy virtue is full, thy doctrine is complete. Among mortal men there has not been thine equal. All kings honor thee. Thy statutes and laws have come gloriously down. Thou art the pattern of this imperial school. Reverently have the sacrificial vessels been set out. Full of awe we sound our drums and bells.' The spirit being now supposed to be present, the ceremony is gone through of presenting the appropriate offerings, which consist, according to circumstances, of pieces of satin, wine, salted tiger's flesh, dried fish, dried and minced venison, minced hare, minced fish, a pure black bullock, a sheep or a pig. The officiating mandarin then reads the following prayer: 'On this month of this year, I, the emperor, offer a sacrifice to the philosopher K'ung, the ancient teacher, the perfect sage, and say, O Teacher, in virtue equal to heaven and earth, whose doctrines embrace the past times and the present, thou didst digest and transmit the six classics, and didst hand down lessons for all generations. Now in this second month of spring (or autumn), in reverent observance of old statutes, with victims, silks, spirits and fruits, I carefully offer sacrifice to thee. With thee are associated the philosopher Yen, continuator of thee; the philosopher Tsang, exhibitor of thy fundamental principles; the philosopher Tsze-sze, transmitter of thee; and the philosopher Mencius, second to thee. Enjoy thou the offerings.' As will be inferred from this prayer, the image of Confucius does not stand alone, but is surrounded by images of his principal disciples, while in a hall at the back of that dedicated to him are ranged those of his ancestors. Occasionally different emperors have visited his tomb in Shan-tung, at which time the imperial pilgrims have worshiped with extraordinary solemnity at his shrine in the adjoining temple. K'ang-he, the most celebrated both as a ruler and a scholar of the emperors of the present dynasty, went on such a pilgrimage, and 'set the example

"Confucius! Confucius! how great was Confucius!
Before him there was no Confucius;
Since him there has been no other.
Confucius! Confucius! how great was Confucius!"

The religion of the Chinese Empire, with its five hundred millions of people, embracing nearly one-half of the population of the entire globe, is little more than a personal reverence for this illustrious man. Its rites and ceremonies all cluster about his name. An acquaintance with his maxims constitutes the beginning and end of education. For twenty centuries they have been taught in every village school. To the people they are the only creed, the only law. Dr. S. Wells Williams says: " He receives such homage from his fellow-men as no other man has ever had, and which amounts in reality to worship." Yet Dr. Legge, a profound student of Confucius and his system, passes this judgment upon him: " I am unable to regard him as a great man. He was not before his age, though he was above the mass of the officers and scholars of his time. He threw no new light on any of the questions which have a world-wide interest. He gave no impulse to religion. He had no sympathy with progress. His influence has been wonderful, but it will henceforth wane."

What, then, is Confucianism?

Its Central Thought.—Its central thought is *The Kingdom.*

In Christianity also we hear of a kingdom, by which

of kneeling thrice in the dust, before the image of the sage.' "—*Confucianism*, pp. 163-165.

is variously meant the prevalence of virtue in human lives (Luke 12 : 20, 21 ; cf. Rom. 14 : 17), the influence of divine grace preceding the manifestation of the divine glory among men (Matt. 13), or the rule of the righteous Lord in his heavens (Matt. 8 : 11) and over his redeemed earth (Rev. 12 : 9, 10). To secure the complete establishment of this kingdom is the prime purpose of every follower of Christ (Matt. 6 : 33). Its name is The Kingdom of God. But the kingdom of which Confucius dreamed, and toward which he constantly and most earnestly directed the minds of his pupils and followers, was of a much more material sort. It was purely a kingdom on earth and of the earth. Its name was China.

"It so happens," says Dr. Matheson, "that this Chinese Empire, with its feudal ranks and its conservative institutions, is itself the object of Chinese worship. The belief in millenarianism—that is to say, the expectation of a kingdom of heaven upon earth—has in all ages of the world found some place in the religious instinct. The vision of such a kingdom has never been wholly absent from the lives of men. It glittered before the eyes of the Parsee; it shone in the imagination of Plato; it dominated the mind of the Jew; it sustained the heart of the early Christian. China, too, had her kingdom of heaven on earth, but with a difference. To the Parsee, to the Platonist, to the Jew and to the Christian the heavenly kingdom was something still to come; to the Chinaman it was something which had already come. The Chinese Empire reveals to him the spectacle of a complete millenarianism—of a kingdom which exists no longer in a vision of the future, but in the actual experience of the passing hour. He believes that the social system in which he lives and moves is pervaded by a mysterious divine life."[1]

Further, the system of Confucius teaches "that by pursuing the plain and practical duties of the hour man can actually make this world itself the kingdom of God—that the harmony of the universe is to be found, not in some transcendental, timeless sphere, but in the completed results of those seemingly trivial acts which make up the moral history of the individual human soul." (It will be seen that the Chinese philosopher is not without disciples in this day; the Agnostics are thinking his thoughts after him.)

Characteristic Features.—This being the central thought in the system of Confucius, what are its characteristic features? They are three:

I. *Filial Piety.*—The system sets out with the idea of social order as prerequisite to the ideal government. Its basis of obligation rests on the secular power.[2] In most other religions the leading idea is God. There is no God in the religion of China. It is purely political. The aim of Confucius was to reform the government of China, which he conceived might be best accomplished by the reviving of certain healthful principles which had prevailed in the traditional Golden Age.

---

[1] *Faiths of the World.*

[2] "The Chinese does not first ask where Spiritual Intelligence dwells, and then confess that to this he must submit. But he starts with the belief in government or society, and then demands that all study or intelligence should be applied to the preservation of it."—F. D. MAURICE, in *Religions of the World,* p. 86.

He therefore avoided all reference to God and eternal things.[1] "While we know so little about life," said he to one of his disciples, "how can we know anything about death?"[2] He would not allow himself to indulge in fruitless dreams. The wrongs and tyrannies in the work-a-day world were real. Peace, safety, prosperity, these were substantial blessings to be sought for and enjoyed. What need of a heaven afar off if by these a heaven could be made on earth? The Chinese people have a proverb which runs in this wise:

"The Buddhist priests declare their Fo in the abyss to be;
Say Lao's followers, ' Paradise lies in the Eastern Sea;'
But great Confucius' pupils look on real things around;
Before their eyes the airs of spring, fresh blowing, brush the ground."

The Lao referred to in this proverb is Laoutsee, an old man who believed in a Supreme Deity and was wont to philosophize about the future. To him Confucius listened with respectful attention, but afterward

[1] "What he heard of divine unseen, mysterious powers above man or above nature, or even in man and in nature, of some thing or person beyond the earthly emperor or the earthly father, he by no means denied. Whatever faith his countrymen had respecting the invisible world he would have wished to confirm. But he did not see his way in such inquiries: he could not trace the actual connection between them and practical life."—*Religions of the World*, p. 89.

[2] "On the subject of spirits, as on all matters relating to heavenly beings, Confucius was reticent. His mind was wrapt up in the things of this earth, and he looked upon all such subjects as obscure and unprofitable. That they were worthy of reverence he was ready to affirm, but he considered that constant reference to them was likely to lead to superstition. 'Spirits are to be respected,' he said, ' but to be kept at a distance;' and in reply to a question put to him as to serving the spirits, he answered, ' While you are not able to serve men, how can you serve their spirits?' "—*Confucianism*, p. 81.

spoke of him as a theorist, a transcendental dreamer, who might better draw in his thoughts from misty and remote things to the evils nearer by.

"*What must I Do to be Saved?*"—The answer of Confucius to the question "What must I do to be saved?" was, "Be a good citizen of China."

His theory of government was patriarchal, "the embodiment of filial piety." The state is a large family, of which the emperor is Tien-tze, the great father of all. The humblest beggar in his dominions may claim protection as his child. The first duty of every citizen is reverence for his political father; his second, reverence for his father in the flesh. In no other country on earth are the obligations that flow from filial ties more thoroughly respected than in China. The great commandment, held inviolate by mandarin and slave, is this: *Honor thy father.* Yet this, observe, is a purely political maxim. There is no sentiment about it. The end in view is the conservation of order in the state.[1] To that end the great father, Tien-tze, and all other fathers—who are regarded as his official aids in securing a good government—must have the implicit and unquestioning obedience of every child.[2]

---

[1] "He taught that the sovereign was the father of his people, and as such entitled to the same obedience, mingled with reverence, which is due from a child to its parent. He claimed to a certain degree unlimited authority for the sovereign over the minister, father over the son, husband over the wife, elder brother over younger, and he enjoined kind and upright dealings among friends, thus inculcating as his leading tenets subordination to superiors and virtuous conduct."—Dr. S. WELLS WILLIAMS, in *Schaff-Herzog Encyclopædia*.

[2] "In reply to Tsze-chang's question, 'How should a sovereign act

Worship of Ancestors.—Here we discover the source of that Chinese phenomenon, the worship of ancestors. It is believed that at death three spirits are liberated from the body; one of these occupies the grave, another seeks the invisible world, while the third takes up its residence in a memorial tablet.[1] Thus every home has its ancestral tablets bearing the names of the honored dead. Twice a month with tapers and burning incense

in order that he may govern properly?' he replied: 'Let him honor the five excellent and banish the four bad things.' The five good things are: (1) When the person in authority is beneficent without great expenditure; that is, when he makes more beneficial to his people the things from which they naturally derive benefit. (2) When he lays tasks on the people without their repining; that is, when he chooses the labors which are proper and employs them on them. (3) When he pursues what he desires without being covetous; that is, when his desires are set on a benevolent government, and he realizes it. (4) When he maintains a dignified ease without being proud; that is, whether he has to do with many people or with few, or with great things or with small, he does not dare to show any disrespect. (5) When he is majestic without being fierce; that is, when he adjusts his clothes and cap and throws a dignity into his looks, so that, thus dignified, he is looked at with awe. The four bad things are: (1) To put the people to death without having instructed them; this is called cruelty. (2) To require from them suddenly the full tale of work without having given them warning; this is called oppression. (3) To issue orders as if without urgency at first, and when the time comes to insist upon them with severity; this is called injury. (4) And, generally speaking, to give pay or rewards to men, and yet do it in a stingy way; this is called acting the part of a mere official."—*Confucianism*, pp. 136, 137.

[1] "It is a great misfortune for a Chinaman to die in a foreign land away from home, for then he is deprived of the benefits of the offerings of his relatives and descendants. We see, therefore, why it is that the Chinese in California send home the bodies of their countrymen who die there. They have a fund for that purpose. The dead would take vengeance upon them if they did not perform the filial act."—C. C. COFFIN.

the inmates of the home bow down before them. This is the universal custom of the empire. It is the natural outgrowth of the patriarchal idea in society and the state. The living are in bondage unto the dead. And this is one of the mighty forces used in upholding and perpetuating the government. It casts a halo of superstitious awe around the names of the forefathers, and gives to filial reverence the highest place among the virtues. Thus the word of the emperor, the great father, becomes as the oracles of God.

II. *Veneration for Learning.*—The second characteristic of the Chinese religion is veneration for learning. This necessarily follows the proposition of Confucius that a political reformation could be accomplished only by returning to the wisdom of the former ages. The compilation of the sacred books was the immediate result of that thought. There are nine of these books.

The Sacred Books.—(I.) *The Five King*, or canonical volumes.

1. The Shu-king, or Book of Ancient History, giving the history of China from the earliest times to 720 B. C.

2. The Shi-king, or Book of Ancient Poems, comprising three hundred and eighty-five odes. The following, translated by Dr. Legge, will serve as an example; it is entitled "A Pastoral Ode: an industrious wife awakens her husband at early dawn:"

> "'Get up, husband, here's the day!'
> 'Not yet, wife, the dawn's still gray.'
> 'Get up, sir, and on the right
> See the morning star shines bright.

Shake off slumber, and prepare
Ducks and geese to shoot and snare.

'All your darts and lines may kill
I will dress for you with skill.
Thus a blithesome hour we'll pass,
Brightened by a cheerful glass,
While your lute its aid imparts,
To gratify and soothe our hearts.'"

3. The Li-king, or Book of Ancient Rites and Ceremonies, containing rules of conduct for all occasions. This book is the Chinese standard of etiquette. It was the uniform custom of Confucius to lay great stress on the importance of decorum, which he himself illustrated in all his actions. "He did all," says Professor Douglas, "with the avowed object of being seen of men and of influencing them by his conduct. In the presence of his prince we are told that his manner, though self-possessed, displayed respectful uneasiness. When he entered the palace or when he passed the vacant throne his countenance changed, his legs bent under him and he spoke as though he had scarcely breath to utter a word. When it fell to his lot to carry the royal sceptre he stooped his body, as though he were not able to bear its weight. If the prince came to visit him when he was ill, he had himself placed with his head to the east, and lay dressed in his court-clothes with his girdle across them."

4. The Yih-king, or Book of Changes, relating particularly to divination and similar mystic arts. "This book," says Alexander F. Tytler, "which has been held as a mysterious receptacle of the most profound know-

ledge, and is on that account allowed to be consulted only by the sect of the learned, is now known to be nothing else than a superstitious and childish device for fortune-telling or divination. It is a table on which there are sixty-four marks or lines, one half short and the other half long, placed at regular intervals. The person who consults the Yih-king for divining some future event takes a number of small pieces of rod, and, throwing them down at random, observes carefully how their accidental position corresponds to the marks on the table, from which, according to certain established rules, he predicts either good or bad fortune.

5. The Chun-tsiu, or Spring and Autumn, so called because, as Confucius says, "its commendations are life-giving as the spring and its censures life-withering as autumn." It is a record of political events from 720 to 480 B. C.

(II.) *The Four Shoo*, or writings. These are collections of the wisdom of Confucius and his disciples.

1. The Lun-Yu; Analects, or Table-talk of Confucius. The following extracts will serve to illustrate the character of this volume:

"The Master saith, Shall I teach you what knowledge is? When you know a thing, to maintain that you know it, and when you do not know it, to confess your ignorance,—this is knowledge."—"With coarse rice to eat, water to drink and my bended arm for a pillow I may be happy; but riches and honor without virtue are as a floating cloud."—"Extravagance leads to insubordination, and parsimony to meanness."

2. The Ta-Hio, or Great Learning, by Tsang-Sin, a disciple. The following is an example: " The ancients who sought to establish virtue throughout the empire began by ordering well their own estates. Wishing to establish virtue in the state, they began by regulating their own household. Wishing to establish virtue in the household, they began by looking to themselves. Wishing to cultivate their individual characters, they began by rectifying their hearts."

3. The Chung-Yung, or Doctrine of the Mean. The following is an extract: " The Master saith, Perfect is the virtue which is according to The Mean. How rare have been the people who could practice it!"—" If there be no stirrings of joy or anger, grief or pleasure, the mind is in Equilibrium. If those feelings be awakened to act in due proportion, the mind is in Harmony. This Equilibrium is the root of human action, and this Harmony is the proper path for all."

4. The Works of Mencius, the Master's most illustrious disciple. The following will illustrate the general character of this book: " Mencius said, The perfect fruit of benevolence is the service of one's parents; of righteousness, the service of one's elder brother; and of wisdom, the service of those two things and abiding in them."—" I love life and I love righteousness. If I cannot have both, I will let life go and choose righteousness."

These volumes are, for the most part, in prose, monotonous, sombre, gray, with neither freshness nor life. To us Anglo-Saxons, who have mercury in our veins, the proverbs of the most sagely ancient teacher and his sublimely wise disciples are as dull as an almanac; but the Mongolian sits hour after hour upon his bamboo mat following the lines with his long fingernails, his eyes half closed, oblivious of the bustling world, murmuring over and over again the celestial words.

For two thousand years or more these sacred volumes have been the substratum of Chinese literature. They are the principal textbooks in all institutions of learning. There is no possibility of political preferment without a thorough familiarity with The Five King and The Four Shoo. The literati are the ruling class. There is no promotion except for scholarship. Once in three years there is an examination of candidates for degrees. No student can be entered as a candidate unless he has previously studied the whole system of Confucius. The successful competitors in the course of time become the rulers of the empire.[1] Thus it is evident that China, commonly regarded as a monarchy, is really an aristocracy—an aristocracy of learning. We, in their eyes, are barbarians because of the light value we put upon scholarship. Ours, they say, is an aristocracy of birth or of riches—that is, of accident—but theirs is an aristocracy of worth. Here,

[1] "The bachelors, or those who are successful, are triennially sent for renewed examination in the provincial capital before two examiners deputed from the general board of public education. The licentiates, thus sifted out, now offer themselves for final examination before the imperial board at Pekin. Suitable candidates for vacant posts are thus selected. There is no one who is not liable to such an inquisition. When vacancies occur they are filled from the list of approved men, who are gradually elevated to the highest honors."—DRAPER's *Intellectual Development of Europe*, ii. 396.

indeed, is something for us to learn from the people of far Cathay.

III. *Conservatism.*—The third characteristic of this religion is conservatism. It is scarcely strange that a nation sitting at the feet of Confucius should wrap itself up in a complacent aversion to progress, for his favorite precept was, "Walk in the trodden paths." China has been at a standstill for twenty centuries. It is the only land on earth of which it cannot be said,

> "The old order changeth, giving place to new,
> And God fulfills himself in many ways,
> Lest one good custom should corrupt the world."

No Progress.—" In China," it has been significantly said, "whatever is gray with age becomes religion." Other nations have learned to worship the rising sun, but Confucius stood with his face toward the past, teaching his followers to revere whatever is old and dead. The language of China is written in square characters just as it was twenty centuries ago. The people dress as they did then. Innovation is treason.[1]

[1] "It will be seen that in government, as with everything else, Confucius strove with all his might to carry his countrymen back to the ideal times of Kings Wan and Woo. He refused to recognize the changes which were foreshadowed by the growth of new and vigorous states and by the decrepitude of the imperial kingdom of Chow, and attempted to bolster up that which was already falling to pieces, and to suppress the aspirations of those who, as must have been obvious to every one but himself, were destined to fight for the mastery over the ruins of the royal house. The sum of his teachings may be described in his own words: 'Follow the seasons of Hea. Ride in the state chariots of Yin. Wear the ceremonial cap of Chow. Let the music be the Shaou, with its pantomimes. Banish the songs of Ch'ing and keep far from specious talkers.'"—*Confucianism*, pp. 138, 139.

One of the Manchu emperors recently sent out an edict against the binding of the feet, but the low mutterings of an insurrection forced him to withdraw it. A strip of land between Shanghai and Woo-Sung was bought up some years ago by foreign residents, who proceeded to build a railway between those points; but the government of Peking tore it up. Thus the whole policy of the state is repressive—to stand still, to abide among the sepulchres of ancient days, poring over the parchments of the sages.

"In arts, in manners, in the physical features of its inhabitants, in mental and moral portraiture, in language and in religion, China has been of all lands the most untouched by time. It has resisted alike the inroads of matter and of mind. Like other countries, it has been subjected to the incursions and the conquests of barbarians, but, in a manner unknown to other countries, it has assimilated its conquerors to its own civilization. It has been subjected to spiritual invasion; foreign religions, like foreign tribes, have tried to settle on its soil. But here, too, the result has been the same: the old Confucian faith has not forbidden the advent of the new, but it has gradually succeeded in drawing it nearer to itself. A civilization which has thus been able not only to resist new temporal influences, but eventually to appropriate these influences to itself, most certainly presents a spectacle of conservatism which is unique in the history of the world." [1]

Not Properly a Religion.—These, then, are the three distinguishing features of Confucianism: filial piety,

[1] *The Faiths of the World*, p. 63.

reverence for learning and conservatism. The reader has, without doubt, come to the conclusion that there is little or nothing of religion in this system. The word "religion" is best taken in its original sense, "a binding back," the thought being of a restoration of the soul to the everlasting truth and love of God. But Confucianism points no higher than a man's head. It practically says, "A principle of order is the one thing worthy of reverence; we can dispense with God."[1] It has been justly called a prosaic belief dignified with the name of a religion. It may be remarked, in passing, as a most singular circumstance, that a philosophy whose very life is in the patriarchal idea should wholly omit to reverence or even recognize Him who is Abba, the Father of all.

There is, however, a solitary spot in China where homage is paid to the Deity. Near by the city of Peking is a temple over whose gateway is inscribed, "To the Supreme Ruler of the Universe." Once every year with magnificent parade the emperor comes hither alone and offers a bullock on the altar. But the people have no part nor lot in this ceremony. They are literally "without God," yet not without gods.

Popular Idolatry.—Polytheism is ever the boon companion of atheism. The multitudes of the people, while professing Confucianism, do not hesitate to patronize at the same time the shrines of Buddhism and Taoism.

---

[1] "It has been questioned whether Confucius even did not doubt the existence of a divine Power, and regard the universe as a vast self-sustaining mechanism; but he undoubtedly gave occasion to his disciples for such a belief by his silence upon the subject and his use of the indefinite term 'heaven.'"—S. WELLS WILLIAMS.

Therefore, though their great master taught them to worship nothing, the empire swarms with gods.

Results.—What are the results? What are the practical fruits of Confucianism in this populous empire where it has prevailed for these two thousand years?

1. *No Independence of Thought.*—Its first effect is seen in an utter absence of independent, progressive thought. The people of China have so long been reading the dull, iterative maxims of the sages that their minds are benumbed. Not even the most venturesome thinker dares to pass beyond "the established boundary-line of precedent." Their ideas are rusty and mildewed, and, like their faces, their houses and their junks, are all made after one pattern. They are doing as Confucius bade them, walking in the old paths.

2. *No Ambition.*—It has killed hope and ambition and all the nobler impulses of the heart. For Confucianism is a low form of materialism; it cuts the soul's wings. The inhabitants of China are a sordid race. They are taught in the sacred books that the seat of the understanding is the stomach; and their lives are passed, accordingly, in toiling for meat that perisheth.

> "To be content's their natural desire;
> They ask no angel's wings nor seraph's fire."

The career of their great teacher is their ideal of life. "At fifteen," he says, "I had my mind bent upon learning; at thirty I stood firm; at fifty I knew the celestial decrees; at seventy I kept the law."

3. *No Good Cheer.*—The people of China rarely sing: they know nothing of romance; the golden glow of

life has been supplanted by plain matter of fact. Their religion has made them a race of washermen and coolies, dull, plodding and as heedless of eternity as moles. There is a mighty truth in the old fable of Prometheus; the fires that give brightness and fervor to human life must be brought down from God. And if there be no God? Then there can be no light, no burning of the soul with eager longings, no life beyond one's tools and daily bread. Thus it is said of the disciples of Confucius that all stars shine to them in the heavens behind; none beckon before. Verily, "a hundred years" of our Anglo-Saxon hope and vigor are worth "a cycle of Cathay."

4. *No Common Morality.*—And what has been the result of this system on the outward morals of China? It is the land of the opium-smoker, that lowest and most bestial of inebriates. It is the land of infanticide; for "What is the good," they say, "of rearing daughters?" It is the land of concubinage and slavery. Woman is not the helpmate, but the slave, of man. Confucius thought it an unpardonable weakness to bemoan the death of his faithful wife; she was only a woman.[1] It

---

[1] "He (Confucius) permits divorce for any one of seven reasons: 'When a woman cannot live in peace with her father-in-law or mother-in-law; when she cannot bear children; when she is unfaithful; when, by the utterance of calumnies or indiscreet words, she disturbs the peace of the house; when her husband has for her an unconquerable repugnance; when she is an inveterate scold; when she steals anything from her husband's house,'—in any of these cases her husband may put her away."—*Cyclopædia of Biography,* p. 418.

"The failure to recognize the sanctity of the marriage bond is a great blot in the Confucian system. It has in a great measure destroyed domesticity, it has robbed women of their lawful influence, and has

has been said that the life of a Chinese woman is a continuous wail from her cradle to her grave. This— though the five sacred books were flawless, and though the schools were a thousandfold more numerous than they are—would stamp the Chinese Empire as a barbarous land.

Of all the nations of the earth, China affords the best illustration of the inadequacy of a written code of morals.[1] The man who would live up to the pre-

degraded them into a position which is little better than slavery. 'Men, being firm by nature,' said Seun-tsze, 'are virtuous, and women, being soft, are useful.' This saying justly represents the estimate commonly held of the relative standing of the two sexes."—*Confucianism*, p. 128.

"A slavish submission is a woman's highest duty, and no better description can be given of the various fates awaiting sons and daughters than that quoted from the Book of Poetry, where the poet forecasts the future of King Seuen:

'Sons shall be his (the king's); on couches lulled to rest
   The little ones, enrobed, with sceptres play;
Their infant cries are loud as stern behests;
   Their knees the vermeil covers shall display.
As king hereafter one shall be addressed;
   The rest, our princes, all the states shall sway.
And daughters also to him shall be born:
   They shall be placed upon the ground to sleep;
Their playthings tiles, their dress the simplest worn;
   Their part alike from good and ill to keep,
And ne'er their parent's heart to cause to mourn—
   To cook his food and spirit malt to keep.'"

Ibid., pp. 124, 125.

[1] Toward the close of the seventeenth century the emperor K'ang-he issued sixteen maxims, founded on the teachings of the sage, for the guidance of the people, whose morality "had for some time been daily declining, and whose hearts were not as of old." He summed up, as it were, all the essential points in the Confucian doctrine, and thus he wrote:

cepts of Confucius would be, indeed, a "superior man."[1] But there is apparently no endeavor to adjust the life

"1. Esteem most highly filial piety and brotherly submission, in order to give due prominence to the social relations.

"2. Behave with generosity to the branches of your kindred, in order to illustrate harmony and benignity.

"3. Cultivate peace and concord in your neighborhoods, in order to prevent quarrels and litigations.

"4. Recognize the importance of husbandry and the culture of the mulberry tree, in order to ensure a sufficiency of clothing and food.

"5. Show that you prize moderation and economy, in order to prevent the lavish waste of your means.

"6. Make much of the colleges and seminaries, in order to make correct the practice of the scholars.

"7. Discountenance and banish strange doctrines, in order to exalt the correct doctrine.

"8. Describe and explain the laws, in order to warn the ignorant and obstinate.

"9. Exhibit clearly propriety and yielding courtesy, in order to make manners and customs good.

"10. Labor diligently at your proper callings, in order to give settlement to the aims of the people.

"11. Instruct your sons and younger brothers, in order to prevent them from doing what is wrong.

"12. Put a stop to false accusations, in order to protect the honest and the good.

"13. Warn against sheltering deserters, in order to avoid being involved in their punishments.

"14. Promptly and fully pay your taxes, in order to avoid the urgent requisition of your quota.

"15. Combine in hundreds and tithings, in order to put an end to thefts and robbery.

"16. Study to remove resentments and angry feelings, in order to show the importance due to the person and life."—*Confucianism*, pp. 167-199.

[1] "'The superior man forms a leading feature in the Confucian philosophy. Nine things he strove after: in seeing to see clearly, in hearing to hear distinctly, in expression to be benign, in his demeanor to be decorous, in speaking to be sincere, in his duties to be respectful, in

to such teachings. One who has long labored as a missionary in China says: " The literati, among whom we might expect to find a pure morality if anywhere, are inveterately addicted to lying, treachery and extortion. Among the rulers justice is unknown. Bribery and oppression constitute the universal practice among the officials of every grade. Avariciousness sways the heart of all classes. There is no mode of deception and fraud, no trick nor art in trade, no quackery and no jugglery, in which the Chinese are not perfect adepts. Deception and lying are so common that they have almost lost the consciousness that they are wrong. Backbiting and quarreling, slandering and cursing, intrigues and broils, are universal. Pilfering and theft, extortion, robbery and piracy, suicide, infanticide and murder, lotteries and gambling-shops, opium-

doubt to inquire, in resentment to think of difficulties, when he saw an opportunity for gain to think of righteousness. Three things he avoided: in youth, when the physical powers are not settled, he avoided lust; in manhood, when the physical powers are in full vigor, he avoided quarrelsomeness; in old age, when the animal powers are decayed, he avoided covetousness.

"The superior man was righteous in all his ways; his acts were guided by the laws of propriety and were marked by strict sincerity. Being without reproach, he was also without fear, and, having studied deeply, his mind was untroubled by doubt or misgiving. Nothing put him out of countenance, for wisdom, humanity and valor were his constant companions. Of the ordinances of Heaven, of great men and the word of sages he alone stood in respectful awe, and this not out of servility, but because he possessed sufficient knowledge to comprehend the wisdom embodied in those powers. Mere eloquence had no effect upon him, and he was careless about the animal comforts of this life. He laughed at want, for his aims were directed toward 'the heavenly way,' not toward eating; and for the same reason wealth and poverty were not causes of anxiety to him."—*Confuciunism*, pp. 88, 89.

dens, are common everywhere." A missionary of the English Church says: "Romans ch. 1 and Ephesians ch. 4 apply fully to the Chinese. Their great idolatrous gatherings in the city, and especially in the country districts, are accompanied by wickedness of every kind. They are a much worse people than they look."[1]

All this in spite of the fact that Confucianism avows itself to be distinctly a moral system. Confucius taught the Golden Rule in the negative form: "What you do not like when done to yourself, do not that to others."[2] The five cardinal virtues of his system are—(1) Benevolence, (2) Duty, (3) Decorum, (4) Knowledge, and (5) Faith. But morality is a dead thing if piety has not quickened it, and moral precepts, however wise and good, can take no vital hold on a people who decline to think of God.

We must judge Confucianism by its fruits. Of all the false religions, none is more deadening in its influence on the moral nature. Between two systems so radically unlike as Confucianism and Christianity it is scarcely possible to institute a comparison. The latter is a religion binding back the soul to God; the

[1] Presbyterian *Foreign Missionary Magazine*, Feb., 1874.

[2] "It does not seem to us that in uttering this precept Confucius really rose above his usual governmental theory—really meant to suggest more than a law for the well-being of the state. The thought in his mind was probably this: If you do evil to others, you may be sure they will retaliate on yourself the same form of evil, for revenge in kind of injury is an instinct of humanity. Such retaliations can end in nothing but political anarchy; avoid them for the sake of good government, and in order to avoid them shun that which may cause them."—*Faiths of the World*, p. 72.

former is a code of secular maxims and injunctions having for its only ends the well-being of society and the state. The one bids us look up and away to those things which are unseen and eternal; the other absorbs all thought and effort in the present hour. The one, as with a two-edged sword, lays bare the soul's defilement, then points to Calvary and the flowing blood that cleanseth; the other finds sin a dark, inevitable fact, and says, "There is no remedy; the dying must die."

No remedy? No help? Lord, deliver us from a philosophy of despair, and help us ever more and more to love the glorious gospel which giveth hope as an anchor to the soul both sure and steadfast, taking hold of that within the veil.

IX.
ISLAM.

I. *The Sacred Books:* The Koran.
II. *Theology:* The Creed.
   (1) *There is One God.*
       Central Thought: Kismet.
   (2) *Mohammed is his Prophet.*
       The teachings of Mohammed in respect to sin, death, resurrection, judgment, heaven, hell, etc.
III. *Ethics:* A Ceremonial System.
   "*What shall I do to be saved?*" Observe the Five Pillars of Practice.
IV. *Jurisprudence:* A Politico-religious System.
   War, Slavery, Polygamy, etc.
V. *Fruits of the System:* Sensuality, Cruelty, etc.

IX. ISLAM.

The Kaaba.—When Adam and Eve were expelled from Paradise they came in their wanderings to the edge of the Arabian desert—so runs the tradition—and there built the Kaaba in precise imitation of the temple wherein they had worshiped in the Garden. It was subsequently swept away by the Flood, but an angel revealed its site to Hagar and Ishmael, who quenched their thirst at its well Zem-Zem. A neighboring tribe of Amalekites, attracted by the waters, pitched their tents there and called the settlement Mecca. They strengthened the hands of Ishmael in the rebuilding of the Kaaba, and to their assistance came the angel Gabriel, bringing from Paradise a semicircular stone which to this day reposes in an outer corner of the wall, smoothed and blackened by the devout kisses of sinful men.

Birth of Mohammed.—In the Year of the Elephant, A. D. 570, there was joy in the house of the venerable Abdallah, the custodian of this black stone. A child was born who, opening his eyes to the light, was heard distinctly to exclaim, "God is great, and I am his prophet!" The air was full of portents. The sacred fire of Zoroaster, which had been jealously guarded for centuries, was extinguished by the dawning of the brighter light. The evil spirits betook themselves to the abyss of darkness. In due time the child received the name Mohammed, " the praised." At three years of age he experienced what might be called a change of heart, the angel Gabriel opening his breast and squeezing out the black drop of sin. Left motherless at six, he fell into a habit of brooding and grew morbidly fond of silence and solitude. He suffered, moreover, from some malady—probably epilepsy or hysteria—which rendered his mind peculiarly impressible. In early manhood he was employed as cameldriver by a rich merchant's widow, Hadijah, who, enamored of his manly beauty, became his wife. Her wealth exalted him among the noble sons of Ishmael, and for her conjugal devotion she was given an immortal place among the four perfect women. In leading her caravans he came into contact with the Jewish and Christian communities of Arabia, thus acquiring a limited knowledge of their Scriptures and traditions, which he afterward put to a most effective use.

Descent of the Koran.—At the age of forty he retired to a cave in the desert, three miles from Mecca, where he dreamed strange dreams and saw wonderful visions.[1] One night Gabriel appeared before him hold-

---

[1] "He was visited by supernatural appearances, mysterious voices accosting him as the Prophet of God: even the stones and trees joined in the whispering. He himself suspected the true nature of his malady, and to his wife Chadizah he expressed a dread that he was becoming insane. It is related that as they sat alone a shadow entered the room. "Dost thou see aught?' said Chadizah, who, after the manner of Arabian matrons, wore her veil. 'I do,' said the prophet. Whereupon she uncovered her face, and said, 'Dost thou see it now?'—' I do not.'

ing a silken scroll and commanding him to read in the name of the Lord. Mohammed answered that he had never learned to read; whereupon the angel shook him thrice, uttered certain cabalistic words, and, lo! the inscription became clear as light. This is known as the prophet's "call." The words uttered by the angel were these:

> "Read! in the name of thy Lord: in the name of the Lord,
> Who created man from a drop of congealed blood.
> Read! for the Lord is the generous One
> Who hath given the Writing,
> And teacheth the ignorant to read it."

This writing on the silken scroll was the first installment of the Koran, the heaven-sent Book. At the conclusion of his interview with the angel the face of Mohammed was of a ghastly hue and covered with perspiration like beads of silver, his ears were filled with the sound of bells and his limbs trembled under him. In his desperation he was about to commit suicide when, faithful husband that he was, it occurred to him to take counsel of Hadijah. On hearing what had occurred, she forthwith did obeisance and declared him verily a prophet of God. Thus she won for herself an immortal name as the first convert of Islam. The next

—'Glad tidings to thee, O Mohammed!' exclaimed Chadizah; 'it is an angel, for he has respected my unveiled face; an evil spirit would not.' As his disease advanced these spectral illusions became more frequent; from one of them he received the divine commission. 'I,' said his wife, 'will be thy first believer;' and they knelt down in prayer together. Since that day nine thousand millions of human beings have acknowledged him to be a prophet of God."—DRAPER'S *Intellectual Development of Europe*, i. 330.

to yield allegiance was the freedman Zaid; the next, Mohammed's cousin Ali; the next, Abu-bekr, and others slowly followed. The people of Mecca gave little heed or credence to the pretensions of their townsman. He was indeed a prophet without honor among his own. At the end of five years he had less than fifty followers, and many of these were of the servile class.[1]

Persecution.—Whether we regard him as knave, fanatic or sincere reformer, it is impossible not to admire the patient continuance of this man. He was troubled on every side, yet not distressed; perplexed, but not in despair. Driven out by the people of Mecca, he resorted with his scant following to a cave in the suburbs, where for three years they "suffered all the privations of a beleaguered garrison." At this time, for his encouragement—so the record runs—the prophet was carried upon a winged steed to Jerusalem, where he met the holy convocation of prophets, and, being lifted into the seventh heaven, communed with God.

The Hejira.—At length, in the year 622, he fled to Medina, taking his disciples with him. This flight is called "The Hejira," and marks the beginning of the

---

[1] "The incarcerations and tortures, chiefly by thirst in the burning rays of the sun, to which these humble converts were subjected to induce their recantation and adoration of the national idols, touched the heart of Mohammed, and by divine authority he permitted them, under certain circumstances, to deny their faith so long as their hearts were steadfast in it. Thus: 'Whoever denieth God after he hath believed, except him who shall be compelled against his will, whose heart continueth steadfast in the faith, shall be chastised' (Koran, Surah xvi.)."—*Islam,* p. 76.

Mohammedan era. The fugitives, being pursued, took refuge in a ravine on Mount Thaur. In this solitude the heart of Abu-bekr failed him, and he said, " They be many that fight against us; we are only two."— " Not so," answered the prophet; " we seem but two, but Allah is a third among us." Their pursuers came to the mouth of the cavern and peered in, but a divinely-commissioned spider had there woven its web and a pair of brooding wood-pigeons forbade further search. After three days the faithful ventured forth and resumed their journey. On reaching Medina their leader was received with glad acclamations as a prophet of God.

Islam.—Now began the organization of Islam. The call to prayer was uttered from the minarets; the Crescentade was proclaimed. And here we mark a transformation in Mohammed's character. He was no more, henceforth, the pure-minded, kindly-disposed, long-suffering dreamer of dreams, but a red-handed fanatic and sensualist.[1] So true is it, as one of the old poets wrote, that when Ambition comes to court Dominion,

> " all the hireling equipage of virtues,
> Faith, Honor, Justice, Gratitude and Friendship,
> Is discharged at once."[2]

It was now announced by the prophet that Islam was

---

[1] " The peaceful preacher of righteousness spent the last ten years of his life in training an army of fanatical warriors. His character became brutalized, his life sensual. He appealed to divine sanction for his licentiousness. The early purity of his soul vanished: he changed into a man of cunning and of blood."—DR. LEES, in *Faiths of the World*, p. 312.

[2] " He (Mohammed) adds another, and perhaps the greatest, illustra-

to be propagated by the sword. No quarter must be given to unbelievers. " Fight against them until there be no idolater left to oppose us, and until the only religion shall be that of Allah the true God."[1] In 623 a company of Mohammedan followers, going out from

tion to the long list of noble souls whose natures have become subdued to that which they worked in—who have sought high ends by low means—who, talking of the noblest truths, descend into the meanest prevarications, and so throw a doubt on all sincerity, faith and honor. Such was the judgment of a great thinker—Goethe—concerning Mohammed. He believes him to have been at first profoundly sincere, but he says of him that afterward 'what in his character is earthly increases and develops itself; the divine retires and is obscured; his doctrine becomes a means rather than an end. All kinds of practices are employed, nor are horrors wanting.' Goethe intended to write a drama upon Mohammed to illustrate the sad fact that every man who attempts to realize a great idea comes in contact with the lower world, must place himself on its level in order to influence it, and thus often compromises his higher aims, and at last forfeits them."—CLARKE'S *Ten Great Religions*, p. 468.

[1] " In 631, Mohammed issued an important command, the crowning-stone of the system he had raised, which shows at once the power he wielded and the strong hold his doctrines had already taken throughout Arabia. Refusing to be present himself during the ceremonies of the pilgrimage, he commissioned Ali to announce to the assembled multitudes in the valley of Mina that at the expiration of the four sacred months the prophet would hold himself absolved from every obligation or league with idolaters—that after that year no unbeliever would be allowed to perform the pilgrimage or to visit the holy places; and, further, he gave direction that either within or without the sacred territory war was to be waged with them, that they were to be killed, besieged and laid in wait for 'wheresoever found.' He ordains, however, that if they repent and pay the legal alms they are to be dismissed freely; but as regards 'those unto whom the Scriptures have been delivered (Jews and Christians, etc.) they are to be fought against until they pay tribute by right of subjection and are reduced low.' "—*Islam*, p. 178.

Medina, waylaid a merchant caravan bound for Mecca and plundered it. That day the Moslem tiger had its first taste of blood, and it has ravaged the earth from then until now. The city of Mecca fell, A. D. 630, before an army of ten thousand led by Mohammed in person; the three hundred and sixty-five idols of the Kaaba were cast down, and from the summit of that venerable shrine Allah was proclaimed the only God. Thenceforth the future of the new religion was assured. From every quarter the sheiks of the Ishmaelitic tribes came flocking to the standard of Islam.

The Prophet's Death.—The prophet died A. D. 632.[1] The 12th of Rabi (corresponding to our June 8th) is observed as a triple anniversary, marking his birth, hejira and death. At his grave the following prayer was offered by Abu-bekr: "Peace be unto thee, O prophet of God, and the mercy of the Lord and his blessing! We bear witness that the prophet of the Lord hath delivered the message revealed to him, hath fought for the true religion until God crowned it with

---

[1] "About the 8th of June, 632, he had regained sufficient strength to make a final visit to the mosque. Viewing with joy the devotion of his followers, who on the news of his illness had assembled in crowds, he proclaimed that he had made lawful to them only what God had approved; that each one of them must work out his own acceptance with God, inasmuch as he himself had no power to save them; and, after discharging some small claims, he returned exhausted and fainting to Ayesha's room. With his head on her lap he prayed for assistance in his last agonies and for admission to the companionship of God. Ayesha tried in every way to soothe the sufferings of his last moments. Ejaculatory words at intervals escaped his lips: 'Eternity of Paradise,' 'Pardon,' 'The glorious associates on high,' and then all was still. The prophet of Mecca was dead."—*Islam*, p. 184.

victory, hath fulfilled the injunction to worship the Only One, hath drawn us unto himself and been kind and tender-hearted toward all the faithful, hath sought no recompense for declaring the true faith, and hath not sold it for a price at any time. Amen! amen!"[1]

Conquest.—The prophet was dead, but his work of conquest was not suspended. His sharp sword still flashed in the air. The Arab tribes, previously at war with each other, now rallied and went forth unitedly to overcome the world. Led on by the indomitable Khaled, "the Sword of God," they pushed their way northward over Syria, entered Africa and possessed themselves of the countries lying along the Mediterranean; crossed into Europe, where they subjugated Spain and a considerable portion of France; driven

[1] "Had he no relentings at the visible approach of the end? Was he to go to the grave untouched by all the calamities he had brought upon mankind, the blood he had shed, the multitudes he had beguiled? He had no touch of remorse for any of these things; rather, he continued firmer in his course than ever—seemed more persuaded of the genuineness of his mission and uttered prophecies of the universal extension of his faith. 'When the angels ask thee who thou art,' he said as the body of his son was lowered into the tomb, 'say, God is my Lord, the Prophet of God was my father, and my faith was Islam.' Islam continued his own faith till the last. He tottered to the mosque where Abu-bekr was engaged in leading the prayers of the congregation, and addressed the people for the last time. 'Everything happens,' he said, 'according to the will of God, and has its appointed time, which is not to be hastened or avoided. My last command to you is that you remain united; that you love, honor and uphold each other; that you exhort each other to faith and constancy in belief and to the performance of pious deeds: by these alone men prosper; all else leads to destruction.' A few days after this there were grief and lamentation all over the faithful lands."—WHITE'S *Eighteen Christian Centuries*, p. 159.

thence by Charles Martel, who smote them hip and thigh at the battle of Poictiers, A. D. 732, they faced about and swept over Persia and Afghanistan; moved on into China, where there are at present four millions of Moslems; and, advancing upon the territory of the Greeks, raised the Crescent over the towers of Constantinople; thence they renewed from the East their attempt upon Europe, from which they were finally driven back by Sobieski, who overwhelmed them in a bloody engagement under the walls of Vienna, A. D. 1683.

The territory of Islam extends to-day "from the Pacific Ocean at Peking to the Atlantic in Sierra Leone, over one hundred and twenty degrees of longitude, embracing one hundred and seventy-five millions of people."

The name "Islam," by which this religion of Mohammed is characterized, is from a root signifying "to be at rest." The name means therefore submission to the divine will.

I. *The Sacred Books.*—The Mohammedans say there are four foundations of the faith—namely:

1. The Koran, or Scriptures of God.

2. Hadith, or Traditional Sayings of Mohammed. These are regarded by the great Sunni sect as having no less authority than the Koran itself.

3. The Ijma, or Consensus of the Fathers, held to be final authority in questions not definitely settled by the Koran and traditions.

4. The Quias, or Reasonings of the Learned, a text-book for Mohammedan schools.

The Koran.—Of these foundations it will be necessary to consider only the Koran. This is believed to be something more than an inspired book—nothing less indeed than the uncreated and eternal word of God. There have been other revelations, but this is held to contain the sum and substance of them all. The original text, known as "the mother of the Book," is said to have been in heaven from the beginning; in fullness of time it was revealed to Mohammed by a process of "handing down" called *tanzil*, and was recorded by his disciples on palm-leaves, white stones, leather, the shoulder-blades of sheep and camels and the breasts or memories of men. A year after the prophet's death the various portions of the book thus "handed down" were collected and published by the freedman Zaid. It is wholly in Arabic, and curses are invoked upon the impious wretch who shall presume to translate it.

Its Contents.—The Koran is not quite as large as our New Testament. It is made up of visions, legends, plagiarized and distorted Bible-stories,[1] apocryphal tra-

[1] "It cannot be doubted that Mohammed found opportunity for prosecuting his study of the Jewish histories, for he reproduces the minute details of the stories of Moses (Surah xxviii.), of Joseph (Surah xii.) and of others, though all are more or less mixed up with legends and apocryphal additions of his own. In his treatment of the Scriptures he shows no comprehensive grasp of Old-Testament teaching; his knowledge is purely superficial, touching only the outside shell of facts, and these are often distorted and strained to suit his own purposes, and abound in fanciful and incongruous details and fables. Thus he tells the story of the 'Seven Sleepers,' dormant in the cave for three hundred and nine years, to illustrate God's care of those who avoid idolatry (Surah xviii.); the golden calf in the wilderness is made to low

ditions, dogmas, moral maxims and civil laws. These are divided into one hundred and fourteen chapters, called "surahs," with such titles as "The Cow," "Thunder" and the like. Each surah begins with the words, "In the name of the merciful and compassionate God."[1]

(Surah xx.); the children of Israel are seduced to idolatry by a Samaritan; Joseph is stated to have been sorely tempted by the 'Egyptian's wife,' and the women of Egypt cut themselves for the love of his beauty (Surah xii.); Joseph satisfies his father that he is still alive in Egypt by sending him an inner garment, the smell of which Jacob recognizes and is by it cured of his blindness; the odor of the vest is borne on the air to the aged patriarch from Egypt to Canaan; the people of the 'City near the Sea' are changed into apes for fishing on the Sabbath (Surah iii.); Abraham, for speaking against idolatry practiced round him, is cast into a burning pile, but God makes the fire cold (Surah xxi. 69); the winds are said to have been subject to Solomon and to have run at his command; the latter asserts himself to have been taught the language of birds (Surah xxvii.), and talks with a lapwing, which expresses its belief in the unity of God; a terrible genius (in orig. *Efreet*) brings to Solomon, in the twinkling of an eye, the queen of Sheba's throne; Job strikes with his feet and a fountain springs up as a liniment for his sores; he is also ordered to beat his wife with rods."—*Islam*, p. 136.

[1] "The Koran in its philosophy is incomparably inferior to the writings of Chakia Mouni, the founder of Buddhism; in its science it is absolutely worthless. On speculative or doubtful things it is copious enough, but in the exact, where a test can be applied to it, it totally fails. Its astronomy, cosmogony, physiology are so puerile as to invite our mirth if the occasion did not forbid. They belong to the old times of the world, the morning of human knowledge. The earth is firmly balanced in its seat by the weight of the mountains; the sky is supported over it like a dome, and we are instructed in the wisdom and power of God by being told to find a crack in it if we can. Ranged in stories seven in number are the heavens, the highest being the habitation of God, whose throne—for the Koran does not reject Assyrian ideas—is sustained by winged animal forms. The shooting stars are pieces of red-hot stone thrown by angels at impure spirits when they approach too closely. Of God the Koran is full of praise, setting forth, often in

Its Literary Character.—The book is written in poetic form, or, to speak more accurately, in rhymed prose. The prophet has an exalted opinion of poetry.

> "Beneath God's throne a dazzling treasure lies,
> Whose opening key is but the poet's tongue;
> Without that key the wondrous hoard's supplies
> Could ne'er be brought on earth to old and young."

There is a wide difference of opinion as to the literary character of the Koran, some Oriental scholars regarding it as a model of excellence, while others (as Professor Nöldeke—see *Encyclopædia Britannica*, under "Mohammedanism"), deem it a "loose," "verbose," "awkward," "slovenly" and altogether inartistic book.

One of its most beautiful chapters is the "Fatiha," or preface, which is rendered by Burton as follows:

> "In the name of Allah the Merciful, the Compassionate!
> Praise be to Allah, who the three worlds made,
> The Merciful, the Compassionate!
> The King of the Day of Fate!

not unworthy imagery, his majesty. Though it bitterly denounces those who give him any equals, and assures them that their sin will never be forgiven—that in the judgment-day they must answer the fearful question, 'Where are my companions about whom ye disputed?'—though it inculcates an absolute dependence on the mercy of God, and denounces as criminals all those who make a merchandise of religion—its ideas of the Deity are altogether anthropomorphic. God is only a gigantic man living in a paradise. In this respect, though exceptional passages might be cited, the reader rises from a perusal of the one hundred and fourteen chapters of the Koran with a final impression that they have given him low and unworthy thoughts; nor is it surprising that one of the Mohammedan sects reads it in such a way as to find no difficulty in asserting that 'from the crown of the head to the breast God is hollow, and from the breast downward he is solid; that he has curled black hair, and roars like a lion at every watch of the night.'"—DRAPER'S *Intellectual Development of Europe*, i. 342.

Thee alone do we worship and of thee alone do we ask aid.
Guide us to the path that is straight—
The path of those to whom thy love is great,
Not those on whom is hate,
Nor those that deviate. Amen."

The second surah, called "The Verse of the Throne," is regarded by the Moslems with peculiar reverence, and is inscribed on the walls of mosques and worn as an amulet upon the breast. It is as follows: "God, there is no God but He, the Living, the Self-subsistent. Slumber takes him not, nor sleep. He is what is in the heavens and what is in the earth. Who is it that intercedes with him save by his permission? He knows what is before them and what is behind them, and they comprehend not aught of his knowledge but of what he pleases. His throne extends over the heavens and the earth, and it tires him not to guard them both, for he is high and grand."[1]

One of the most impressive surahs is the hundred and first, entitled "The Striking," and having reference to the last judgment: "In that day we shall be like moths scattered abroad, and the mountains shall become like carded wool of various colors driven by the wind. Moreover, he whose balance shall be heavy with good works shall lead a pleasing life, but as to him whose balance shall be light, his dwelling shall be in the pit of hell. It is a burning fire."[2]

Its Authority.—The authority of the Koran is held to be final and absolute in questions pertaining not only to theology, but also to science, philosophy and

[1] LEES. [2] STOBART.

civil government. The book must not be touched with unwashen hands, and the eyes of an unbeliever must never gaze upon it. The Moslem living reveres it as a veritable fetich, and dying clasps it to his bosom as a passport to the regions of the blest.

> "I saw a Moslem work upon his shroud alone
>   With earnest care, even as the silkworms weave their own.
>
> "In his illness it always near his bedside lay,
>   And he wrote Koran-verses on it night and day.
>
> "When with that sacred script it was filled from side to side,
>   He wrapped it round his body and in calmness died.
>
> "In that protecting robe, now buried in the ground,
>   Still may he know the peace he in its writing found." [1]

II. *Theology.—The Creed, or " Kalima."*—The most succinct statement of the Mohammedan belief is found in the *Kalima*, which may be said to correspond to our "Apostles' Creed." It is as follows: *La Ilah illah Allah; wa Muhammad Rusoul Allah*—"There is no god but God, and Mohammed is his prophet." The two propositions of this creed are co-ordinate and equally binding on the Moslem mind and conscience. Dr. Lees says of this Kalima, "It expresses both the power and feebleness of Islam." Gibbon says, "It asserts an eternal truth and an eternal lie."

1. "*The Eternal Truth.*"—"There is no god but God." Here is the truth of truths. Thomas Carlyle, contemplating this article of the Mohammedan faith, was moved to say, "We call Mohammed's creed a kind of Christianity." Herein he found the strength of the

[1] ALGER.

whole system: "Out of all that rubbish of Arab idolatries, argumentative theologies, traditions, rumors and hypotheses of Greeks and Jews with their idle wire-drawings, this wild man of the desert with his wild sincere heart, earnest as death and life, with his great flashing natural eyesight, had seen into the kernel of the matter. Idolatry is nothing: 'These wooden idols of yours, ye rub them with oil and wax, and the flies stick on them; these are wood, I tell you! They can do nothing for you. They are an impotent, blasphemous pretence; a horror and abomination, if ye knew them. God alone is; God alone has power; he made us, he can kill us and keep us alive; *Allah akbar*, God is great! Understand that his will is the best for you; that howsoever sore to flesh and blood, you will find it the wisest, best; you are bound to take it so; in this world and the next you have nothing else that you can do.'"

Is it a Kind of Christianity?—But, Carlyle to the contrary, Mohammedanism is not "a kind of Christianity," rather it is as far as possible from it. The two cardinal doctrines of the Christian religion are the incarnation and the atonement. Both of these are distinctly contradicted in the Koran. In the most precious of its surahs, said to be of more value than all the remainder of the book, occurs this statement:

> "Say there is one God alone?
> God the eternal.
> He begetteth not, is not begotten,
> And there is none like unto him."

It is obvious from this that the monotheism of Islam

is not Christian monotheism. The prophet has indeed no conception of our doctrine of the tripersonal One. He looked on the Trinity as tritheism. He seems to have believed that the three persons of the Christian's Trinity were God, Jesus and the Virgin Mary.[1] He therefore pronounced against it: "They misbelieve who say, 'Verily, God is the third of this,' for there is no God but one; and if they do not desist from what they say, there shall touch those who misbelieve among them grievous woe." Again: "The Christians say, 'Messiah is the Son of God.' They take their doctors and monks for lords. God fight them, how they lie! They are bidden to worship but one God; and there is no God but He." And again: "The Messiah, Jesus, the son of Mary, is but the apostle of God, and the word of God which he cast into Mary and a Spirit from God. Believe, then, in God and his apostles, and say not 'Three.' Have done! it were better for you. God is only one." In Surah xix., relating to the birth of Jesus, it is said that when Mary's kindred charged her with incontinence the child upon her arm defended her saying, "Verily, I am the servant of God. He hath given me the book of the gospel and hath appointed me a prophet. And he hath made me blessed and dutiful toward my mother. This is Jesus, the son of Mary, the word of truth concerning whom they doubt. It is not meet for God that he should have any son. God forbid!"

---

[1] DR. HENRY H. JESSUP: "There is reason to suppose that Mohammed inferred from the Mariolatry prevalent in his time that the Trinity consisted of the Father, the Son and the Virgin Mary."

In like manner—as we shall see more particularly farther on—the doctrine of the atonement as held by Christians is denied by Mohammed in most explicit terms. We affirm, therefore, that Mohammedanism as a system of belief has nothing whatever in common with the distinctive creed of the Christian religion. The claim of fellowship which is sometimes made seems, therefore, a trifle gratuitous on the part of persons whom the Mohammedans themselves are wont to stigmatize as "infidels" and "Christian dogs."

Opposed to Idolatry.—The monotheism of Islam is opposed to every form of idolatry. It will be remembered that the first act of the prophet on entering Mecca in triumph was to overthrow the images in the Kaaba.[1] As long as he lived the driver of Khadijah's caravans was beating down as with his camels' hoofs the "abominations" of the sons of Ishmael. "The belief," says Maurice, "that nothing in the earth, nothing in the heavens, not even light, is a symbol of God —that not even man himself can be looked upon in any other character than as a minister of the one Supreme Being,—evidently inspires every enterprise. In

[1] "One day, whilst sitting by the Kaaba, he uttered in the hearing of his opponents words of compromise regarding their gods Al-Lat and Al-Ozza and Manah, that 'their intercession might be hoped for with God.' These words were listened to with surprise by the idolaters who were present, and a reconciliation seemed possible; but within a few days the concession he had made was by the prophet attributed to a suggestion of the Evil One, was uncompromisingly withdrawn and the idol-worship condemned and reprobated, thus: 'What think ye of Al-Lat and Al-Ozza and Manah, that other third goddess? They are no other than empty names, which ye and your fathers have named goddesses' (Surah liii.)."—*Islam*, p. 80.

the strength of it they destroy temples, idols and priests, plunder cities, make slaves of their inhabitants, turn their children into soldiers of the Crescent."[1] The God of Islam is enthroned in the supreme place, above all principalities and powers of earth and heaven—an awful Presence abiding solitary and alone. Only God is great!

> "A King, who by the public mouth was named the Great,
> Was on his station's frailty wont to meditate.
>
> "Against all arrogance as a protecting gate
> This phrase he oft repeated: *Only God is great.*
>
> "Those words he bade them on the palace-wall ingrain,
> Whose fragrant columns, crumbling, to this day remain.
>
> "City and realm are sunk, but travelers relate
> You still may read that motto: *Only God is great.*"

The Absolute Will.—The God of Islam is the apotheosis of pure Will. There is no love or true mercy or sympathy in him. The Mohammedan system is called by Palgrave "a pantheism of force." The Koran gives ninety-nine names of God, but "Father" is not among them. The very closest relation of the believer with God is expressed in the word *islam*, or submission to his will. "Verily," said the prophet, "there is none

[1] "It was a mercy of God," continues the same writer, "that such a witness, however bare of other suppoiting principles, however surrounded by confusions, should have been borne to his name, when his creatures were ready, practically, to forget it. The first Mohammedan conquest, the continued dominion, prove the assertion 'God is' to be no dry proposition, but one which is capable of exercising a mastery over the rudest tribes, of giving them an order, of making them victorious over all the civilization and all the religion which has not this principle for its basis."

in heaven or on earth but shall approach the God of mercy as a slave." How far, how infinitely far, removed is this from the filial intimacy of those who by the spirit of adoption are admitted into the glorious liberty of the children of God! The God of the Moslems, as Palgrave observes,[1] "is one in the totality of omnipotent and omnipresent action which acknowledges no rule, standard or limits, save one sole and absolute will. He himself, sterile in his inaccessible height, neither loving nor enjoying aught save his own and self-measured decree, without son, companion or councilor, is no less barren for himself than for his creatures; and his own barrenness and lone egoism in himself is the cause and rule of his indifferent and unregarding despotism around."

> "One God the Arabian prophet preached to man;
> One God the Crescent still
> Adores through many a realm of mighty span—
> A God of power and will—
>
> "A God that, shrouded in his lonely light,
> Rests utterly apart
> From all the vast creations of his might,
> From nature, man and art;
>
> "A power that at his pleasure doth create,
> To save or to destroy;
> And to eternal pain predestinate,
> As to eternal joy."[2]

Central Thought: Kismet.—The Moslem's belief in

[1] Quoted by DR. LEES, in *The Faiths of the World*.
[2] "The Mohammedans accept the doctrine of God's absolute predestinating decree, both for good and evil, for man's obedience and disobedience, for his future happiness and misery, and also that these

Fate grows out of his conception of God. All things are controlled by an infinite Will. There is no changing the supreme purpose concerning us. What is to be must be. Prosperity and adversity alike are met with a stolid front: "*Kismet*—it is the divine will." All things that come to pass were written on stone tablets from the beginning. The day of a man's death is inscribed on his forehead, and he can do nothing to avert or postpone it. Hence the desperate valor of Moslems on the battle-field.

> "Fate is a hand. It lays two fingers on the eyes,
> Two on the ears, one on the mouth, and silent cries,
> 'Be ever still!' Then down in endless sleep man lies."

This Mohammedan doctrine of predestination makes God an unreasoning and hateful autocrat and man an impotent creature in his terrible grip. "When God resolved to create the human race he took into his hands a mass of earth, the same whence all mankind were to be formed, and in which they after a manner pre-existed; and, having then divided the clod into two equal portions, he threw the one half into hell, saying, 'These to eternal fire, and I care not!' and projected the other half into heaven, adding, 'And these to Paradise, and I care not!'" On this Palgrave eternal and immutable decrees cannot by any wisdom or foresight be avoided. Carried to its extreme, this doctrine saps the foundation of free will, renders men blind to the teaching of the past, apathetic in the present and indifferent to the future. It makes prayer an empty form, destroying as it does all dependence upon an overruling Providence, and, pitiless as the grave, takes away alike the power of avoiding sin and of escaping its punishment—making even the power and mercy of the Almighty subject to the fiat of an inexorable Fate."—*Islam*, p. 97.

says : " In a word, he burns one individual through all eternity amid red-hot chains and seas of molten fire, and seats another in the plenary enjoyment of an everlasting brothel, between forty celestial concubines, just and equally for his own good pleasure and because he wills it." This may be called, literally, predestination with a vengeance.

2. "*The Great Lie.*"—The second article of the Islamic creed is, " Mohammed is God's prophet." This is the sublime falsehood for which holy wars without number have been waged—a falsehood for which there is no ground nor extenuation whatever in the life and character of Mohammed—a falsehood which, like a granite pillar,[1] has upheld Islam for thirteen centuries, only to crumble at length under the silent influence of clearer light, leaving that imposing fabric to suffer the common fate of all spurious systems of religion.

Sin.—In addition to the two fundamental doctrines of the Kalima already mentioned, there are other important tenets. The Moslems believe in sin; not, however, in that kind of sin which is described as "any want of conformity unto or transgression of the law of God." The conviction of sin felt by a Moham-

[1] " It is, without doubt, one of the most noticeable circumstances in the history of his religion that his own person should have been so much bound up with it; that every caliph or sultan who has reigned over any tribe of his followers should have reigned in his name; that the recollection of a man should have so much more power than even the book which Mussulmans regard with such profound reverence; that the honor of a human chieftain should so markedly distinguish a religion which looks upon man as separated by an immeasurable distance from the object of his worship."—F. D. MAURICE, in *Religions of the World*, p. 20.

medan is due to a consciousness of having come short of his complement of meritorious observances. He has not cried *Allah il Allah* an hundred times since daybreak, as he should have done, or he has failed to make the requisite number of prostrations, or he has not cursed the infidel with sufficient gusto.

"*What shall I Do to be Saved?*"—The only possibility of deliverance from the dire consequences of such shortcoming is in doing better for the future.[1] The Moslem is for ever "turning over a new leaf." There is no room in his religion for any such thing as forgiveness, though the prophet in his last hours cried out for it: "Allah! grant me pardon—pardon and an eternity in Paradise!" The Christian doctrine of redemption is wholly repudiated, and there is no other

---

[1] "The joys of Paradise are to be obtained only by the rigid performance of all the observances of the faith; and the value of the believer's works are to be weighed by a hard taskmaster rather than a loving Father, the dread of whose displeasure, more than the smile of whose favor, is to be the motive or principle of action."—*Islam*, p. 191.

"The Koran repudiates the idea of any vicarious sacrifice for sin, teaches expressly that each soul must account for itself to God, and, denying the truth of Christian redemption, lays upon each individual the task of atoning for his own sin, of securing pardon and of rendering himself meet for admission to Paradise. Self-righteousness, the merit of good works and of a rigid attention to the prescribed formularies and ceremonies of their faith, with God's mercy to supply any deficiency,—these constitute the scheme of salvation prescribed in Islam."—*Ibid.*, p. 232.

"In proposing self-righteousness as the means of salvation Islam is admirably adapted to flatter the pride of man; and in this particular especially is it antagonistic to Christianity, which, excluding the merit of man's works, calls for inward holiness, not outside form, and summons the humble, contrite sinner in deep abasement to the foot of the cross as his only hope of pardon, his only source of peace."—*Ibid.*, p. 237.

rational ground of forgiveness. The Moslem is left, of a truth, to work out his own salvation with a great fear and trembling, because he works without God. His own hand or none must save his guilty soul from the flaming pit.

Death.—At death soul and body are buried together. A few hours later the grave is visited by two angels, who cause the deceased to sit up and answer for himself. If he can sincerely avow belief in the Kalima, he is allowed to rest in peace; otherwise, he is beaten and turned over to the mercy of dragons until the last day.

Resurrection.—The resurrection is sure. It will occur at the sounding of the trumpet of the angel Israfil. Out of their graves everywhere the dead, great and small, shall then come to judgment.[1]

---

[1] " There is, however, much diversity of opinion as to the precise disposal of the soul before the judgment-day: some think that it hovers near the grave; some, that it sinks into the well Zem-Zem; some, that it retires into the trumpet of the Angel of the Resurrection; the difficulty apparently being that any final disposal before the day of judgment would be anticipatory of that great event, if, indeed, it would not render it needless. As to the resurrection, some believe it to be merely spiritual, others corporeal, the latter asserting that the os coccygis, or last bone of the spinal column, will serve, as it were, as a germ, and that, vivified by a rain of forty days, the body will sprout from it. Among the signs of the approaching resurrection will be the rising of the sun in the west. It will be ushered in by three blasts of a trumpet: the first, known as the blast of consternation, will shake the earth to its centre and extinguish the sun and stars; the second, the blast of extermination, will annihilate all material things except Paradise, hell and the throne of God; forty years subsequently the angel Israfil will sound the blast of resurrection. From his trumpet there will be blown forth the countless myriads of souls who have taken refuge

Judgment.—One of the most striking surahs of the Koran, called "The Folding Up," thus pictures the events of the dreadful last day:

therein or lain concealed. The day of judgment has now come. The Koran contradicts itself as to the length of this day, in one place making it a thousand, in another fifty thousand, years. Most Mohammedans incline to adopt the longer period, since angels, genii, men and animals have to be tried. As to men, they will rise in their natural state, but naked—white-winged camels with saddles of gold awaiting the saved. When the partition is made the wicked will be oppressed with an intolerable heat, caused by the sun, which, having been called into existence again, will approach within a mile, provoking a sweat to issue from them, and this, according to their demerits, will immerse them from the ankles to the mouth; but the righteous will be screened by the shadow of the throne of God. The Judge will be seated in the clouds, the books open before him, and everything in its turn will be called on to account for its deeds. For greater despatch, the angel Gabriel will hold forth his balance, one scale of which hangs over Paradise and one over hell. In these all works are weighed. As soon as the sentence is delivered, the assembly in a long file will pass over the bridge Al-Sirat. It is as sharp as the edge of a sword and laid over the mouth of hell. Mohammed and his followers will successfully pass the perilous ordeal, but the sinners, giddy with terror, will drop into the place of torment. The blessed will receive their first taste of happiness at a pond which is supplied by silver pipes from the river Al-Cawthor. The soil of Paradise is of musk. Its rivers tranquilly flow over pebbles of rubies and emeralds. From tents of hollow pearls the houris, or girls of Paradise, will come forth, attended by troops of beautiful boys. Each saint will have eighty thousand servants and seventy-two girls. To these some of the more merciful Mussulmans add the wives they have had upon earth, but the grimly orthodox assert that hell is already nearly filled with women. How can it be otherwise, since they are not permitted to pray in a mosque upon earth? I have not space to describe the silk brocades, the green clothing, the soft carpets, the banquets, the perpetual music and songs. From the glorified body all impurities will escape, not as they did during life, but in a fragrant perspiration of camphor and musk."—DRAPER'S *Intellectual Development of Europe*, vol. i. p. 345.

"When the sun shall be folded up,
And the stars shall fall;
When the mountains shall be moved,
And the she-camels shall be left uncared for,
And the wild beasts shall be huddled together;
When the seas shall boil;
When the souls and bodies of the dead shall be reunited,
And the leaves of the Book shall be unrolled;
When the heavens shall be stripped away like a skin,
And hell shall be made to blaze,
And Paradise shall be brought near;—
Then every soul shall know what it has done."

On that day all souls will be required to pass over the bridge Sirat, which is sharper than a sword's edge and finer than a hair. " In passing over it the feet of the infidel will slip and he will fall into hell-fire, where his feet will be shod with shoes of fire, the fever of which will make his skull boil like a cauldron; but the feet of the Moslem will be firm and will carry him safely to Paradise, where palaces of marble full of delights, amid groves and gardens, await his coming."

Heaven.—The heaven of Islam is a place of eight divisions, as follows: (1) The Garden of Eternity, (2) The Abode of Peace, (3) The Abode of Rest, (4) The Garden of Eden, (5) The Garden of Refuge, (6) The Garden of Delight, (7) The Garden of the Most High, (8) The Garden of Paradise. All these are places of innumerable sensual joys—shadowy groves, fountains, fruits "hanging low so as to be easily gathered," and wives *ad libitum.*

Hell.—The Mohammedan hell has seven apartments, to wit: (1) Gehenum, for Moslems on their way heavenward; (2) Laswa, full of furious flames, for Christians;

(3) Hutama, a similar place for Jews; (4) Sahir, a place of torment for Sabians; (5) Sagar, for Magians, (6) Gahim, a red-hot furnace for idolaters; and (7) Hawia, a bottomless pit for hypocrites. All these are chambers of inexpressible pain. "Verily," says the Koran, "those who misbelieve in our signs we will broil with fire; whenever their skins are well done, then we will change them for other skins, that they may taste the torment. Verily, God is glorious and wise."

El-Aaraf.—Between heaven and hell there is an intermediate place, called El-Aaraf, which is simply a partition-wall whereon sit—so that they may look both ways—the souls of mortals who, like Rob Roy, are "o'er good for banning and o'er bad for blessing."

Spirits.—The upper and nether regions are peopled with angels. The four chiefest of the blessed ones are Gabriel, the messenger of revelation; Michael, the friend of the Jews; Azrael, the angel of death; and Israfeel, the angel of resurrection. The archangel of the region of darkness is Eblis, whose business is "to tempt man to disobedience." Aside from these, the earth is peopled with genii, who play all manner of pranks among the living and haunt the cities of the dead.

III. *Ethics.*—As the future happiness of the Moslem depends wholly on the performance of certain duties, it is important to know what those duties are. To begin with: they have little or no connection with the great principles which are expressed in the moral law. A disciple of Mohammed may be a thief, a liar, a sensualist and a murderer, and still be a very good Mo-

hammedan. The sum-total of duty is a strict observance of the ritual. Dr. Henry H. Jessup says: "One who fulfills the ritual in whole or in part is a good Moslem, though not to be believed under oath. Dr. Eli Smith of Beirut was said by an Arab to be a very holy man, 'But, poor man! he had no religion;' that is, no observance of an outward ritual. The good works of Islam are of the lips, the hand and outward bodily act, having no connection with holiness of life. An Arab highway-robber and murderer was once brought for trial before a Mohammedan pasha, when the pasha stepped down and kissed his hand, as the culprit was a dervish or holy man who had been on several pilgrimages to Mecca and had been known to repeat the name Allah more times than any other man."

The Five Pillars.—The Five Pillars of Practice, called *Deen*, are as follows: (1) Repeating the creed, or Kalima. (2) Observing the five stated periods of prayer—viz. before sunrise, just after mid-day, before sunset, after sunset and at nightfall. At these periods the call is heard from all the minarets: "*Allah il Allah! God is great! I bear witness that there is no god but God! I bear witness that Mohammed is the prophet of God! God is great! There is no other god but God!*"[1]

[1] "THE CALL TO EVENING PRAYER.

"One silver crescent in the twilight sky is hanging,
    Another tips the solemn dome of yonder mosque;
And now the muezzin's call is heard, sonorous clanging,
    Through thronged bazaar, concealed hareem and cool kiosk:
'In the Prophet's name, God is God, and there is no other.'
On roofs, in streets, alone or close beside his brother,

On hearing that cry the people, wherever they may be, perform their oblations with water or sand, prostrate themselves and silently go through their devotional ritual. Prayer is called "the key of Paradise." It consists chiefly in repeating the hundred names and other magical portions of scripture. The most meritorious act of devotion is the repetition of Al-Fatiha, the opening surah of the Koran. (3) Keeping the thirty days' fast of Ramadan. During this holy month no Moslem is allowed to eat, drink, or smoke from dawn, when there is light enough to distinguish between a black and a white thread, until sunset. During the nights, however, he may do pretty much as he pleases. The fast terminates with the festival of Eed-al-Fitr, or breakfast, which is celebrated with great rejoicing. (4) Performing the legal alms. The common saying is, " Prayer carries us halfway to God, fasting brings us to his door, but alms admit us." The system of almsgiving, aside from relieving the necessities of the poor,[1] furnishes the material strength of the Mos-

> Each Moslem kneels, his forehead turned toward Mecca's shrine,
> And all the world forgotten in one thought divine."
> ALGER'S *Oriental Poetry*, p. 137.

[1] *A Sermon on Charity*, said to have been preached by Mohammed: "When God made the earth it shook to and fro till he put mountains on it to keep it firm. Then the angels asked, 'O God, is there anything in thy creation stronger than these mountains?' And God replied, 'Iron is stronger than the mountains, for it breaks them.'—'And is there anything in thy creation stronger than iron?'—'Yes, fire is stronger than iron, for it melts it.'—'Is there anything stronger than fire?'—'Yes, water, for it quenches fire.'—'Is there anything stronger than water?'—'Yes, wind, for it puts water in motion.'—'O our Sustainer, is there anything in thy creation stronger than wind?'—'Yes, a

lem government. (5) The pilgrimage to Mecca.[1] This
is required of all believers: if they would make sure

good man giving alms: if he give it with his right hand and conceal it
from his left, he overcomes all things. Every good act is charity: your
smiling in your brother's face, your putting a wanderer in the right
road, your giving water to the thirsty, is charity; exhortation to another
to do right is charity. A man's true wealth hereafter is the good he
has done in this world to his fellow-men. When he dies people will
ask, What property has he left behind him? But the angels will ask,
What good deeds has he sent before him.'"

[1] The following vivid description of the departure for Mecca is by
REV. T. P. HUGHES in *The Missionary Gleaner:* "The *mahmal* is a
velvet canopy which the pilgrims convey to and from Mecca. It is a
square frame of wood with a pyramidal top, with a rich covering of embroidered velvet, surmounted with silver balls and crescents. As far as
I could ascertain, the canopy was empty, it being merely carried with
the pilgrims as an emblem of royalty. The origin of the ceremony is
said by some to be as follows:

"'Shegur-ud-durr, a beautiful Turkish female slave, who became the
wife of Sultan Salah, on the death of his son caused herself to be proclaimed queen of Egypt, and performed the pilgrimage in a magnificent
hodaq, or covered litter, borne on a camel. For several successive years
the empty *hodaq* was sent with the caravan of pilgrims for the sake of
state. Hence, succeeding princes of Egypt sent with each year's pilgrimage a kind of *hodaq* (which received the name of *mahmal*) as an
emblem of royalty, and the kings of other countries followed their
example.'

"At seven o'clock in the morning all the leading officers of state
assembled in a portico erected below the citadel to receive the two
Egyptian princes, a vacant seat being left for the viceroy. The officers
were all dressed in French uniform with the usual Turkish fez cap—the
only persons in turbans being two Mohammedan moulvies. The roads
were lined with troops, and as the royal party arrived the bands struck
up the Egyptian national air. There were a number of European visitors, including the American ambassador from Berlin, one English peer
and an English member of Parliament.

"After the arrival of the princes there was a pause in the ceremonial,
and the uninitiated in Egyptian etiquette were on the tiptoe of expectation. Were they waiting for the khedive? After a few minutes a car-

of Paradise, they must, at some time during their lives, make the seven circuits of the Kaaba, say their prayers within its confines and kiss the black stone.

Such is the Mohammedan idea of religion. It is purely a ceremonial system. It suggests no such thing as regeneration or other spiritual change, nor any real communion with God. There have, of course, been Moslems who have passed beyond and above the narrow and sordid limits of Islam—who have seen through the fraud and emptiness and have dreamed of better things. Witness the refreshing spirituality of the following by a Sufi poet, entitled "The Religion of the Heart:"

riage drove up in regal state, and there stepped forth an old Mohammedan priest. It was the Sheikh-ul-Islam, the archbishop and lord chancellor of Egypt. Of course royalty must be kept waiting for this representative of orthodox Islam. The whole assembly rose and received the venerable old man with becoming respect, and then the signal was given for the mahmal procession to move on.

"Amidst the din of fifes and drums and the wild Egyptian national air, the shouts of the dervishes, 'Allah! Allah! Allah!' and the tinkling of bells, the canopy, which was borne upon the back of a fine tall camel, approached the sheikh and the royal princes. The procession was headed by a fat, long-haired, brawny fellow (a dervish), almost naked, who incessantly rolled his head to and fro, shouting 'Allah! Allah! Allah!' The mahmal was surrounded by a guard of horsemen, and the people kept running round it, shouting in the most frantic manner. When it came opposite the princes, they, in company with the Sheikh-ul-Islam, approached it with the greatest veneration and touched it, uttering some pious ejaculation. This was done by all the officials; then the procession moved on, and encamped outside the city gate until the next day, when the caravan left to perform the haji, or pilgrimage to Mecca. The merits of it are so great that *every step taken in the direction of the Kaaba* (the great shrine at Mecca) *blots out a sin, and he who dies on his way to Mecca is enrolled on the list of martyrs.*"

"Beats there a heart within that breast of thine?
Then compass reverently its sacred shrine:
For the true spiritual Kaaba is the heart,
And no proud pile of perishable art.
When God ordained the pilgrim rite, that sign
Was meant to lead thy thought to things divine:
A thousand times he treads that round in vain
Who e'en one human heart would idly pain.
Leave wealth behind; bring God thy heart—best light
To guide thy wavering steps through life's dark night.
God spurns the riches of a thousand coffers,
And says, 'My chosen is he his heart who offers.
Nor gold nor silver seek I, but above
All gifts the heart, and buy it with my love;
Yea, one sad, contrite heart, which men despise,
More than my throne and fixed decree I prize.'
Then think not lowly of thy heart, though lowly,
For holy is it, and there dwells the Holy.
God's presence-chamber is the human breast;
Ah, happy he whose heart holds such a guest!"[1]

The fact remains, however, that with the vast majority this system is a dry and empty shell. To the question, "What shall I do to be saved?" the invaria-

[1] From ALGER's *Oriental Poetry*. In the following may be found a similar reference to the spirituality of true worship:

"THE UNWALLED HOUSE OF GOD.

"The holy Nanac on the ground, one day
Reclining, with his feet toward Mecca lay.
A passing Moslem priest, offended, saw,
And, flaming for the honor of his law,
Exclaimed, 'Base infidel, thy prayers repeat!
Toward Allah's house how dar'st thou turn thy feet?'
Before the Moslem's shallow accents died
The pious but indignant Nanac cried,
'And turn them, if thou canst, toward any spot
Wherein the awful House of God is not.'"

ble answer is, Do your duty; that is, Stand by the Five Pillars and submit to the divine will.

IV. *Jurisprudence.*—In this religion we find a combination of the secular and spiritual power. Dr. Jessup says: "It is a politico-religious system. The sultan is the caliph or successor of Mohammed. He is the prophet, priest and king of the Mohammedan world. The laws of the empire are based on the Koran, the decisions of the imams and Mohammedan tradition. In Turkey the imperial army is a religious army, the great national festivals are religious festivals, testimony is a religious act, and Mohammedanism is thus intrenched in the very political and civil organization of the empire." Back of this close wedlock of Church and State we find in the Koran an elaborate legal code.

War against the Infidel.—The first civil injunction of the Koran is aimed at the extermination of the infidel: "When ye encounter the unbelievers, strike off their heads!" This is in marked contrast with the spirit of the gospel of Christ, who said, "Love your enemies, bless them that curse you, do good to them that hate you, and pray for them which despitefully use you and persecute you."[1]

Slavery.—By the Koran law slavery also is made to rest on divine authority. In countries where Islam

[1] "Light and darkness are not more opposed than the loving dictates of the gospel and the vengeful spirit of the Koran, in which hatred and oppression take the place of love and forgiveness of injuries, and the denunciations of the prophet contrast with the voice of the Good Shepherd, which speaks of peace and good-will to all mankind."—*Islam,* p. 238.

prevails it is absolutely impossible that there should be freedom or equality among men.[1]

Polygamy.—Polygamy also is upheld and advocated. The prophet himself practiced it. Frederick D. Maurice says: " Polygamy is no accident of Mohammedanism: a careful consideration of the system will show that it must fall to pieces the moment any reformer shall undertake to remove this characteristic of it." In consequence of the debasement of the marriage relation the condition of woman among the Moslems is wholly lamentable. She is regarded as a lower order of being, unreasoning and incapable of self-control, never the helpmate, but the slave, of man.[2]

[1] "The religion of Islam is an outward form, a hard shell of authority, hollow at heart. It constantly tends to the two antagonistic but related vices of luxury and cruelty. Under the profession of Islam polytheism and idolatry have always prevailed in Arabia. In Turkistan, where slavery is an extremely cruel system, they make slaves of Moslems in defiance of the Koran. One chief being appealed to by Vambery (who traveled as a dervish), replied, ' We buy and sell the Koran itself, which is the holiest thing of all. Why not buy and sell Mussulmans, who are less holy?' "—CLARKE'S *Ten Great Religions*, p. 478.

[2] " It may be well to consider what the teaching of the Koran is on the subject. In the fourth Surah, entitled ' Women,' among various directions regarding their years of orphanage, inheritances, chastity and the forbidden degrees, permission is given to the faithful ' to take two or three or four, and not more,' women as wives, and in addition to these, as concubines, the slave-girls ' which their right hands possess ' (Surah lxx.), that is, purchased or made captive in war. In reality, the number of wives is practically unlimited, as the Koran allows an almost unchecked power of divorce and exchange. The action of the husband, who is expressly stated to be superior to the wife, is nearly uncontrolled. He may repudiate his wives without any assigned reason and without warning—may, if apprehensive of disobedience, rebuke, imprison and strike them (Surah iv.); and against this the dishonored spouse has almost no means of redress. Exposed to the tyranny of her

As somewhat of good is to be found in every religious system, we here discover not a few healthful pre-

husband and treated as a kind of plaything—a being formed for lust and labor, to be capriciously flung aside on the least provocation or in a moment of anger or for mere dislike—she is worse than a slave."—*Islam*, p. 150.

In this connection it will be interesting to note the efficacy of recent missionary work in the zenanas. The following (from the Presbyterian *Foreign Missionary*) is a translation of a Mohammedan proclamation issued in Lahore in 1866:

"MUSSULMANS ON ZENANA MISSIONS.

"We have received a translation of a proclamation that has been issued to the Mussulman population of Lahore. We believe that it is not confined to Lahore, but has also made a stir in Amritsar and Sialkot. It bears remarkable testimony to the efficacy of the work done in zenana schools. It runs as follows:

"'THE SOCIETY FOR THE PROMOTION OF ISLAM.
"'*Education of Women*.
"'In the name of God the merciful and gracious.'
"'O believers, save yourselves and your families from the fires of hell.'
"'O readers, a thing is taking place which deserves your attention, and which you will not find it difficult to check. Females need such education as is necessary to save them from the fires of hell. The Quran and the traditions teach this necessity, and two great philosophers say, "Home is the best school;" but to make it so women must be taught. We are doing nothing, but are trying to destroy our children. Although we are able to teach our own girls, yet wherever you go you find zenana mission-schools filled with our daughters. There is no alley or house where the effect of these schools is not felt. There are few of our women who did not, in their childhood, learn and sing in the presence of their teachers such hymns as "He to Isa, Isa bol" ("Take the name of Jesus"), and few of our girls who have not read the Gospels. They know Christianity and the objections to Islam, and whose faith has not been shaken? The freedom which Christian women possess is influencing all our women. They, being ignorant of the excellencies of their own religion, and being taught that those things in Islam which are really good are not really good, will never esteem their own religion.

cepts touching the well-being of men in their civil and social relations.[1] A strict prohibition is placed upon

"'Umar, one of Mohammed's four bosom friends, was fond of reading the books of Moses and the Gospels, but Mohammed forbade him, saying, "These may lead you in the wrong way." How much more danger, then, is there in our little daughters reading them!

"'There are multitudes of missionaries in the land whose object is to destroy your religion. They see that the condition of a country depends on the condition of the women, and therefore they send women to teach ours to work and read, and at the same time to sow the seeds of hatred to Islam.

"'Christian women teach Mohammedan women that they should have the liberty which they possess, and the Mohammedan teachers in these schools, who are only nominal Mohammedans, by pretending to teach the Quran draw our daughters into these schools, and then teach them the gospel and hymns. For a little while they may teach the Quran, but when the missionary lady comes in they hide it under a mat or throw it into some unclean place, into which if a man had thrown it he might have been sent to prison. And as long as the lady is present they teach Christianity and expose Mohammedism. Can we be pleased with such instruction as this? O believers, why not teach your children Christianity instead of your own religion?

"'How far has this religion influenced our women? So far has the love of liberty extended among our daughters and daughters-in-law that they get into carriages with these teachers, go to the Shalamar garden, bathe in the tank, sit at table and eat, and then make a quantity of tea disappear.'"

[1] "In the midst of all these revelations there occur here and there excellent moral sentiments to which no exception can be taken. Thus the duty of helping the poor, of relieving the needy traveler and of doing justice to the orphan is insisted on. The love and honor due to parents from their children, the performance of covenants and the use of just weights form part of the believer's duty. Liberality is commended, profuseness condemned. The prophet points out how, at the end of the world, our words, our thoughts—nay, the very use of our eyesight—will be brought into account; and he states how desirable it is for the true believer to love God, to pray to him and to walk humbly in his sight (Surah xvii.). On the occurrence of such sentiments in the Koran it may be well to remember that no civilized heathen nation ever

the exaction of usury, another on infanticide, another on gambling and another on the use of intoxicating drink. Thus, while the Mohammedans are in most points an ungodly people, they are, as a rule, free from these particular sins.

V. *Fruits of the System.*—It need scarcely be said that a system which so broadly divorces morality and religion can have but one result—namely, utter moral and spiritual demoralization. The author of *Gesta Christi* says: "In fact, the many false and evil elements of Mohammedanism have made it one of the curses of mankind. It has spread abroad the spirit of cruelty and lust, and under it are found the unnatural vices. It could not rise above its source. It illustrated or exaggerated everywhere the vices of its leader. It left behind it, whether in Spain, Sicily, Egypt or Bagdad, anarchy, corruption and horrible social evils."[1]

existed in which just, beautiful and sublime sentiments were not known and recorded in its sacred books."—*Islam*, p. 138.

[1] *L'Afrique* has answered the apologists of Islam in a strain which we have thought quite worthy of a translation. It says: "It cannot be denied that the Mohammedan religion has had the effect of improving in some measure the usages and customs of its negro proselytes. Thus, the prohibition of strong drink has been salutary; they have become neater, more respectable and more industrious. It could not be otherwise, for contact with a more civilized people—and such we consider the Arabs to be—would naturally produce these effects. The Arabs have also communicated a desire for trade to the inhabitants of Soudan, developing commercial activity, which the people who are still heathen do not possess. On the other hand, has the Mohammedan religion abolished the many practices so offensive and revolting to morality? Has it cured that sanguinary plague of Africa, the slave-trade? Has it caused a cessation of the continual wars between state and

Sensuality.—The universal vice of the Moslems is sensuality. In this they are encouraged by their book, which distinctly says, "Your wife is your field," and by the example of their prophet, who took to himself eleven wives and numberless concubines.[1] The institu-

state? Does it interdict polygamy? Does it permit the entrance of foreigners and of the torch of Christianity? We are forced to answer all these questions in the negative. Can a good influence be exercised by a people who consider the negro race simply as so much prey and a source of profit—a people who practice slavery openly, and whose national traits are those of the most eager and the most fierce hunters of men? All travelers agree in asserting the contrary."

The following words of King Mtesa, quoted by H. M. Stanley, show also the estimate made of the Mohammedan character by a discerning native: "The Arabs come here for ivory and slaves, and we have seen that they do not always speak the truth, and that they buy men of their own color and treat them badly, putting them in chains and beating them. The white men, when offered slaves, refuse them, saying, 'Shall we make our brothers slaves? No, we are all sons of God.' I have not heard a white man talk a lie yet. Speke came here, behaved well and went his way home with his brother Grant. They bought no slaves, and the time they were in Uganda they were very good. Stanley came here and would take no slaves. And when I think that the Arabs and the white men do as they are taught, I say that the white men are superior to the Arabs, and I think, therefore, that their book must be a better book than Mohammed's."—Presbyterian *Foreign Missionary*, June, 1880.

[1] "On a certain day, Mohammed, entering unexpectedly the house of Zeid, had a momentary glimpse of the charms of his beautiful wife and uttered a cry of passionate admiration. The circumstance was reported, and the disciple by an immediate divorce enabled the prophet to add a new bride to his harem. By these marriages—for he had then six living wives—the legal number allowed to the faithful had been overstepped, and, moreover, his alliance with the wife of his adopted son was considered highly improper, if not incestuous. But Mohammed had an easy and effectual method of silencing present scandal and avoiding further complication by an additional surah to the Koran; thus: 'O Prophet, we have allowed thee wives, and also the slaves which thy right hand possesseth, and any other believing woman if she give her-

tion of home, as it is established and fostered under the benign influences of the gospel of Christ, yielding such blessing and peace, is unknown in the Mohammedan world. The harem yields the highest type of earthly happiness, as understood by Mohammedans, and one of the most splendid surahs of the Koran contains a promise of seventy-two black-eyed houris to the meanest of the prophet's followers on reaching the other world.

Cruelty.—It is usually the case that sensuality goes hand in hand with cruelty. They are twin vices. The Mohammedans are the most cold-blooded and implacable people on earth. The hand of Islam, the Ishmaelitic faith, is against every man. It is related that after the battle of Badr one of the prisoners who were brought before the prophet cried out, "There is death in thy glance!" Another of them, on being ordered for execution, asked in anguish, "Who will take care of my little girl?" The prophet answered "Hell-fire," and commanded him to be immediately slain. In this religion war is a divine ordinance, a sacrament. It is written in the Koran, "O Prophet, stir up the faithful to war! As to those who fight in defence of the true religion, God will not suffer their works to perish, but will lead them into Paradise." The pathway of Islam all along the centuries has been red with blood. In the great Mohammedan university in Cairo,[1] where ten thousand

self and the prophet desireth to take her to wife. This is a peculiar privilege granted thee above the rest of the believers' (Surah xxxiii.)."— *Islam*, p. 161.

[1] For a most interesting sketch of this great university see the Presbyterian *Foreign Missionary* for January, 1878.

students are assembled to study the Koran and prepare themselves to propagate the true religion, a prayer is offered every evening which is thus translated by Dr. Jessup: "I seek refuge with Allah from Satan the accursed! In the name of Allah the Compassionate, the Merciful! O Lord of all creatures! O Allah! destroy the infidels and polytheists, thine enemies, the enemies of the religion! O Allah! make their children orphans and defile their abodes! Cause their feet to slip; give them and their families, their households and their women, their children and their relations by marriage, their brothers and their friends, their possessions and their race, their wealth and their lands, as booty to the Moslems, O Lord of all creatures!"

It is obvious that a religion of this character cannot withstand the benignant influences of advancing civilization. It belongs to dark ages and benighted lands. Its methods are distinctly barbaric. Its Yemen blade will prove no better than a willow withe against the sword of the Spirit, which is the word of God,[1] and

---

[1] "Strong only as a military theocracy, Islam as a creed was a mixture of fatal apathy with sensual hopes, and did but repeat the same mechanical formula with lips of death. Checked in Europe by a long line of Christian heroes from Charles Martel to John Hunniades, and from Hunniades to Sobieski, its aggressive power was broken. It now acts only as a gradual decay in every nation over which it dominates. The traveler in Palestine may be shocked to see even the fair hill of Nazareth surmounted by the white-domed wely of an obscure Mohammedan saint; but he will be reassured as he notices that in every town and village where Christians are there are activity and vigor, while all the places which are purely Islamite look as if they had been smitten as with the palsy by some withering and irreparable curse."—FARRAR'S *Witness of History to Christ*, p. 114.

which no power of earth can resist or withstand. Here is the contrast:

> "Mohammed's truth lay in a holy book;
> Christ's in a sacred life.
>
> "So while the world rolls on from change to change,
> And realms of thought expand,
> The letter stands without expanse or range,
> Stiff as a dead man's hand.
>
> "While as the life-blood fills the growing form,
> The spirit Christ has shed
> Flows through the ripening ages fresh and warm,
> More felt than heard or read."[1]

The green banner of Islam and its garments rolled in blood must presently be folded and laid away, for Shiloh comes; the early twilight of his appearing already overspreads the earth.

[1] Lord Houghton, quoted by Dr. Lees.

X.
THE TRUE RELIGION.

Conclusions from the foregoing Survey:
    I. The Religious Instinct is Universal.
    II. There is Truth in all Religions.
        (1) As to God; (2) As to Morals; (3) As to the Essential Christ.
    III. All the Religions thus far considered are Vitally Defective.
    IV. All of these are Unfit for Universal Diffusion.
    V. Three Necessary Characteristics of the True Religion :
        (1) Pleroma; (2) Faultlessness; (3) Power to Save.
    VI. Christianity has these Characteristics.

The Cardinal Truths of Christianity:
    (1) As to God.
    (2) As to Man.
    (3) As to Man's Relations with God.
        " What shall I do to be saved ?"
    Christian Morals.

Central Truth: Christ :
        (1) As the Manifestation of God; (2) As the Sin-bearer; (3) As the Ideal Man.

Christianity the True Religion.

X. THE TRUE RELIGION.

WE want a definition of "Religion." There are various theories as to the origin of the word. By some it is alleged to be an offshoot from *re-legere*, "to read over"—*i. e.* to form an opinion or system of opinions from the things which have been written touching the great spiritual problems. By others— and with equal plausibility—it is thought to have come from *re-ligare*, "to bind back"—*i. e.* to restore the soul to its original relation of friendship with God. The first of these derivations places the emphasis on creed; the second, on cultus, by which is meant the expression of one's creed in worship and conduct of life. A combination of both, however it may offend the principles of philology, will yield the best definition of *religion*[1]—to wit: a creed *plus* a

[1] "'Religio est, quæ superioris cujusdam, naturæ, quam Divinam vocant, curam ceremoniamque affert.'—CICERO.

"Professor Whitney of Yale says: 'A religion is the belief in a supernatural being or beings whose actions are seen in the works of creation, and in such relations on the part of man toward this being or beings as prompt the believer to acts of propitiation and worship and to the regulation of conduct.'

"Professor Köstlin of Halle says: 'Religion means the conscious relation between man and God, and the expression of that relation in human conduct.'

"According to Mr. Herbert Spencer, religion may be defined as an '*a-priori* theory of the universe;' and there is, the writer tells us, a

cultus. If a system can be found presenting a faultless and comprehensive creed and system of belief, with appropriate forms of worship and a code of morals, not merely as parchment symbols, but inscribed deep on the tablets of the inner man and vitally manifested in the "walk and conversation," that must be, *par excellence*, the true religion (James 1 : 22–27). It is our belief that these conditions are met fully and only by the religion of Jesus Christ.

Conclusions from our Survey.—From our survey of the great systems we arrive at certain conclusions, as follows:

I. *The Religious Instinct is Universal.*[1]—For

subsidiary and unessential element in religion—namely, the moral teaching—'which is in all cases a supplementary growth.' 'Leaving out,' he says, 'the accompanying moral code, which is in all cases a supplementary growth, religion may be defined as an *a-priori* theory of the universe.' But it is clear that this definition would not be universally accepted, for we find Mr. Matthew Arnold saying in his *Literature and Dogma* that 'Religion, if we follow the intent of human thought and human language in the use of the word, is ethics, heightened, enlightened, lit up by feeling; the passage from morality to religion is made when to morality is applied emotion; and the true meaning of religion is not simply morality, but morality touched by emotion.' Mr. Max Müller has defined religion more simply as the *sensus numinis*, the sense of our dependence upon something (or some one) else. 'All nations join, in some way or other, in the words of the Psalmist: "He hath made us, and not we ourselves."' "—KEARY'S *Outlines of Primitive Beliefs*, p. 4.

[1] "Religion is a universal fact. It is found among all nations. However ruined, alienated, degraded they may be, there exists in all a universal instinct, seeking its satisfaction and manifesting itself in religious forms and ceremonies. 'You may see states,' says Plutarch, 'without walls, without laws, without coins, without writing; but a people without a god, without prayer, without religious exercises and sacrifices, has no man seen.' For a consciousness of the existence of God everywhere

> "E'en in savage bosoms
> There are longings, yearnings, strivings
> For the good they comprehend not."

In St. Paul's presentation of the status of the pagan nations (Rom. 1 : 19, 20) he says that God hath manifested unto them the things which may be known concerning him; "for the invisible things of him since the creation of the world are clearly seen, being perceived through the things that are made, even his everlasting power and divinity." Thus they have both the holy aspiration and the sufficient response. As the hart panteth for the water-brooks, so does the universal heart of man pant after God. Everywhere we find this thirst for the living God. Nor has he ever or anywhere left himself without a witness. All nature is an open book of theology, the air is resonant with voices of divine invitation;

> "And as the waxing moon can take
> The tidal waters in her wake,
> And lead them round and round to break
> Obedient to her drawings dim,

exists, and man cannot think of God without attributing to himself some kind of relation toward him."—LUTHARDT'S *Fundamental Truths of Christianity*, p. 147.

"Columbus at first indulged in the error that the natives of Hayti were destitute of all notions of religion, and he had consequently flattered himself that it would be the easier to introduce into their minds the doctrines of Christianity—not aware that it is more difficult to light up the fire of devotion in the cold heart of an atheist than to direct the flame to a new object when it is already enkindled. There are few beings, however, so destitute of reflection as not to be impressed with the conviction of an overruling Deity. A nation of atheists never existed."—IRVING'S *Columbus*, vi. chap. 10.

> So may the movements of his mind,
> The first great Father of mankind,
> Affect with answering movements blind,
>   And draw the souls that breathe by him."

The false religions are the "movements blind" with which the world has answered the "dim drawings" of God. It is thus that the nations "haply feel after him" (Acts 17 : 27).

II. *Truth in all Religions.*—We find, therefore, a modicum of truth in every one of the religions of the globe. It is by no means necessary that in our effort to exalt Christianity as the one true religion we should characterize all other systems as false *in toto*. The divineness of the human soul is heard speaking more or less distinctly through them all.

(1) *God.*—Here is God himself, dimly outlined, perhaps, like Michael Angelo's picture of the Almighty behind the huge clouds of chaos, nevertheless the veritable One. There is a profound and blessed truth in the words with which the archangel in *Paradise Lost* is represented as addressing Adam on his expulsion from the garden:

> "Yet doubt not but in valley and in plain
> God is, as here, and will be found alike
> Present; and of his presence many a sign
> Still following thee, still compassing thee round
> With goodness and parental love, his face
> Express, and of his steps the track divine."

We Christians must not arrogate to ourselves all of the divine presence and guidance. If I mistake not, we have discovered in each of the sacred books a silhouette, if nothing more, of the face of God.

(2) *Morals.*—We have discovered traces also of " his track divine;" that is, the path of righteousness. Each of the false religions has its code of moral maxims, not a few of which are substantially identical with those of the Christian system. Let it be remembered that a moral code is the resultant of a belief in God. It is uttered forth not by the still small voice of Calvary, but by the thunders and trumpet-blasts of Sinai; it is heard, therefore, not merely in Christian lands, but to the uttermost parts of the earth. The fundamental principles of virtue are the common heritage of all races. It need, then, occasion no surprise when we hear the familiar maxims of the moral law proceeding from the lips of pagan oracles,[1] nor even when we read the

[1] " In communicating his revelation to man, God may have made, and certainly did make, use of pre-existing elements, of ideas already familiar to those whom he addressed. It may have been that for some points of difficulty man had already fashioned true answers, or such at least as were not far from the truth. These the revelation would confirm by a declaration of their conformity with truth, a happy guess would be turned into certainty, while error would be eliminated and misapprehension corrected. It was not necessary that everything should be done from the beginning; we are not to expect to find in a divine revelation everything entirely new and strange. There may have been, as Mr. Buckle says, excellent moral precepts propounded and acted on before the introduction of Christianity; was it necessary, therefore, that Christianity should ignore and pass them by, or that it should supersede everything which had already commended itself to the conscience of mankind? Rather would we expect it to acknowledge and embody such precepts, adding to them an authority which they had not previously possessed. There may, in like manner, have been conceptions which, to some extent, interpreted and satisfied the religious need; it was not necessary that these should be discarded, but that they should

Golden Rule in the annals of Confucius, which were written five centuries before the Christian era.

(3) *An Essential Christ.*—Nor is this all. Alas for the pagan world if the whole measure of its truth is contained in these dim outlines of a holy God and a broken table of law! But there is something further in these false systems of religion which we cannot have overlooked—to wit, the suggestion of a Christ—dim, indeed, sometimes, as a spectre walking in a dream, but still an "essential Christ," one who shall somehow deliver the world from the consequences of man's ill-doing and usher in a golden age. The word of hope addressed by Hermes to Prometheus chained to the rock had in it a prophecy of the glorious gospel of redemption by vicarious death almost as plain as that which glowed on the fire-touched lips of Isaiah: "Thy suffering can never end until a god shall appear as thy substitute in anguish, ready to descend in thy behalf into the midnight realms of Hades and the gloomy depths of Tartarus." And the fourth Eclogue of Virgil, written on the occasion of the birth of Pollio's son, seems like an inspired welcome to Shiloh:

> "The last great age, foretold by sacred rhymes,
> Renews its finished course; Saturnian times
> Roll round again; and mighty years, begun
> From their first orb, in radiant circles run.

be made the foundation and the means of further enlightenment; nor, as Max Müller says, should 'any doctrine seem the less true or the less precious because it was seen not only by Moses or Christ, but likewise by Buddha or Laotse.'"—ALEXANDER STEWART, in *Catholic Presbyterian*, i. 6.

> The base, degenerate, iron offspring ends,
> A golden progeny from heaven descends.—
> See! laboring nature calls thee to sustain
> The nodding frame of heaven and earth and main.
> See to their base restored earth, seas and air,
> And joyful ages from behind in crowding ranks appear."

It is not for us to say whether such anticipations of a great Deliverer are lingering echoes of the protevangel of Eden (Gen. 3 : 15), or the expressions of an intuitive conviction that a good God will not leave a sin-stricken world to suffer an irremediable doom; in any case, we rejoice to know that even the nations that lie in darkness and the shadow of death are not wholly Christless. They have slender clues of gospel truth, which, were they followed, would lead bewildered souls out of the dark labyrinths into the light. Thus, God is exonerated and the nations are without excuse (Rom. 1 : 20) if, becoming vain in their imaginations, they choose the unbroken night rather than the endless day.[1]

III. *All the False Religions are Vitally Defective.*—We have found that all these religions, notwithstanding their contingent of truth, are vitally defective. As

---

[1] "We ought to hail with gratitude, instead of viewing with suspicion, the enunciation by heathen writers of truths which we might at first sight have been disposed to regard as the special heritage of Christianity. In Pythagoras and Socrates and Plato, in Seneca, Epictetus, and Marcus Aurelius, we see the light of heaven struggling its impeded way through clouds of darkness and ignorance; we thankfully recognize that the souls of men in the pagan world, surrounded as they were by perplexities and dangers, were yet enabled to reflect, as from the dim surface of silver, some image of what was divine and true; we hail with the great and eloquent Bossuet, '*the Christianity of nature.*' 'The divine image in man,' says St. Bernard, 'may be burned, but it cannot be burnt out.'"—FARRAR's *Seekers after God*, p. 182.

James Freeman Clarke says: "In every instance we can touch with our finger the weak or empty side." It is true that all nations have a more or less clear conception of Deity; yet, left to themselves, they have, after the manner of Confucius, grown weary of gazing into nebulous depths, and therefore dispensed with God altogether; or, like the Hindus, have enlarged and rarefied the dimly-outlined Presence until it has become an all-pervading Something or Nothing, without life or personality; or else, their foolish hearts being darkened, they have changed the glory of the incorruptible One into the images of men and birds and four-footed beasts and creeping things. Thus the heathen, themselves being their own witnesses, knowing God, have not, in any of their religions, glorified him as God. It is true also that not a few of the sound principles of morality are found among them; but they are like the proper remedies on the shelves of a quacksalver: here are salutary balms and balsams side by side with solutions of toads' gall and powder of serpents' fangs, and all manner of foolish and deleterious nostrums. It were better, mayhap, for the sick to die in the course of nature than to be thus drugged with mingled truth and error.

It would be a pleasure, at this point, to feel assured that the benighted nations in their extremity are greatly helped, possibly delivered, by such of their dreams and visions as declare an "essential Christ;" but, alas! the very blood upon their sacrificial altars becomes a mere fetich, the symbol being put for the thing symbolized, and the rising smoke of their oblations hides the sun.

IV. *The False Religions Unfit for General Diffusion.—* These various systems are, all alike, unfit for general diffusion. They are man-made and ethnic.[1] They dis-

---

[1] "Now, we are met at once with the striking and obvious fact that most of the religions of the world are evidently religions limited in some way to particular races or nations. They are, as we have said, *ethnic*. We use this Greek word rather than its Latin equivalent, *gentile*, because *gentile*, though meaning literally 'of or belonging to a race,' has acquired a special sense from its New-Testament use as meaning all who are not Jews. The word 'ethnic' remains pure from any such secondary or acquired meaning, and signifies simply *that which belongs to a race.*"—CLARKE'S *Ten Great Religions*, p. 15.

"We find that each race, besides its special moral qualities, seems also to have special religious qualities, which cause it to tend toward some one kind of religion more than to another kind. These religions are the flower of the race; they come forth from it as its best aroma. Thus we see that Brahmanism is confined to that section or race of the great Aryan family which has occupied India for more than thirty centuries. It belongs to the Hindus, to the people taking its name from the Indus, by the tributaries of which stream it entered India from the north-west. It has never attempted to extend itself beyond that particular variety of mankind. Perhaps one hundred and fifty millions of men accept it as their faith. It has been held by this race as their religion during a period immense in the history of mankind. Its sacred books are certainly more than three thousand years old. But during all this time it has never communicated itself to any race of men outside of the peninsula of India. It is thus seen to be a strictly ethnic religion, showing neither the tendency nor the desire to become the religion of mankind.

"The same thing may be said of the religion of Confucius. It belongs to China and the Chinese. It suits their taste and genius. They have had it as their state religion for some twenty-three hundred years, and it rules the opinions of the rulers of opinion among three hundred millions of men. But, out of China, Confucius is only a name.

"So, too, of the system of Zoroaster. It was for a long period the religion of an Aryan tribe who became the ruling people among mankind. The Persians extended themselves through Western Asia and conquered many nations, but they never communicated their religion.

tinctly bear the image of their creators, and cannot therefore—so long as race-diversities and antagonisms exist—overspread the earth. The intense spirituality of Brahmanism, for instance, which so highly commends it to the transcendental Hindus, makes it repellent for ever to those northern tribes who dwell where the elements are in perpetual strife. The matter-of-fact philosophy of Confucius would have produced among the vivacious and romantic Greeks an insufferable weariness. Thus, the very strength of the ethnic systems debars them from catholic conquest. The religion which is to become universal must commend itself to the universal heart and conscience; to that end its Author must be thoroughly familiar with Jew and Greek, barbarian, Scythian, bond and free. There is only One such—namely, the God and Father of us all.

> " The true religion, sprung from God above,
>   Is—must be—like her fountain,

It was strictly a national or ethnic religion, belonging only to the Iranians and their descendants, the Parsees.

" In like manner, it may be said that the religions of Egypt, of Greece, of Scandinavia, of the Jews, of Islam, and of Buddhism, are ethnic religions. Those of Egypt and Scandinavia are strictly so. It is said, to be sure, that the Greeks borrowed the names of their gods from Egypt, but the gods themselves were entirely different ones. It is also true that some of the gods of the Romans were borrowed from the Greeks, but their life was left behind. They merely represented by rote the Greek mythology, having no power to invent one for themselves. But the Greek religion they never received. For instead of its fair humanities the Roman gods were only servants of the state—a higher kind of consuls, tribunes and lictors. The real Olympus of Rome was the Senate Chamber on the Capitoline Hill."—CLARKE'S *Ten Great Religions*, p. 16.

> Embracing all things with a tender love,
>   Full of good-will and meek expectancy;
>   Full of true justice and sure verity
>   In heart and voice; free, large, even infinite;
>   Not wedged in strait particularity,
>   But grasping all in her vast, active spirit."

V. *Three Necessary Marks of the True Religion.*—This true religion must have three distinguishing marks.

1. *Pleroma*, by which is meant the possession of all excellences. The universal religion, which is to crowd out Islam and Buddhism with all other competitors, must obviously so commend itself to the Moslem and Buddhist as that they shall miss none of the beneficent features of their former faiths. It must therefore be *teres atque rotundus*,[1] a compend and summary of all the excellences of all the religious systems of the world.

2. *Faultlessness.*—In each of the man-made systems we detect points of weakness, theological or ethical flaws. There must be an utter freedom from these in the religion which is to bind the nations all together and back to God.

3. *Power to Save.*—It is not enough that a religion should, like Brahmanism, transport the mind from earthly to unearthly realms; not enough that it should, like Buddhism, bring back the mind from unprofitable dreams to common tasks and duties; nor yet enough

---

[1] "The question emerges at this point: 'Is Christianity also one-sided, or does it contain in itself all these truths?' Is it *teres atque rotundus*, so as to be able to meet every natural religion with a kindred truth, and thus to supply the defects of each from its own fullness? If it can be shown to possess this amplitude, it at once is placed by itself in an order of its own."—*Ten Great Religions*, p. 24.

that, like the inspiriting mythology of the Norseman, it should perpetually broaden the horizons of our freedom. The religion of the Greeks led them into porches of philosophy and the vast galleries of the liberal arts, while that of the Egyptians brought them, reverently hoodwinked, into interminable labyrinths of spiritual mystery. The philosophy of Confucius maps out an earthly kingdom abiding in the sunshine of perpetual peace, while Islam unsheaths the sword to propagate the iron rule of an infinite sovereign whose figure overshadows all. Thus each has its own work. Each performed its office in presenting a partial outline of many-sided truth, a fragmentary code of morals, or a single feature—perchance grim and distorted—of an infinite and every way glorious God. The true religion, however, must accomplish all that is performed by all of these and something more—ay, vastly more. It must show itself to be the power of God unto salvation. Whatever its other achievements, this must be its *chef d'œuvre*: it must furnish a complete and satisfactory answer to the question, " What shall I do that I may have eternal life ?" It must show itself able to deliver human souls from the shame, bondage and penalty of sin.

VI. *Christianity has these Marks.*—It is claimed that the foregoing conditions are fully met in the religion of Jesus Christ. If that claim be established, it stands that Christianity is of divine origin and must ultimately become the religion of the whole earth. The following diagram, showing the leading excellences and defects of the false systems, will abridge our labor at this point:

I. The Fetich.

Good Features.	Bad Features.
Central Thought: Man not his own Master.	Chance, as distinguished from Providence.
A Belief in the Unseen.	Abject Superstition.

II. The Religion of Egypt.

Central Thought: Reverence for Life.	Zoölatry, or worship of life.
Immortality: The *Ka*, or Soul.	Mystery, a *religio bifrons*.
The *Maat*, or Moral Code.	

III. Zoroastrianism.

Central Thought: Conflict.	Dualism, the devil coequal with God.
The Four Laws: Piety, Purity, Veracity, Industry.	Hopelessness.

IV. Brahmanism.

Diaus-Pitar, "Our Father in Heaven."	*Central Thought:* Caste.
Spirituality.	Spiritual Pride.
	Pantheism.
	Transmigration.
	No Personal Responsibility.

V. Buddhism.

Central Thought: Self-culture.	*Karma;* or, The Law of Consequences.
The Noble Eightfold Path:	*Nirvana;* or, Extinction of the Soul.
1. Right Belief.	Selfishness.
2. Right Feelings.	Sadness.
3. Right Speech.	
4. Right Actions.	
5. Right Means of Livelihood.	
6. Right Endeavor.	
7. Right Memory.	
8. Right Meditation.	

VI. The Religion of Greece.

Central Thought: God in Nature.	A Pantheon of Humanized and Immoral Gods.
The Dignity of Man.	Immorality.
Wisdom the Principal Thing.	Skepticism.

VII. Norse Mythology.

The Al-Fadir.	Nature-worship.
Central Thought: Courage.	A Sordid View of the Future Life.
Love of Freedom.	
Immortality, *Heimgang*.	

VIII. Confucianism.

GOOD FEATURES.	BAD FEATURES.
Central Thought: The Ideal Kingdom.	Practical Atheism.
Filial Piety.	No Good Cheer.
Patriotism.	No Ambition.
The Five Cardinal Virtues: Benevolence, Duty, Decorum, Knowledge, Faith.	No Progress.
Conservatism.	

IX. Islam.

"The Eternal Truth," one God.	"The Eternal Lie," Mohammed is the Prophet of God.
	Unitarianism.
	Central Thought: Kismet.
	Formalism: The Five Pillars of Duty:
	1. Repeating the Creed.
	2. Observing the Stated Seasons of Prayer.
	3. Keeping the Fast of Ramadan.
	4. Performing the Legal Alms.
	5. Making the Pilgrimage to Mecca.
	The Sword.
	Slavery.
	Degradation of Woman.

It appears from this diagram that all the good features of the false systems are to be found in Christianity, and of the bad features not one; that is to say, Christianity has both *pleroma*[1] and faultlessness. One

---

[1] "The word *pleroma* (πλήρωμα) in the New Testament means that which fills up—fullness, fulfilling, filling full. The verb 'to fulfill' carries the same significance. To 'fulfill that which was spoken by the prophets' means to fill it full of meaning and truth. Jesus came, not to destroy the law, but to fulfill it; that is, to carry it out farther. He teaches that love fulfills the law, that the Church is the fullness of Christ, that Christ fills all things full of himself, and that in him dwells all the

thing more remains to be shown in order to establish
its claim to be the absolute religion [1]—namely, that it
offers a satisfactory plan of deliverance from sin.

fullness of the Godhead bodily. One great distinction between Christianity and all other religions is in this pleroma, or fullness of life which it possesses, and which, to all appearance, came from the life of Jesus."
—*Ten Great Religions*, p. 504.

"Christianity differs from all other religions (on the side of truth) in this, that it is a pleroma, or fullness of knowledge. It does not differ by teaching what has never been said or thought before. Perhaps the substance of most of the statements of Jesus may be found scattered through the ten religions of the world, some here and some there. Jesus claims no monopoly of the truth. He says, 'My doctrine is not mine, but His who sent me.' But he *does* call himself 'the Light of the world,' and says that, though he does not come to destroy either the law or the prophets, he comes to fulfill them in something higher. His work is to fulfill all religions with something higher, broader and deeper than what they have—accepting their truth, supplying their deficiencies."—*Ibid.*, p. 492.

[1] "And what, then, is Christianity? It is a world of thoughts which have been working and fermenting in the minds of men up to the present hour; it is an all-affecting change in our mode of thought and observation; it is a transformation of our entire social system; it is a renewal of our inner life; in short, it is a world of effects which are matters of daily experience. Wherever we may be and wherever we may go we encounter this new world of Christianity, even when we do not recognize it, even when we ignore or deny it. But, above all, Christianity is *religion*. The Christian religion is the source from which that stream of blessings flows of which even they who oppose or despise the Christian faith partake. As religion, however, it is connected with all those religions which have preceded it, and that not merely as one of them, but as their truth, their aim—as simply religion. Christianity is the absolute religion, the only true and intrinsically valid religion. Such is the pretension with which it entered the world and which it constantly maintains. This may, perhaps, be called exclusiveness and intolerance, but it is the intolerance of truth. As soon as truth concedes the possibility of her opposite being also true, she denies herself. As soon as Christianity ceases to declare herself to be the only true religion she annihilates her power and denies her right to exist, for she denies

Let us observe how the false religions answer the great question,
"*What shall I Do to be Saved?*"

1. Fetichism ....No answer.
2. The Religion of Egypt...Observe the *Maat*, or moral code.
3. Zoroastrianism ....Repeat the *Patet*.
4. Brahmanism................Be absorbed in Brahm.
5. Buddhism...................Be sublimely indifferent to everything.
6. The Religion of Greece ..No answer.
7. Norse Mythology..........Fight a good fight (right or wrong).
8. Confucianism ....Be a good citizen of the kingdom of China.
9. Islam.........................Do your *duty;* that is, stand by the Five Pillars.

With these let us contrast the answer of Christianity as given in its great doctrine of justification by faith. It is this: Believe in the Lord Jesus Christ, and thou shalt be saved—saved from the defilement, the bondage and the penalty of sin. This is Christianity's masterstroke; and at this point it conclusively and finally demonstrates its superiority over all. "I am not ashamed," said the great cosmopolitan apostle—"I am not ashamed of the gospel of Christ; for it is the power of God unto salvation to every one that believeth; to the Jew first, and also to the Greek" (Rom. 1 : 16).

The Cardinal Truths of Christianity.—Observe, now, the cardinal truths of the Christian religion, which may be briefly considered under three heads:

her necessity. The old world concluded with the question, What is truth? The new world began with the saying of Christ, 'I am the Truth.' And this saying is the confession of Christian faith."—LUTHARDT'S *Saving Truths of Christianity*, p. 20.

(1) *As to God.*—He is declared to be " a spirit, infinite, eternal and unchangeable in his being, wisdom, power, holiness, justice, goodness and truth." Dr. Robert Flint says: " Christianity, alone of religions, gives a clear, self-consistent, adequate view of God. It presents him as the one God, eternal, infinite, omnipotent, omniscient; as perfect in wisdom, in righteousness, in holiness; and yet as merciful, gracious, full of goodness and love; a true Father in his feelings and actings toward men; the God and Father of Jesus Christ, in whose character and sacrifice his moral glory has found the highest revelation of its purity and beauty, its attractiveness and tenderness."

(2) *As to Man.*—He is set forth as the crowning work and masterpiece of the divine creation; he was made in the image and after the likeness of the infinite One: put to the test, which was necessary for his confirmation in virtue, he ignominiously fell from his high estate and became alienated from God; but he was not left without hope, for no sooner had he fallen than the possibility of a restoration was placed before him. " Christianity, alone of religions," says Dr. Flint, " addresses itself to man as he really is and in the whole extent of his being, overlooking no weakness, cloaking no sin, making no false concessions, yet denying no legitimate supports, and appealing in due order and degree to faith, reason, affection and will."

(3) *As to the Relations of Man with God.*—Restoration is brought about through the vicarious suffering of a Mediator, the Theanthropos, who, being man that he may be able to suffer, and God that he may suffer

enough, bears the world's sins in his own body on the tree. The condition affixed to the offer of salvation through this great atonement is faith in Christ crucified. He that believeth in the Lord Jesus Christ shall be saved. "Christianity, alone of religions," again says Dr. Flint, "discloses and promises to man a complete communion with God. It shows the perfect union of the divine and human in the person and life of its Founder. It offers, on the basis and surety of a divinely-accomplished and divinely-accepted atonement, full reconciliation with God to every one who will repent and turn from his sins." [1]

Christian Morals.—The resultant of this faith in Christ crucified is a godly life. The moral code of Christianity, like its plan of salvation, is adapted to all classes of people in all possible relations to the very end of time. It is calculated to build up a happy

[1] "Whether we look at the character of Christ in its unapproachable elevation of purity and loveliness, or at the manifestation of God's love in his incarnation and atoning death; whether we look at the influence which these have exerted in moulding the world's history through eighteen centuries, or at the power they have shown themselves to possess of sustaining and guiding the believer's life and of ministering to his comfort and peace,—we feel we are in the presence of that which is unique because it is alone divine. Christianity is the only system which has dared to probe to the bottom of the wound of which humanity is so sadly conscious, because it alone was provided with a perfect remedy. It can present the ideal at which men should aim without detraction, because it alone can hold out a prospect of its realization. It can exhibit the extent to which men fall short of this ideal in all its awfulness, because it alone bridges the fatal gulf. In other religions we have man seeking God—feeling after him if haply he might find him: here only is God seeking man in the fullness and freeness of redeeming love."—ALEXANDER STEWART.

home, a pure society and a just government. It enlarges the heart of a man, giving him a commission of love to the antipodes, and thus fits him for a place in the universal neighborhood, the kingdom of God.

The Central Truth of Christianity.—The central truth of the Christian religion is Jesus Christ.[1] He is first, midst, last. He is all and in all. For other foundation can no man lay than that is laid, which is Jesus Christ (1 Cor. 3 : 11).

(1) *Christ as the Manifestation of God.*—He is represented as the manifestation of God. The Word was made flesh and dwelt among us (and we beheld his glory, the glory as of the only-begotten of the Father), full of grace and truth (John 1 : 14). For in him dwell-

---

[1] "But if I say Christianity, I thereby say Jesus Christ. Christianity appeared in the world, not as a system of philosophy, not as a code of morality, but as an actual fact—the fact of the person Christ Jesus. All depends on him. With him Christianity stands or falls. It cannot be separated from him. It was not his precepts, but his person and his testimony concerning himself, which brought about the crisis in Israel. He himself made his whole cause depend upon his person. We cannot separate it from him. Rationalism has attempted to separate Christianity from Christ, and to reduce it to a mere morality. But experience has proved the attempt impossible. Jesus Christ does not bear the same relation to Christianity as Mohammed does to Mohammedanism, or as any other founder of a religion to the religion he has founded; but he is himself Christianity. To speak of Christianity is to speak not of doctrines and precepts, but of Jesus Christ. Christianity is indeed a summary of truths, a new doctrine, a philosophy if you will, a new view of the world, a new explanation of history, a new mode of worship, a new morality, a new rule of life, etc. It is all these, because it is a fact universal in its nature. But all these depend upon the person of Jesus Christ, are given with him and included in him—stand and fall with him."—LUTHARDT'S *Fundamental Truths of Christianity,* p. 256.

eth all the fullness of the Godhead bodily (Col. 2 : 9). In Jesus Christ all the divine attributes are brought within our human ken. " God's general revelation of himself is by fixed laws of order which know no pity, which show no forgiveness, which are indifferent to the interests of individuals, which conceal the divine character in some respects while they reveal it in others. God's special revelation of himself by intervening among these laws in miraculous acts and inspired words brings him nearer to individual hearts, and yet it leaves him far away; for, after all, but signs and sounds have been given, not himself; he is himself still shrouded in darkness, still hidden where no man can approach him. Can he come yet nearer man, that man may draw closer to him? Christianity answers, and its answer is Christ,—the person, the character and the work of Christ." [1]

(2) *Christ as the Sin-bearer.*—But Christ is not merely the manifestation of God; he is set forth also as the sin-bearer, and as such the Saviour of the world. In vain had guilty men, groaning under the burden of their guilt, looked elsewhere for deliverance; in vain had they bowed before their idols and sought counsel at their oracles; the gods were dumb, the oracles were silent, there was no voice nor answer nor any that re-

---

[1] " Christianity fully recognizes the whole revelation of God in man, and represents the completion of the revelation of God as made through a perfect man. The religion of Greece tended to form artists, and that of Scandinavia, warriors; Brahmanism is the religion of priests, and Buddhism of ascetics; but Christianity aims at the production of men, true and complete men, sons of God, perfect as the Father in heaven is perfect."—DR. ROBERT FLINT, in *Faiths of the World*, p. 358.

garded. "At the end of the long ascent of natural development we find ourselves only on a Babel tower, looking heavenward, but with no wings to mount. Here the dreams of optimists and the sanguine hopes of reformers have halted and died. That which the human heart cannot but long for, and catch gleams of in the mute prophecies of nature, yet cannot realize of itself, is at last fulfilled in the redemption of Christ. From this shadowy tabernacle of earth and sky, where the inexorable debt of nature is paid with 'blood of goats and calves,' 'by his own blood he has entered once into the holy place, having obtained eternal redemption for us.'"[1]

(3) *Christ as the Ideal Man.*—Still further, Christ is set forth as the Exemplar of right living. It is not enough that in him we should behold God, nor that through him we should have our sins forgiven: we must have placed before us somewhere an illustration of perfect character, that we may pattern our lives after it. In Christ we mark the perfect Man, and the constant aspiration of the true Christian is that he may be more like him.[2] "It has been reserved," says

---

[1] *The Old Bible and the New Science.*

[2] "Christianity was not only a doctrine, but a life. Oh, let us strive to imitate that life! Take it with you, my young brethren, into the dust and glare of the busy world; amid the struggles and duties of this place of learning now, amid the temptations of great cities and eager lives hereafter, into the country parsonage and the lawyer's chambers, the merchant's counting-house and the soldier's tent. Take but this with you, and, pure, happy, noble, confident, you may smile hereafter when men tell you that Christianity is dead. Do this, and it shall never die; it shall grow younger with years; it shall deepen in faith and wisdom, in dominion and power, in purity and peace; the dew of its

Lecky, "for Christianity to present the world an ideal character which, through all the changes of eighteen centuries, has filled the hearts of men with an impassioned love; has shown itself capable of acting on all ages, nations, temperaments and conditions; has not only been the highest pattern of virtue, but the highest incentive to its practice, and has exercised so deep an influence that it may be truly said that the simple record of three short years of active life has done more to regenerate and soften mankind than all the disquisitions of philosophers and all the exhortations of moralists. It has indeed been the wellspring of whatever is best and purest in the Christian life."[1]

birth shall be as the womb of the morning, and all they who believe and live thereby shall shine as the brightness of the firmament, and as the stars for ever and ever."—CANON FARRAR *to Students of Cambridge University*.

[1] It would be profitable to note the failures of the false religions and philosophies in their endeavor to picture the ideal Man. Canon Farrar says: "The Stoic wise man is a sort of moral phœnix, impassible and repulsive. He is intrepid in dangers, free from all passion, happy in adversity, calm in the storm; he alone knows how to live, because he alone knows how to die; he is the master of the world, because he is master of himself and the equal of God; he looks down upon everything with sublime imperturbability, despising the sadnesses of humanity and smiling with inviting loftiness at all our hopes and all our fears. But in another sketch of this faultless and unpleasant monster Seneca presents us not the proud athlete who challenges the universe and is invulnerable to all the stings and arrows of passion or of fate, but a hero in the serenity of absolute triumph, more tender indeed, but still without desires, without passions, without needs—who can feel no pity because pity is a weakness which disturbs his sapient calm. Well might the eloquent Bossuet exclaim, as he read of these chimerical perfections, 'It is to take a tone too lofty for feeble and mortal men. But, O maxims truly pompous! O affected insensibility! O false and imaginary wisdom, which fancies itself strong because it is hard, and generous because it is puffed up!'"

Just here we observe the vital difference between Christianity viewed as a moral system and all the other religions of the earth. The latter furnish more or less elaborate codes of maxims and precepts, but the former, doing all this, and doing it more satisfactorily, goes farther still and furnishes an illustration of its moral code in the person of a perfect Man.[1] The best morality of paganism is but a mummied body of maxims, fragrant of balms and spices, but without warmth or power; while that of Christianity, being quickened by divine inspiration, is as a living soul. The Golden Rule of Jesus differs from the same precept in its pagan form as Aaron's budded rod from a dry wisp of papyrus. Our Master speaks in Christian ethics as one having authority; and, though other teachers have let fall in fragmentary utterances not a few of the truths enunciated in his gospel, the world is still constrained to admit that man never spake like this Man. The superiority of the Christian system of morals to all others may be clearly perceived in the contrasted characters of the Christian and non-Christian nations.

Grapes are gathered from vines, and thistles from the thistle-bush. The religion of our Lord and Saviour Jesus Christ is the only religion that has ever produced

---

[1] "Yes, the life of Christ is indeed an example, a ὑπογραμμόν, over which the loveliest of saints' lives have been but faintly traced; a glory of which all that is bright among Christians has been but 'a pale image and faint reflection.' Beautiful indeed has been the life of the saints of God, and one has been full of charity, and one of purity, and one of zeal; but *this* life is not a type of any one excellence, but a radiation of them all—not virtuous, but Virtue; not truthfulness, but Truth."
—FARRAR.

a thoroughly enlightened people or a really holy life.[1]

Christianity the True Religion.—We arrive thus at the conclusion that Christianity, alone of religions, is of divine origin, and that, as such, it must supplant all others and possess the earth.[2] The Seed of woman named in the protevangel, though bruised on Golgotha in his struggle with Error, shall yet crush the life out of it. The seed of Abraham, multiplied as the stars of heaven, shall bless all the nations of the earth (Gal. 3 : 16). The caravans of Midian and Ephah, the fleets of Tarshish, the royal armies of the Gentiles, shall bring

---

[1] "The morality of paganism," says Farrar, "was, by its own confession, insufficient. It was tentative where Christianity is authoritative; it was dim and partial where Christianity is bright and complete; it was inadequate to rouse the sluggish carelessness of mankind where Christianity came with an imperial and awakening power; it gives only a rule where Christianity supplies a principle. And even where its teachings were absolutely coincident with those of Scripture it failed to ratify them with a sufficient sanction; it failed to announce them with the same powerful and contagious ardor; it failed to furnish an absolutely faultless and vivid example of their practice; it failed to inspire them with an irresistible motive; it failed to support them with a powerful comfort under the difficulties which were sure to be encountered in the aim after a consistent and holy life."

[2] "Other religions are defective and erroneous, ours is perfect and entire; their systems were esoteric, ours is universal; theirs temporary and for the few, ours eternal and for the race; a handful read the philosophers, myriads would die for Christ; they in their popularity could barely found a school, Christ from his cross rules the world; they could not even conceive the ideas of a society without falling into miserable error, Christ established an eternal and glorious kingdom, whose theory for all, whose history in the world, prove it to be indeed what it was from the first proclaimed to be—the kingdom of heaven, the kingdom of God."—FARRAR'S *Witness of History to Christ*, p. 148.

gold and incense and shall show forth the praises of the Christ of God.

The line of argument pursued in this brief series of essays has been kept strictly within the limits of Comparative Religion: it might be vastly strengthened, were this within our province, by a consideration of the part which Christianity has taken in the enlightenment and uplifting of the nations. We should find it no difficult matter to present an imposing array of *gesta Christi*, for the altars of the gospel are hung—like the fountain-shrine of Lourdes—with crutches and disused bandages, the eloquent testimony of such as believe themselves to have been healed by its medicinal virtue; and its pillars—like those of the ancient temple—are adorned with the golden shields of many who, drinking of its cool waters on the march, have been made strong out of their weakness and enabled to put to flight the armies of the aliens.

The path of the gospel in history is marked on either side with monuments of loving-kindness. It has relieved the poor and suffering, enlightened the ignorant and helped the downtrodden to their feet. It is now nearly nineteen hundred years since Jesus the Christ came from heaven to save our ruined race. We look back over those centuries with wonder and gratitude, for one by one the nations have arrayed themselves under the red-cross banner until Antichrist to-day rules solely in the lands that lie in darkness and the shadow of death.[1]

[1] "When we think of these moral characteristics, and see what the Christian religion has done for the world, see the commentary which eighteen centuries of civilization have written upon the Gospels, see what Europe

We are therefore in a position to say, "As for God, his way is perfect; the word of the Lord is tried; he is a buckler to all them that trust in him" (2 Sam. 22:31).

We rejoice in our confident assurance that the light of this glorious gospel of the blessed God, which has been shining with an ever-increasing radiance since it first arose above Bethlehem, shall continue to shine brighter and brighter unto the perfect day. Lift up your eyes, O believer, and mark the innumerable starry host: even so shall be the fruit of the travail of Emmanuel's soul.

> "For him shall endless prayer be made,
> And princes throng to crown his head;
> His name, like sweet perfume, shall rise
> With every morning sacrifice.
>
> "Let every creature rise and bring
> Peculiar honors to our King,
> Angels descend with songs again,
> And earth repeat the loud *Amen.*"

and America are to-day, and then turn back to Judea, to that haughty, bigoted, exclusive, illiterate, despised race, and see where the religion was cradled, we cannot but think that it was providential in its birth and beneficence. Shakespeare and Newton towered above the average level of society in their time, like Teneriffe above the sea. But when we think of this Jewish boy rising up at the feet of the Pharisees and Sadducees, with the religions of the Ganges on the one hand and that of Olympus on the other, and think what it was he said and wrought and contributed to the world, he towers so high above Shakespeare and Newton that the distance between these and the average level of life in their day, in the comparison, becomes a mere ripple on the surface of the world."—*From an Address by* WENDELL PHILLIPS.

THE END.

www.ingramcontent.com/pod-product-compliance
Lightning Source LLC
Chambersburg PA
CBHW021203230426
43667CB00006B/534